RESCUING
PENNY JANE

Center Point
Large Print

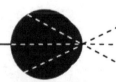

**This Large Print Book carries the
Seal of Approval of N.A.V.H.**

RESCUING PENNY JANE

One Shelter Volunteer,
Countless Dogs, and the Quest
to Find Them All Homes

AMY SUTHERLAND

CENTER POINT LARGE PRINT
THORNDIKE, MAINE

This Center Point Large Print edition
is published in the year 2017 by arrangement with
Harper, an imprint of HarperCollins Publishers.

All photographs courtesy of the author
unless otherwise noted.

The text of this Large Print edition is unabridged.
In other aspects, this book may vary
from the original edition.
Printed in the United States of America
on permanent paper.
Set in 16-point Times New Roman type.

ISBN: 978-1-68324-335-9

Publisher's Cataloging-In-Publication Data
(Prepared by The Donohue Group, Inc.)

Names: Sutherland, Amy.
Title: Rescuing Penny Jane : one shelter volunteer, countless dogs, and
the quest to find them all homes / Amy Sutherland.
Description: Center Point Large Print edition. | Thorndike, Maine :
Center Point Large Print, 2017.
Identifiers: LCCN 2016059626 | ISBN 9781683243359
    (hardcover : alk. paper)
Subjects: LCSH: Dog adoption. | Dogs—Training. | Animal shelters. |
Large type books.
Classification: LCC SF427 .S88 2017b | DDC 636.7/0887—dc23

For all the dogs I've met as a shelter volunteer but especially for Sadie, Sharyn, Bella, Stanley, Happy, Titan, Sullivan, D'Angelo, Digger, Simba, Bertha, Bones, and Holly.

"Heaven is no place for dogs," said Indra. "You have won the supreme reward by your virtuous life—there is no sin in abandoning a dog."

"I cannot do it," said Yudhishthira. "It would be wicked to cast aside one so devoted from a selfish desire for the joys of heaven."

—*Mahabharata*

Contents

RESCUING
PENNY JANE

Prologue:

GOING TO THE DOGS

For our first dog, we wanted a clean slate, to be there from the get-go, from the eight-week mark, when it is love at first sight for the puppy and for you, when you can easily scoop him up with your hands and nuzzle your nose against his soft belly. We had our hearts set so firmly on an Australian shepherd that we never even thought to go to an animal shelter. Instead, on an early spring night in 1998, my husband and I barreled down the highway from Portland, Maine, to a country town in southern New Hampshire. The breeder had told us on the phone that she had three available pups. By the time our car wound up the curving drive to the hilltop farm in the fading light, only one was left: a drowsy, petite female. This one was not up to snuff. She had, the breeder explained, too much white, which spilled down her chest and over each paw, in her otherwise-auburn coat to qualify her as a show dog like her father, the impressive Propwash St. Elmo's Fire, who had a ruff as thick as a lion's mane. The breeder would part with this too-white pup for six hundred dollars. We were thinking she might be our anniversary present to each other.

I have always loved dogs—some might say, especially cat lovers, to a fault. Some people come around to dogs. I, the daughter of several generations of dog lovers, was born with this affection, just as I was with a love for patent leather shoes and swimming pools. I love dogs in the sense that I am aware of dogs' many faults (the great swags of drool, the middle-of-the-night yips, the muddy prints they leave on leather couches and white linen dresses), but they still make my heart leap. I love them in the sense that I consider this deep affection an elemental part of who I am: a writer, a cook, a midwesterner, an eldest child, a tall woman, and a dog lover. When their guileless eyes look into mine, I feel they see the elemental me, not the human, but the being. As Gertrude Stein wrote, "I am because my dog knows me." That makes for a simple equation: no dogs, no me—which sounds about right.

Yet, for years after I left home and Ruby, our family's exuberant Lab mix, I was hopelessly dogless. I couldn't imagine the logistics of having my own pooch as I bounced from one tiny apartment to another, first on a waitress's measly salary and then on a newspaper reporter's slightly measlier salary. All I had was a long list of names for the pups I would have one day: Fancy, Sister, Bunny, and Stella Rondo, the last inspired by my favorite Eudora Welty story, a name that few, if any, dogs could carry off. Eventually I married a man who was as nuts about dogs as I was. We bought a roomy, if weary, old house near an ample park. Landlords no longer controlled our lives. We could afford a veterinarian. Scott, my husband, worked at home. After all the years we'd been forced to wait to get a dog, now that we finally could, we were seized with impatience. We wanted one yesterday.

Sitting cross-legged on the floor lightly patting the dozing pup's small, fuzzy back, we began to fall under that spell that canines unwittingly cast. Images of beach walks and car rides with the young Aussie streamed through my mind. Dogs can too easily seem like yours, even a puppy who's having trouble waking from her early-evening nap. If we didn't take her tonight, the breeder declared, someone was coming in the morning to look at her. We didn't have a dog bed or food or toys or a crate. Our small yard was not fenced.

We named her Dixie Lou Devil Dog, the long name a nod to her show dog pedigree and the Devil Dog for the tantrums she sometimes threw when we tired of Frisbee and attempted to put it away. She woke me with whimpers at 5:00 a.m. each day. I gave up my morning meditation to sit on the floor in my robe and hold up a ragged piece of sheepskin that Dixie Lou loved to pitch herself at over and over. Her puppy teeth cut my hands like razors when we played tug. She insisted I toss her a tennis ball while I cooked dinner. She dug holes in our newly seeded backyard. Dixie Lou made me impossibly happy. Having a dog was one of those rare things in life, like Paris or the Grand Canyon, that were even better than what I had imagined. Way better.

Dixie Lou became our canine training wheels. Scott and I learned how to live with a dog, how to train one, and a good deal about how to think like one, at least a high-energy Australian shepherd who would give her life for the almighty Frisbee. We made some mistakes, despite myriad puppy classes and a library of training tomes. Though we did as books advised and led Dixie Lou over different types of flooring when she was a puppy, to familiarize her with the feel of them on her little paw pads, we somehow skipped linoleum, which is why Dixie Lou trembled at the mere sight of those smooth, synthetic tiles. She moved across them mincingly, like a new ice skater at a teeming rink. This ruined most dog-friendly stores for her, not to mention the vet's office, where she shook and drooled with anxiety. Until Dixie Lou, I had not realized that linoleum lurks around every corner.

We also never thought to introduce Dixie Lou to ceiling fans. When she spotted her first one whooshing away in a hotel hallway, our pup crouched and froze. She peered worriedly at the whirring monster overhead, then pressed herself flat against the wall to avoid walking directly under the turning blades. From then on, whenever Dixie Lou padded into a new room, she'd worriedly lift her eyes to the ceiling and check for spinning blades. I found myself doing the same, even when I was alone.

Two mistakes—that's not so bad. We accommodated those, as well as a few of her other foibles, such as when she sometimes mouthed our arms or nipped at our coats when we tried to put her Frisbee away, what we called a "devil dog attack." We put up with her quirks because each time we walked through the door, Dixie Lou always greeted us as if we were king and queen of the Aussies, peeling back her lips in her strange, toothy grin, snorting loudly, and wiggling her bottom like a hula dancer as she circled our feet. She trailed us around the house, slept until we got up in the morning, and watched TV with us. Dixie Lou and I spent countless hours in the nearby park, where I discovered trails through the thick beach roses, learned the changing rhythms of the tides, and watched full moons set Casco Bay ablaze. After a day of squeezing every second out of every hour at the newspaper, I squandered time with abandon outside with my pup. I came upon baby snakes and plucked puffy milkweed pods for no reason. I found like-minded company during my rambles. I befriended a car mechanic whose clothes were so shabby that I first assumed he was homeless. He would walk Oscar, his amiable, water-loving Rottweiler mix, to the beach each night, even in the winter, for a saltwater dip. I chatted daily with a federal judge whose svelte, chocolate-colored standard poodle wouldn't come when he called. "Zoe," His Honor would plead over and over as his dog galloped in great leggy circles around him. I listened to a sewage engineer's dating woes while I wove my fingers through his old mutt's wiry coat.

My redhead pup shaped my days into a soothing, steady pattern of outings and feedings, but she also reacquainted me, now firmly middle-aged, with an unpredictability that made life fresh in a way it hadn't been since I was a kid. A cat would send us both sprinting, Dixie Lou after the cat, me after her. If I tossed her Frisbee too far into the bay, I might find myself wading in up to my thighs to fetch the disk from the tide's tight grasp. When I saw a ranger headed in our direction, I'd slink down a side trail, even hide behind a bush, to avoid a ticket for having her off leash where I shouldn't. I climbed fences, broke trail for her through thigh-high snow, and wedged myself under parked cars to retrieve tennis balls. I found the old me, the tomboy who once spent whole afternoons looking for crawdads in a stream or throwing mud balls to the neighborhood Irish setters, the me I'd lost to mortgages and deadlines and dinner parties.

• • •

If you love dogs, a dark image may lurk at the back of your mind: all those homeless dogs barking in shelters, all those faces behind kennel doors. The American Society for the Prevention of Cruelty to Animals estimated in 2012 that nearly four million dogs go into shelters every year. They are largely strays and dogs surrendered by their owners. Only a fraction of shelter dogs have been beaten or underfed or both, and confiscated by animal control officers. Wherever they come from, most shelter dogs are adults and are rarely spayed or neutered. Most are mutts, but there is a show ring's worth of pedigrees, too—cocker spaniels, redbone coonhounds, even Newfoundlands, the very breed that so gamely accompanied Lewis and Clark into the unknown.

They all need homes.

Americans have always behaved paradoxically when it comes to canines. We in the land of Rin Tin Tin, Toto, and Benji are a doggy nation, no doubt. You'll find a pooch in one out of three homes. We have, in fact, more dogs than children. We lavish some $52 billion annually on these pups, more than we spend even on alcohol. We open our wallets for puppy pedicures, ecofriendly chew toys, dog strollers, even faux testicles for neutered male dogs. Yet there are people who will unload their dogs on the local shelter when they outgrow their puppy collars or shed on the new sectional couch. Beagles are given up because they bark too much, Great Danes because they are pony-size, border collies because they herd the kids. Worse, people will leave their dogs behind in a park for someone to find or will push them out of the car near a farmer's field to fend for themselves. When I lived in Burlington, Vermont, each spring brought daffodils, longer days, and a wave of stray dogs on the street as the graduating students from the University of Vermont drove off in their Volvos and left their pets behind.

Solid numbers are hard to come by, but the most optimistic estimates say that about a half or so of the dogs in shelters find homes each year. Approximately a third or more of shelter dogs are put down each year, some 1.2 million by the ASPCA's count in 2012. Some of these dogs, the severely ill or dangerous, need to be euthanized, but many do not. There are shelters that still put down dogs because they don't have enough room for them. What would save those animals are homes. There are few tragedies with such an obvious and simple answer. Homes—all we have to do to save these dogs is find them homes. The question is how.

I confess that for most of my life, like most dog lovers, I avoided thinking about that painful question. I confess that, like most people, I have normally avoided any intractable, overwhelming problem. My few turns at do-goodism had not gone well. I flipped pancakes, some thirty at a time, while volunteering at a homeless shelter. I could never make the pancakes fast enough, and the line of ragged, hungry men would eventually trail out the door. Discouraged, I quit. When I was a candy striper at a children's hospital while in high school, I barely made it through the summer before I handed in my uniform because the endless number of bandaged, ailing kids whose families never seemed to visit began to haunt me. After my father died, I made one pathetically small donation to the American Lung Association, triggering an avalanche of mail from charities of every ilk. One person can make a difference, but in my experience it never feels like it when you are that one person. Sometimes it just feels like a pain in the neck.

Then, on the morning of September 11, 2001, I snapped on the television and watched with Dixie Lou by my side as the second tower of the World Trade Center tumbled down. The attacks of 9/11 had the same effect on me as my father's sudden death had seven years before. It drove home the waywardness of life, how it was unpredictable as a wild animal, which made me want to seize it all the more. I'm not much of a dreamer, so my bucket list has always been filled with small potatoes. I eyed one near the top. I had long wanted to walk dogs at the local shelter but had never managed to carve out the time between my job and the demands of wearing out a herding dog every day. Yet I had left the newspaper to write a book on the quirky world of American cook-offs. Now that my time was my own, I could spare a couple of hours once a week for shelter dogs. In some ways it would be penance for having bought the purebred at my feet.

So, one night that fall, I drove along a road that swerved through farm fields and stands of old trees to the Animal Refuge League of Greater Portland, which is actually one town over, in Westbrook. I took a seat on the scuffed floor of a room packed with eager would-be volunteers, nearly all women. We politely listened to a brief talk by the young ponytailed volunteer director and then crowded around her to fill our names in the blocks of a time chart. I elbowed in to sign up for dog walks from 7:30 to 9:30 a.m. on Fridays, an ungodly hour for me. I can rise early enough, but my brain isn't on the clock until 8:00 a.m. Still, I was excited. Before I even leashed one dog, I told all my friends about having signed up. They responded as if I had told them I was going skydiving. "Wow, that's brave," they said in a way that lent "brave" the ring of "insane." Then I got long explanations, accompanied with furrowed brows and sad eyes, as to why *they* could never do that. They would want to adopt all the dogs. Their hearts would break. The shelter, all those miserable barking dogs, would make them suicidal. Me, me, me, they mewed. I wanted to ask, "But what about the dogs?" Instead, I nodded and started to fret. I had been worrying only about the early hour, if I could think straight enough to hook a leash on a wound-up golden retriever. Now I began to worry if I would leave the shelter each Friday sobbing, if it would get all *me, me, me.* Yet, for a mere two hours a week, for the dogs, I thought, I could at least give the shelter a shot.

That is how I unwittingly fell down the rabbit hole of an intractable problem, how my life with shelter dogs began, a far busier but more meaningful life that began to shape itself around a key question: How could more dogs find homes? And I've been chasing down answers to that question ever since I scrawled my name in that time chart more than fifteen years ago. Along the way, I've adopted two troubled dogs, fostered two more, brought home a dozen or so for overnights, and worked with so many at the shelter that I can't remember most of their names, I'm sorry to say. The dogs never stop changing, but the question remains the same: How can I, you, we, as communities, as a society, find more homes for these dogs?

At first I looked for answers only in my own volunteer work, as in "How can I help find this lovely mutt at my feet a home?" Eventually, though, I wanted answers for the vast number of homeless dogs. I looked for answers for them in conversations with leading shelter directors, researchers, people on the ground, trainers, adoption counselors, and caretakers. I searched for the newest thinking and the boldest ideas. In a world that too often relies on anecdotes and myths, I searched for facts. What I learned has been eye-opening and inspiring. Rich Avanzino, the "father" of the no-kill movement, an eternal yet pragmatic optimist, told me that he believes that within his lifetime, every animal in the United States that needs a home will find one. Rich is in his early seventies. Still, he could be right.

Avanzino has often been accused of being unrealistic, but since he became the maverick director of the San Francisco Society for the Prevention of Cruelty to Animals in 1976, the number of cats and dogs euthanized in shelters has dropped from an estimated twenty-four million to just under four million. Shelter dogs have, against all odds, become popular, even a status symbol. In the dog parks of Boston, people proudly introduce their mutts as "rescues," almost as if they were a sought-after breed. The number of no-kill cities, such as San Francisco, Reno, Nevada, and Austin, Texas, has hit two hundred and is growing. An estimated 83 percent of pet owners now spay or neuter their animals. Donations to animal shelters and welfare organizations are at an all-time high. There are many reasons to hope.

If you have avoided thinking about homeless dogs, now is clearly the time to do so. They are not, as it turns out, an unsolvable problem.

To answer a big question you must also answer thousands of small ones. How do you pull a halter onto a whirling juvenile German shepherd in the tight confines of a shelter kennel? How do you persuade a petrified, half-blind pug to let you hook a leash to his collar? How do you convince people looking for a pet to consider a dog's personality before his breed or color? How do you convince people to spay their pets, or to license them, or to train them to come, or that dogs are not people? I have found many answers since that first morning, but back then, I didn't realize that I was on a quest. When I opened the shelter's door and stepped inside, all I was thinking about was how I could hear the dogs barking even though they were two rooms away. Opening the door to the roomful of kennels was like cracking the stadium door at a rock concert. The din rushed at me, pressed against my chest. The franticness alone, a mix of excitement and desperation, made me tense. The dogs were understandably manic. They had been closed in their kennels for thirteen hours, from around 6:00 the night before. I yelled to a shelter staffer, asking which dogs I should walk first. "What?" she hollered back.

Next I learned about the smell. When I opened that door to the kennels, the odor was as strong as an outhouse. It burrowed inside my sinuses. I scrunched my nose and held my breath as best I could. My job, essentially, was to take the pooches for a stroll so the concrete floors of their kennels could be hosed down. Most shelter dogs develop epic bladders and bowels. However, the puppies and young dogs would often leave puddles and little logs with paw prints in them. But it was the dogs with the runs, from the unfamiliar food, the stress, or some dastardly gastric bug, who would leave greasy slicks. Sometimes the dogs would have smeared the poop all over the concrete floor, their bedding, and themselves. The sight was something out of a madhouse, but with a dog happily wagging his tail in the middle of it. As I leashed up some of these dogs, they'd often excitedly jump up on me and leave a dab or two of poop on my jacket sleeve, which I'd notice only later, while standing in line at a coffee shop. Always, I learned, check your coat for brown spots.

I had last been in a shelter in junior high school, when my mom let me pick out a dog, a thick-chested, short-legged terrier mix with black eyes whom I inexplicably named Tang. I picked Tang because he was the only quiet one in his crowded kennel. He was quiet, we learned in the days after we took him home, because he had pneumonia.

On the drive home, I happily held Tang on my lap, but that shelter weighed on my mind: the thundering barking, the mob of dogs crammed as many as six to a kennel with no toys or beds.

I braced myself for something at least a little along those lines when I began volunteering at the Animal Refuge League, but found instead a light-filled room with two long rows of kennels, twenty-four in all. Each dog had his own kennel, along with a blanket and a raised bed. A dusty boom box on the concrete floor played Mozart and Beethoven. There were fenced yards to play fetch in and a sprawling, wooded park behind the shelter for strolling. I trotted dogs on paths that looped through pine forests, along a small, reed-lined stream, and across an unmowed field that glinted gold in the fall. To reach the back door that led to these paths I had to pass the incinerator, where dogs who had been euthanized were cremated, but I had no time to contemplate its dark use. The dogs on their leashes, so eager to get out, pulled me quickly past.

Over those two hours, as the woods warmed up and birds sounded the start of another day, I would walk between six and eight dogs. In the beginning, I sometimes got lost on the park trails, but the dogs, as they so often do, patiently showed me the way. Some wanted to press their noses deep into the dry weeds. Others raced down the muddy trails, and I clung to their leashes, dug in my heels, and leaned back like a water-skier. Some of the puppies just wanted to play, and I would sit cross-legged in the field's tall grass and wrestle with them until, exhausted, they crawled into my lap. The old dogs, with their rheumy eyes and unsteady back legs, were the easiest to walk and often were content just to sit in the sun and be stroked. It was ridiculously simple to make all these dogs happy, if only for twenty minutes. It was ridiculously easy to do something good, to make a difference.

Life can get a little exciting with shelter dogs. An exuberant young pit bull mix made such a mad dash for the marshy stream that he jerked the leash out of my hand. I rushed knee deep into the water to grab hold of him. It was early December. My gloves, shoes, socks, and the bottom of my pants were soaked. By the time we returned to the shelter, the hem of my wet pants had iced up and one foot was completely numb. On another winter morning, I slipped on a patch of ice as I walked a different pittie, Baxter, a one-year-old with a blocky head and a joyful nature. I landed so hard on the frozen trail that the leash sprang out of my hand. As my rear thumped to the cold ground, I saw Baxter's black-and-white backside zoom away from me. Running after a fleeing dog is usually fruitless, though it's exactly what you want to do. Most dogs will only keep running, out of fear or out of fun, thinking you've joined in the hijinks. I sat up and called for Baxter once, again, then a third time as he started to slip out of sight around a bend between a clump of pines. He miraculously spun around and returned, but raced past me, just out of reach, snorting and smiling as he passed. I got on my knees. Again, he buzzed me. This went on for the next five minutes, what was a great game of chicken for Baxter, and, for me, a nightmare during which I had to chirp gamely, "Come, Baxter, come." I had little to work with. When you walk a shelter dog, you are walking a dog you have no bond with. You often have just met. Some are even a little scared of you. Even if they aren't, the command to come is Greek to most. Finally, Baxter got just close enough that I was able to dive to my right and, with an outstretched hand, snag the leash. He yanked hard against it, dragging me a little on my side over the icy grass, but I held tight. Then Baxter dove on my chest playfully and lapped my frosty cheeks with his warm tongue. I sat up and rubbed his ears. I kissed him on his fat head. He would not run off to be creamed by a car, and my life would not be consumed by guilt and self-loathing. We each smiled, though I kept my tongue in my mouth.

To walk shelter dogs, I also quickly learned, you must be not only fast on your feet but also open-minded. Pitties such as Baxter regularly filled the kennels at the Animal Refuge League. Before my first pittie, I was worried about these reputed bad boys of the canine world. I had not been totally immune to the endless news stories about the breed's reputed viciousness and other myths. I had watched a documentary film in which one attacked a female police officer, sinking his canines into her breast, of all places. Still, I mustered my courage. If you are too afraid to walk pitties, there won't be many dogs for you to walk at most shelters. I took out my first, a bruiser with a mostly white coat and the trimmed ears of a fighter, on full alert. I held his leash taut in both hands. I was calm and cool with my commands, using none of my usual happy talk. I watched for the least little bit of body language that signaled he would turn and latch his wide jaw onto my breast. Of course he didn't. He loped along happily, throwing me the occasional sparkly-eyed smiles over his shoulder that seemed to say, "Isn't this fun?" By the end of the walk, I felt a little silly.

I eventually fell hard for the pitties, the way you do for anyone who is unjustifiably misunderstood. I owed it to them, for my own prejudices and for the entire world's. Besides, they grinned goofily through their kennel doors. They were some of the most attentive dogs in the shelter, always eyeing me with a "What can I do for you?" look. Some wagged their tails so hard they loudly thwacked against the tiled walls of their kennels. Unaware of their killer reputations, they nuzzled my legs and sighed when I scratched their broad heads.

The only danger the pitties posed was the same that all strong dogs did. They could pull me this way or that. They could trip me or knock me down when they frantically leapt on me in the kennel as I tried to leash them. That is why you need some muscles to walk shelter dogs. Each time I took one out, we had to pass through three doors, the first being the biggest adventure. It opened into a tiled hallway, where Angry, a feral cat who lived in the shelter and seemed to have a death wish, might be lazily padding by. If that was the case, I would have to dig my weight in to keep some gorilla-size young punk of a dog from lunging at Angry, who would slowly sit down and, I swear, smirk. God help me if the floor had just been mopped.

Past Angry and his taunts and through another door, the incinerator loomed. The shelter staff fired up the dusty metal monstrosity rarely, and did so only early in the morning, gently loading in the limp body of a dog or cat, closing the door, and flicking a switch. Like many shelters that accept all the dogs who come their way, the shelter euthanized the ones they deemed too ill or too dangerous to be put up for adoption. That is why, as I learned in those early days, when you work with shelter dogs, you are bound to break your heart now and again, even if you are as dry-eyed as they come, as I liked to think of myself. Once, I fell in love with a caramel-coated, green-eyed pittie named Sadie. She was small and had a slight point to her muzzle. Some dogs actually improve in a shelter, with regular meals, exercise, and affection. Yet Sadie was one of the ones who did not. When she arrived, she came out of the kennels on a leash well enough, but as the weeks passed, moving her past the other dogs became trickier and trickier. She'd rage and rage at them, charging and roaring. I'd pull her leash tight, brace my arms, and then hurry her along with a hearty "Let's go!" Once outside, she became wiggly and silly like most young dogs. If she wanted a pat, she butted the top of her anvil-shaped head against my shins. I loved her.

One morning, as we were coming back inside, Sadie suddenly shoved her way between my legs and charged with teeth bared at a rangy black dog in his kennel. I grabbed the kennel door with one hand, to keep from falling, and pulled her leash hard with the other. Sadie and I were a knot of legs, leash, and raving dog that I couldn't seem to untangle. Trying to get at the black dog, Sadie clacked her jaws madly right between my calves. She could so easily have bitten me accidentally. For the first time, I was scared. I had never heard the growl of a dog bent on destruction. The sound was monstrous, heart-rattling, nothing like the few "dogfights" I had seen in the park near our house. I regained my footing somehow and dragged Sadie away from the mutt's kennel and into her own. By the time I unhooked her leash, she was wagging her tail and butting her head on my shin. I was breathing hard. I kneeled to pet her, but also to calm my racing heart. On my way out, I told a staff member about the incident, so she could warn other volunteers. The very next day, a volunteer's thigh got between Sadie and a dog in a kennel. Sadie, I was told, bit the woman hard enough to send her to the emergency room. Between that and my misadventure, the shelter staff decided that Sadie had become too dangerous to handle. My copper-colored girl was put down. I was sorry I had said anything, but there was no way I could not have.

There were other, smaller dark moments. A few dogs, understandably, dug their paws in when you headed back into the shelter. You could coax some with handfuls of greasy treats, but others you had to drag across the concrete floor. Some dodged and weaved at the end of their leashes as I pulled them along. Some collapsed in a heap, which, if they were too hefty for me to lift, became a real problem. I couldn't leave them while I went for another set of arms. I would have to wait until someone happened by. Like a prison guard, I had to shove a dog or two into their kennels and slam the door quickly with a thud. They'd rush the kennel door, throw their paws hysterically up against the chain link, and peer at me wild-eyed, pleading.

There were also dogs who languished for months, such as a shepherdy mutt named Spuddy, whose ribs pushed against his whitish-blond coat. He couldn't gain weight and had the runs no matter what the vet did. Many mornings, Spuddy was coated with poop from his black nose to the end of his curled tail. You had to hose him down outside before you could walk him. Though he seemed to be shrinking away, Spuddy was easy to walk, loved to nuzzle—which, once I hosed him off, I was happy to do—and held his tail high on the trails. At times, he looked befuddled but never discouraged.

Some mornings I would arrive to find dogs who had been adopted smiling at me once again from behind their kennel doors. They had been returned. If the pooches came back quickly, they were usually no worse for the wear. They would paw at me gleefully, greeting an old friend. It bothered me that people had given up on them after a night or two, but it did not bother the dogs. For them, it was just another passing adventure. Yet, if they were in their adoptive homes for a few weeks or months, they often came back to the shelter looking confused and anxious, and sometimes their behavior problems would have worsened or they would have developed new ones. They were afraid of men or would growl over their dinner. Some dogs came back twice their size, as if they had been fattened for slaughter. None of this would help get them adopted again.

What I came to hate most was the offhand neglect I witnessed. I rarely saw badly abused dogs, but ones who were no longer wanted by their owners came in daily. These pets often had not been exercised or trained or neutered. People dropped off dogs who didn't even know their names. One day, a cocker spaniel arrived who was deaf because his repeated ear infections had not been treated. I soon realized that the sinister dogfighters, twisted animal abusers, and deranged hoarders of the world were actually less common than I'd assumed. Not that they don't do far more than their fair share of harm to canines, but our kennels were filled with the cast-off pets of people who were good neighbors, devoted parents, college graduates, churchgoers, former Eagle Scouts, even self-professed dog lovers. The confused-looking new arrivals, who'd only hours before had a home, made the imbalance of our ancient friendship clear. Perhaps we can get by without dogs, but they, unfortunately, can't get by without us.

This should have given me a stomachache but surprisingly it didn't. I did avoid the front desk, where people dropped off their pets, for fear I might slap someone across the face—such as the woman who made her young, sobbing son stand by her as she handed over the family cat. "I told you if you didn't help this would happen," she announced to the boy in front of the entire room.

Maybe I should have slapped her.

My undersize biceps expanded, I'd come home with bruises I couldn't account for, and I got a fat lip I was oddly proud of. Still, by far, most of the walks were uneventful, and I often found myself listening to the chickadees chirp or considering the way the morning light played down the slope of a German shepherd's back. Walking shelter dogs could be almost meditative at times, as we silently shared the simple pleasures of companionship and the wealth of the great outdoors. When my mother came for her annual summer visit, I took her to the shelter to show her how much fun it was. She ended up sobbing after we walked a chunky black Lab with a slight limp. "What will happen to him?" she worried when we put him back in his kennel. On the drive home, she told me, "I don't know how you do it."

In fact, not only could I do it, but I found that the weeks I couldn't go to the shelter, I missed it terribly. I loved the liveliness, the constant flow of new faces and all their stories, most with happy endings. I was not tempted to adopt any of the dogs, because they streamed through the shelter like a river, in the side door and, sooner or later, out the front door. They leapt into the backseat of car after car and drove off with new families and most likely to better lives. In the meantime, I met all types of pups: slack-mouthed giants; spinning, whippety things; and brassy herding types. I liked that the dogs never saw me as a "good" person. There was none of the awkwardness that comes with helping humans, of that uneasily unbalanced relationship. We just went for walks and had some fun. I didn't need a thank-you. Their ample, infectious joy, which filled me every Friday morning, was more than enough. I drove off after my two hours and eight dogs anything but depressed. I was, surprisingly, exhilarated.

That feeling has never gone away, and that's why, all these years later, I find myself on a subzero night piloting a lean, acrobatic pittie named Greg across the icy streets of Boston. It's why I'm still looking for answers, for him and for all the other homeless dogs. It's why I wrote this book.

Dixie Lou

1

STRAYS

Random events, coincidences, can suddenly make you realize you need a dog or, in our case, a second dog.

After a long day on a favorite beach, as Scott, Dixie Lou, and I padded barefoot across a parking lot still hot from the day's sun, a middle-aged couple rushed toward us. "Can we pet your dog?" the woman called breathlessly. We set down beach chairs and heavy baskets stuffed with sodden, sandy towels by our car so they could, but Dixie Lou was never one to hold still for love. With arms outstretched, the man and woman in their bathing suits and flip-flops trailed our dog as she circled our station wagon with a tennis ball in her mouth. Our Aussie snorted and wiggled her bottom good-humoredly. Once or twice, as Dixie Lou changed course and slipped past their legs, the couple got to run their sunburned hands down her warm back. Then the threesome would circle in the other direction as Scott and I watched. As they lapped our car, the couple told us they had had an Aussie who died. They had loved her intensely, as we did Dixie Lou. I asked when they had lost their pup, assuming it must have been recently, given their obvious desperation to lay their hands on our Aussie.

The woman's face tightened. "Five years ago," she said. They were still brokenhearted, she said, too heartbroken to get another dog.

Scott and I looked at each other. We didn't want to be them. Dixie Lou was only four, but all of a sudden we felt the press of time. On the drive home we decided we needed a second dog soon. This new one would be a shelter dog. After walking them, the natural next step was to bring one home. Besides, we were ready for a dog who might be full of other people's mistakes. We would look for a herding-type dog, who often fare poorly being boxed up in a shelter. They spin in their kennels, bounce anxiously off the doors. Few people can handle a herder's exuberance and work drive. Dixie Lou had proved we could. By the time we pulled into our driveway the plan was set.

I began to keep an eye out at the shelter for a border collie or another Australian shepherd or a blend of either. The rest of the summer drifted by. Each Friday, I would find the kennels filled with the usual pitties and Lab mixes, along with a few random purebred dogs. The head kennel worker, a woman with big eyes and a husky voice, would tell me of border collies who had come and gone since I was last there. Finally, one early September morning, I came upon a seven-month-old border collie mix staring uneasily through his kennel door. He was all black but otherwise had the trim waist, the curlicue tail, and the loose, long coat of the breed. He also had the alert eyes—too alert in his case. The sign on his kennel said his name was Busy Bee. He trembled when I looked at him. He licked his lips. He was scared of people. Otherwise he was perfect.

Who would want such a petrified pup? I thought. Maybe not even me. I could safely take a week to consider Busy Bee and all his nervousness. Though we hadn't even decided to adopt him, Scott and I began to debate what we would change his name to. We discussed which training classes to sign him up for. As so easily happens with dogs, our fates and his easily twined in our minds, though Scott had yet to meet the scared pup. The next Friday, I came in and found a transformed dog. Busy Bee wiggled when he saw me. He tossed his front paws on his kennel door to greet me, which is when I noticed a sign that said he'd been adopted. My dog was going home with someone else. "Why didn't we just get him?" Scott asked when I got home. "They took our dog."

A few weeks later, another waifish border collie mix appeared, almost magically. I had walked dogs for two hours and was ambling down the row of kennels saying good-bye to each. Suddenly I came upon this demure-looking dog I hadn't noticed all morning. She had sidled up close to her door so that, with her sad, dark eyes, she could see down the row of kennels. When I paused in front of her, she fled to her bed at the back of her kennel. She tucked her tail tight between her legs and looked at me over her shoulder. This dog was the reverse of Busy Bee. She had all the markings of a border collie, the white socks and tail tip, but her coat was short like a Lab's. A neat white line ran between her eyes, bisecting her small face. Her muzzle was squarish, like a hound's. Her ears flopped.

As I opened the door and went in, she pinched her dark eyes. I slid down on the floor to make myself smaller and less threatening. She kept her distance. Her white-tipped tail fluttered. After she gave me a few more nervous looks, I let her be. There was no name or age mentioned on her kennel door. There was a red sticker, which meant that only the staff could handle her, not volunteers. I had accidentally broken the rules by entering her kennel.

It wasn't exactly love at first sight, more a kind of illogical determination that overtook me not to the make the same mistake twice, which is when you often make a different kind of mistake. I put a hold on her at the front desk. I asked her name. Bumble Bee: she was Busy Bee's sister. "It's fate," I told the shelter worker at the front desk. It was, though fate is its own animal, a wild, unpredictable one with its own mind.

• • •

Bumble Bee had a story, a dramatic one, but it was vague at best. She was born amid the fury of a Maine February on a small farm in Cornish, a village close to the New Hampshire border. As the story went, she and her mother, Honey Bee, who resembled an oversize beagle, and her brother, the lovely Busy Bee, lived under the farmhouse's porch. There the small family could hide from the winds and the snow, but not from the cold's sharp bite. A litter of two is small for a dog, who typically has four to six. Maybe some pups had succumbed to temperatures that easily slipped below zero. That any of them, born utterly helpless, blind, survived the fierce wind chills seems nearly impossible. Honey Bee must have been a good mother.

Maybe the mother was the farmer's pet, but an outside one. Maybe he fed them. Yet given how terrified the pups were of humans and of being indoors, they had likely spent their early months wandering through the leafless apple orchards and dormant fields or snuggling up tight against Honey Bee for as long as they could to stay warm. The Bees were akin to barn cats, living along the edges of the farm, outliers who were mostly left to fend for themselves.

The Bees were something that has become a relative rarity in the United States: stray dogs. Long gone are the days when it wasn't that

43

unusual to have a stray just show up in your suburban backyard, the way Curly, my childhood dog, did in 1959. The sweet shepherd mix (who actually resembled an Aussie, I realized later) had no collar. He did have mange. My mother gave him special baths for weeks, during which his skin bled and his fur came out in her hands. When his coat grew back, it was lush and wavy and won him his name. For the next eighteen years he chased sticks, did battle with the boxer down the street, roamed our freshly minted neighborhood, and scanned driveways for parked cars with open doors. Having found some station wagon left so, Curly would sometimes climb in and take a nap.

Today a roving pet dog, never mind a car sitting in a driveway with its door open, can inspire a rash of panicky 911 calls. How times have changed. Not all that long ago, when life was harsher yet in some ways more relaxed, strays, or "tramps," as they were called, wandered many American cities and towns. Life on the street, picking through a city's plentiful garbage, was considered the natural, if unfortunate, state of a canine. Yet strays also had their good points. They could be put to work—say, hooked up to a ragpicker's small wagon for a day and then let loose come sunset, maybe with a handful of food. They cleared the streets of trash and killed rats. Two strays in 1860s San Francisco were such expert ratters that the press followed the adventures of Bummer and Lazarus, medium-size mutts who lived outside a saloon and, as one reporter put it, "wagged with one tail." When a new dogcatcher nabbed Lazarus, an angry mob swarmed the pound, demanding his release. Soon Lazarus rejoined his best friend, Bummer, and the city declared the two mutts exempt from the stray ordinances. Off they ran. They reportedly stopped a runaway horse pulling a cart. They also ransacked shops and picked fights with other dogs. Bummer killed a sheep or two. Lazarus died in 1863—like many strays, from poison. A year later a drunk kicked Bummer down a staircase hard enough to kill him. Bummer was still popular enough that the drunk was thrown into jail, and Mark Twain, then a young newspaperman, penned an obituary for the stray who died "full of years, honor, disease and fleas."

Though Bummer and Lazarus won hearts, few other stray dogs did. When homeless dogs were picked up, it was not to help them but because they woke people with their barking, pooped on the sidewalk, and harassed the horses, cows, pigs, and chickens that crowded city streets. Stray dogs, like rats, were considered pests. They were also considered a health hazard. People wrongly believed that rabies was caused by hot weather and that panting was an omen of the disease. During the "dog days" of summer, when Sirius, the Dog Star, flickered in the heavy, humid sky,

New York City police were ordered to shoot all unmuzzled dogs on sight. Anyone could earn a bounty for killing a stray. People who had pet dogs were wise to keep them inside until the combustive heat and hysteria had fizzled.

This was the status quo for strays when my hero, the long-faced failed playwright Henry Bergh, founded the ASPCA in 1866. Bergh did not start the association to help homeless dogs, as I had once assumed. He launched the country's first humane organization primarily to help the over-worked, often abused workhorses who dropped dead in the streets by the thousands every year. Yet Bergh did not ignore the city's many homeless dogs. He also protested their treatment at the city pounds, where dogs were routinely clubbed to death or drowned in the East River. He also spoke out against how corrupt the pounds were. Workers earned only as much as they collected in redemption fees, and many resorted to kidnap-ping and ransoming pet dogs. Despite this, Bergh turned down the city's request that the ASPCA take over management of the pounds, fearing that City Hall would not pay the organization what it would cost to do so.

After Bergh died in 1888 the ASPCA did take on management of the city's pounds. It raised funds to run them by charging a one-dollar fee for dog licenses, and the staff were paid a salary—no one had to kidnap a dog to make a living. The ASPCA became not only a professional operation, but also an effective one. In its early years, it rounded up and euthanized more strays than the city had previously. The organization was applauded for clearing New York's streets of bothersome strays. It also euthanized these dogs more humanely, by gassing them. This was progress, and in short order, private animal welfare societies around the country followed the ASPCA's lead and took on animal control services. This model survived for most of the next century, though Bergh's fears proved true. New York, like most cities and towns, never covered the costs of collecting strays or running the pounds, and humane societies were forced to fund-raise to pay for the services they'd taken on. Worse, though they were animal welfare organizations, they euthanized millions of homeless cats and dogs in the decades that followed, a practice that earned shelters a reputation they are still living down.

When I talk to shelter leaders, I get mixed messages about stray dogs. Some think they are a problem of the past. One says to me, "Strays?" incredulously, as if I'm the biggest ninny he's ever talked to. He's right that the number of strays that were once picked up by legions of animal control officers has dropped dramatically. Still, some leaders, especially shelter directors in major cities or bedraggled rural counties, think strays remain a serious problem, and a puzzling one to boot. Strays still make up possibly half of the dogs going into shelters nationally, as many as two million. That sounds like a problem, maybe even a crisis, but it's a crisis most of us never see.

A stray dog is basically a loose dog, or "a dog running at large," which has a comically criminal tone to it, as if the dog might hold up a bank. A dog can be "at large" for all kinds of reasons. It could be someone's pet who is allowed to go where he pleases and see what adventures the day brings. All our family pets roamed up through the 1980s, the last hurrah for dogs wandering middle-class suburban neighborhoods. We opened the front door for our merry, lovely Lab mix, Ruby, whenever she stood by it with expectant eyes and a wagging tail. Each afternoon, she'd amble down to my youngest brother's elementary school and wait for him outside. We found out that a woman blocks and blocks away would feed our mutt pancakes on her back porch. Ruby ruined countless touch football games by running off with the ball, a trail of little boys in pursuit squealing her name to the heavens. We stacked the footballs she brought home in the garage, where neighborhood kids could come reclaim them. Ruby was also regularly picked up by the neighborhood cop. He would open the door to his cruiser, and in our lovely girl would step. Ruby loved car rides. The cop knew our address and would drive her home, which is why our scofflaw luckily never went to the pound. My mother would apologize, yet again, and pay the ticket, which she considered a small price for Ruby's freedom. Life was more casual then, maybe too much so, but Ruby had a good run of stealing footballs, eating pancakes, and walking my kid brother home from school every day—and maybe even holding up a bank or two. Who knows? So much of her life was her own.

Life seems anything but casual now, when you can get a ticket for walking your dog off leash even when she's right by your side, as I have learned the hard way. Yet there are still holdouts who let their pets run, typically in poorer, urban neighborhoods or in the country, most of which Maine is. Next to no one lets his dog roam in Portland, but many do in the farming communities, the old mill towns, and the shaggier villages that make up the sprawling state. That explains why nearly all the strays at the Animal Refuge League of Greater Portland are collected by their owners, who sheepishly pay the fine and go home, where they probably let their dogs out the kitchen door again. Some of these dogs may have gotten loose inadvertently, escaped fences, broken loose from their leashes somehow, or slipped out a tear in a screen door, as Dixie Lou did once. These kinds of "strays" have families who want them back.

A stray could also be a village dog or a community dog, an animal whom people might feed, even pet, but whom no one truly "owns." That has been the fate of most dogs throughout history and still is in many foreign countries. I've seen them sleeping along or even in the road in Mexico, wandering some poor farms in Spain, and sunning themselves in the town squares of Havana. In this country, if I wanted to see village dogs, I'd go to a Native American reservation, such as the Pine Ridge Reservation in South Dakota, home of the Oglala Lakota tribe. In fact, you could find every kind of stray at Pine Ridge, where countless dogs run loose on the country's largest reservation. Pine Ridge's treeless, wind-swept expanse comprises some of the poorest counties in America. Where life is hard for humans, you can be sure it is hard for dogs.

Wherever they come from, most of the dogs that fill most shelters are abandoned pets. These dogs are truly homeless, the ones in greatest need of a shelter's help. These are the dogs I know best, dogs like Sandy, who was the color of onyx, with a bald tail and the rough coat of having lived on the run for at least two years. Someone had fed her, even built a little shed for her, at a storage facility far south of Boston. That is why when Sandy came into the shelter, she wasn't in such bad shape, with just some arthritis, a touch of kidney disease, and, like most long-term strays, heartworm. The vet guessed she was eleven. Whatever her age, Sandy had an old soul. At first she flinched when people reached over her head, but then she became a social butterfly, a sign that she had been someone's pet at some point. As friendly as Sandy could be, she didn't seem so in the kennels, where she barked and barked, raising her graying muzzle high as if calling someone, something, maybe an old owner, maybe the stars she had spent so many nights under. She reminded me of Buck in Jack London's *The Call of the Wild*, a dog who hadn't left all his wolfishness behind. Most people visiting the kennel did not make the literary connection. After six months of Sandy carrying on, unnerving most would-be adopters with that crazy howl, an elderly man, raw from having just lost his wife, finally saw the old soul beyond the ruckus and took her home.

A feral dog is another kind of stray. They are the descendants of abandoned pets like Sandy. These former pets mate and have puppies, who then grow up never knowing life in a human home. The Bees were a perfect example. The mother, Honey, who must have been someone's pet at some point, given how comfortable she was with people, was left to fend for herself and then got pregnant. Her pups, Busy and Bumble, spent their months outside with their mother away from people. Puppies can easily adjust to life with another species, even a towering one with long,

51

insect-like appendages such as ours, if they are handled and cuddled. If they have not been, humans become as scary as Martians. Busy's and Bumble's fear of humans was a sure sign of their being feral, or what is also called unsocialized. Now I understand the ramifications of that, but the day I drove Bumble Bee home, I had no idea. In fact, I wasn't even aware of the existence of feral, or unsocialized, dogs. Back then, a stray was a stray to me. A stray was like Curly. Now I know better.

Mindy Naticchioni is, if only by default, a specialist in stray dogs. Those are the only kind of dogs you'll find at the Cuyahoga County Animal Shelter, about ten miles south of downtown Cleveland. The newish building with a handsome rotunda can be found amid a stretch of country littered with truck dealerships and vacant office buildings. The surrounding fields of trees and tall grasses look like they may still have the final say on this land. Inside the shelter, dogs bark their greetings loud and clear from the expansive adoption floor, and their roaring chorus might be more overwhelming if it weren't for the light pouring through the high windows overhead. These dogs, wagging at their kennel doors, if a tad thin or worn looking, come from all over the sprawling county that hugs Lake Erie's southern shore. Many come from downtown Cleveland, where people often ditch their pets in the city's many parks. Others come from empty houses and warehouses of East Cleveland, which in 2016 became the first city to file for bankruptcy in Ohio. Pitties that are picked up as strays in municipalities that ban them are sent here to the safe haven of Cuyahoga.

Wherever they come from, most of the dogs at the county pound are young, medium to extra-large, unneutered males, mostly pitties but also German shepherds and Rotties or mixes of those. That is why Naticchioni's facility regularly plucks little dogs, what she calls "fou-fous," from Cleveland's overflowing city shelter, which takes in as many as seventy-five dogs a week. The fou-fous add some variety to the shelter floor, can be housed two to three in a kennel, and fly out the door. "We can move a Chihuahua like it's on fire," she says. One week, Cuyahoga took in forty-six dogs from the city, half of them fou-fous, including an emaciated five-year-old dachshund they named String Bean. String Bean had wandered into a neighbor's yard. The neighbor reported him as a stray so that animal control could essentially save the dachshund from his owner. Naticchioni sent String Bean to a clinic and then on to a foster home to put on some weight.

Next to none of the strays who land in Cuyahoga is feral. There have been so few that Naticchioni says she can remember each one, such as Gigi and

Major, two fluffballs of black fur who had to be trapped. The young dogs had to spend weeks fostered with a trainer to learn how to be pets, which against all odds they did. Unlike Gigi and Major, Cuyahoga's strays are overwhelmingly pets who have been dumped. Many of them have the raggedy bald patches of mange from living outside on their own. A growing number of them have heartworm. Some have medical conditions the vets have never seen before, such as the dog with a strange genetic mutation that gave him a bony kind of bill like a platypus, and another who had an elongated clitoris. "That might make her hard to adopt out," Naticchioni tells me.

No matter what the strays are like, Naticchioni must take them. Any city or county facility is legally compelled to accept every stray who arrives at its door. Any private nonprofit shelter that contracts with a city or county to provide animal control has to do the same. Once a stray is picked up by an animal control officer or brought in by a good-hearted citizen, it has to go somewhere. That is how shelters can end up euthanizing for space, to make room for the dogs they are legally obliged to take in by putting down the dogs they were already legally obliged to take in—as insane as that sounds. When Naticchioni became director at Cuyahoga in 2013, that's exactly what she was afraid she'd have to do.

This isn't the career Naticchioni planned. She

did work part-time as an adoption counselor for a year at the Cleveland Animal Protective League while finishing her college degree in human resources. Then she landed a job at a trendy clothing chain for teens, traveling the country and fixing broken stores. She worried about cratering sales receipts, cranky store managers, and disheveled sweater displays. When she had righted one wobbly store, she'd go on to the next. Nobody's life was at stake. In her free time, she volunteered at the APL training the dogs. A private nonprofit, the APL is not obliged to take in strays and can turn owner surrenders away if its kennels are full. The APL never, ever has to euthanize for space. Before Naticchioni became director at Cuyahoga, the county shelter did so regularly. That was only one of its problems, according to an audit. That's why she took the job. The shelter was broken. Dogs obviously aren't T-shirts, but Naticchioni still thought she could fix it.

Naticchioni has to take every stray, but on any given day, she never knows how many that might be. The "stray season," Naticchioni tells me, begins around Easter. If that April week is uncharacteristically balmy, along with the early tulips will come seventy-five dogs. That number will settle down to the usual fifty dogs a week through the long days of summer, with another spike in dogs on the Fourth of July, unless it's a rainy Independence Day. As fall cools and dries the air, the number of strays begins to wax. The season ends with one last burst Thanksgiving week, when a bedraggled army of old dogs totters in. Naticchioni wonders if the Turkey Day strays appear because people gussy up their houses for the coming feast and houseguests, maybe install new wall-to-wall carpeting, and then turn out their creaky, incontinent pets.

At any given week in the year, though, the number of dogs can suddenly spike. When her kennels start to fill, it happens quickly, like a rogue wave rolling out of a calm sea. Twenty dogs will arrive one day. Another 20 will show up the next. She has kennels for 132 dogs in total. When she's down to 10 open ones, she and her staff start working the phones looking for room in other shelters and with rescue groups. As a last resort, she can put dogs in offices or meeting rooms. They can go into what's called "wires." That means tucking dogs in crates in the hall-ways, which is, at best, a very temporary solution. Crates are harder to clean than kennels. Stress and disease crest. Soon the halls will fill with the sound of dogs hacking from kennel cough. But if it comes to wires, and it has only twice so far, so be it, Naticchioni says. Better that than her worst fear, which hasn't come true yet. She has yet to euthanize one dog for space since she took the job.

In Ohio, as in every state, a stray dog is

presumed to be a lost pet. State law requires that the dog must be held for a requisite number of days before it is made adoptable. Massachusetts requires seven days. Maine calls for six, though the Animal Refuge League of Greater Portland will keep them for seven. If the dog is in Ohio, it's three days, not including the day the dog comes in, making the hold, in effect, four days. The hold starts anew every time an animal is transferred to another facility. If a dog is transferred twice, that could add up to nearly two weeks of limbo. All these strays waiting out the clock create a bottle-neck of dogs. They can't even be neutered or spayed. The dogs just sit there, which costs money. Worse, the stray hold prolongs a dog's time in a shelter, which is stressful and can make the dog's behavior worsen. Shelters, according to their own policy or state law, will keep dogs with ID tags, licenses, or microchips beyond the stray hold while they try to track down the owner. One shelter vet told me that she dreads finding microchips in a collarless dog. Many times those microchips lead to an out-of-date address or phone number, as it did with Biko, a cheery puggle I once walked. His chip was registered to no current address. The microchipping company had been sold several times over, and the last phone number listed for it was for a fax. Still, Biko had to sit in a kennel for a week before he could be put up for adoption.

The holds are obviously worthwhile if a dog is just loose or lost, but how many strays are? That's what Emily Weiss of the ASPCA wanted to know. Weiss, who oversees research at the ASPCA, is one of the shelter world's few rock stars. In fact, when I heard her speak at a conference in Daytona, Florida, Weiss looked as if she were on her way to a gig, with her chunky silver jewelry and muscle shirt. Weiss earned a PhD in animal behavior and for years worked with zoo animals, making their often-dull lives less dull. Along the way, she moonlighted with shelters, where she finally went to work full-time because, she believed, she could help far more animals that way.

When Weiss gives talks, she often recounts the story of her first dog, Benny, whom she adopted in college. Benny was a blue-tongued, chunky, orange chow mix. One of his bottom canine teeth poked out over his top lip. Being a sizable and unneutered dog, Benny had little future in a shelter of the 1980s. Still, there were requirements to adopt him. So Weiss forged a landlord's approval and took a photo of someone else's fenced yard, which she presented as her own. Her ruse worked, and she took Benny home to her unfenced yard, where the landlord had no idea she'd gotten a dog. As Weiss always says, "Benny was the bomb," until thirteen years later, when he died in her lap. Obviously, Weiss doesn't always like to follow the rules, and Benny is exhibit A as to why.

At the ASPCA, Weiss has used her scientific mind to worm out the truth behind the shelter world's assumptions, conventions, and taboos, such as adopting a pet to put under the Christmas tree. Weiss and her team found that pets given as gifts were no more likely to be returned to a shelter. She and her team checked to see if the numbers backed up the belief that black dogs are harder to find homes for than dogs of other colors. The numbers said no. Black dogs made up, in fact, the highest percentage of adoptions. To answer the question of how many strays are actually lost dogs, Weiss and her team called a thousand households across the country that had lost a dog. How, the researchers asked them, had they found their wayward pups? Half had tracked down their pets as I had when Dixie Lou slid through that tear in the screen door: by scouring the neighborhood while hollering her name. The dogs who just materialize at the kitchen door or wander up the driveway as if to say, "What's the big deal?" account for 20 percent. About another 20 percent were found by a neighbor or were returned home because they had an ID tag or a microchip. Only a fraction, a mere 6 percent of the frantic owners, located their missing pets at a shelter. What this study means for shelters is what many suspect: 90 percent or more of the strays pacing their kennels are not lost. No one is looking for them. They are nearly all abandoned, which renders stray holds, at best, pointless. That is why some shelter leaders, including Naticchioni, want those holds shortened, but age-old conventions, not to mention state laws, die hard.

At Cuyahoga, a mere one in ten of the dogs is claimed by his owner. Naticchioni says those owners typically show up within the first twenty-four hours. After that, even if the staff have reached an owner on the phone, chances are slim someone will come for a dog. Naticchioni can't do anything about the owners who won't come or about the holds, but in the retail world, she learned how to move merchandise. Before Naticchioni, Cuyahoga spayed and neutered the dogs as they came off their holds in the order they had arrived at the shelter—first come, first served. Now the ones who will be adopted quickest are fixed first. That's what happened to the fou-fous who came from the city pound. They'd come in on a Monday. Their stray hold was up on Friday, and they were fixed and ready to go. Over that weekend, all twenty went home. As the fou-fous drove off with their new families, the now-empty kennels were readied for the strays who were sure to come next and who had nowhere else to go.

I knew some of Bumble Bee's story, though it was vague. The shelter seemed certain about her age:

eight months. They also told me she'd bitten the animal control officer who had captured her, which gave me no pause for some reason. Her family arrived without names. A shelter staffer dubbed them the Bees. That was all I knew, and Bumble Bee couldn't tell me anything. A dog's muteness, a trait that can make him such an ideal constant companion, especially for a writer, can work to his disadvantage. Strays come with little or no story. They are nameless and ageless. They might as well have amnesia. The dogs who are dropped off by their owners often arrive with their exact age and their history. The shelter staff can ask if a dog snaps at toddlers or quakes at thunder or yaps the day away. Even dogs who are confiscated typically come in with a little information, if only bad things, such as they were stuffed in a crate with six other dogs or had their muzzles taped closed or lived only outside with a dirty water bowl. A stray is a mystery.

This leaves shelter and rescue workers to decipher a stray's personality with behavior evaluations and their own gut reactions. That can be tough in a shelter, where most dogs are understandably rattled. Anxious or scared ones can be especially hard to read, as, like anxious or scared humans, they can become aggressive or withdraw into their fear. Either behavior will cloud the little bits that make them who they are: relishing a belly rub, preferring wading to swimming, or having a penchant for warbling loudly in the car. These things made Bumble Bee Bumble Bee, but I wouldn't know that for months, and the shelter workers certainly had had little idea what this farm pup was like other than that she was petrified and had bitten someone. Later, when I ran into the shelter director, she told me that Bumble Bee had been the "scarediest dog" they'd ever seen.

That was somewhat obvious when we met her that sunny October morning, a Saturday, the day of the week that breaks with the most promise, the day I took Scott to meet her. Bumble Bee tucked her tail between her legs and kept her head low as the deep-voiced kennel manager led her to a yard where we could get to know one another. As soon as Bumble Bee was let off her leash, she darted to the far end of the yard. She nosed the soft mud and glanced at us a couple of times, I think to see if we'd left. We cooed, "Bumble Bee, Bumble Bee." We kneeled on the soft, wet earth and proffered treats in our outstretched palms. Nothing doing.

"I don't know," Scott said. I agreed.

We had brought our Aussie with us. The kennel worker told us that Bumble Bee had been uninterested in other dogs so far. Queen Dixie Lou considered herself above other canines and could hardly be bothered to sniff one. We debated bringing her in. We were about ready to go, but what was another five minutes? After a stretch of rain, the day was fresh, almost balmy. What was the rush? A fine day can lead you to take a chance.

When we led Dixie Lou into the yard, Bumble Bee ran to her. She wagged her now-upright tail merrily. The two dogs licked each other on their mouths. They wiggled and shimmied around each other, happily sniffing here and there. Her Majesty Dixie Lou even good-naturedly pawed Bumble Bee on the nose. We smiled the way you do watching people hug hello in airports. We took the twosome for a walk. The moment we hit the trail, Bumble Bee's tail curled into a neat loop, the white tip nearly brushing her back. As she stepped along the trail peppered with fallen leaves, her little black face relaxed. She, unlike Dixie Lou, who always strained on her leash like a carriage horse, didn't pull at all, just gracefully stepped along. The two dogs walked side by side over the root-woven paths in the fading heat of the fall day.

Evolution may have short-wired the human brain when it comes to dogs, to allow us to bond to them with unreasonable speed. By the end of the fifteen-minute walk, we had mostly made up our minds. We considered thinking on Bumble Bee overnight, but what did we really need to think about? And that would mean another long, forlorn night in the shelter kennel for this shy critter who, during our brief outing, had come to seem like "our" dog. That seemed irresponsible, even cruel. Wandering through the pines, Scott and I each holding a leash, we found no other way to end the story than to become a foursome. A home, our love, what we thought was our estimable dog know-how—that would do the trick. So we made the same mistake that humans make over and over, especially with homeless dogs: we oversimplified a canine and over-estimated the power of our love alone to heal her.

I handed over my credit card to cover the hundred-dollar adoption fee, signed some paper-work, and instantly went from volunteer to adopter.

We weren't even out of the parking lot before we ran into a hitch. Bumble Bee wouldn't climb into our station wagon. She froze. Her dark eyes tightened. We knew enough not to pick her up or pull her in. I got the kennel manager to come out to the parking lot to lift her onto the back seat, and off we went.

We let her spend most of that first day, a warm early October one, in the backyard. She nosed through some of the ornamental grasses and rhododendrons, but mostly, unlike a typical adolescent dog, she lay still in the lush grass looking sad and confused, her oversize pink shelter collar hanging loosely from her neck. She'd had a shock, we told ourselves sitting on our porch. She would settle in.

When the four of us went for a long walk in the

ample park near our house, she held her curled tail high again, and her face relaxed as it had on our earlier outing. Her worried expression also softened at the sound of kibble clattering into a bowl. As Bumble Bee dug her muzzle deep into her food bowl in our kitchen, I patted her bony shoulders. She flinched but didn't stop munching or move away. Then she ran up our steep, wooden back staircase. She peered down at me helplessly from the second-floor landing. She seemed clueless as to how to come back down. I called to her. She just whined and barked. When I walked upstairs to get her, with Dixie Lou beside me, Bumble Bee ran from us. Maybe, I thought, this dog had never been on stairs.

I followed her through the second-floor hall to the front staircase, which, with its two landings, I thought might be easier for her to descend. Several times I marched up and down the stairs, raising my knees high, as Dixie Lou followed me as if to say, "Look, easy as pie." Bumble Bee watched with her tail tight under her legs and then receded back down the hall. I gave up and went to make lunch as her barks echoed upstairs. Eventually, I heard the light, slow click of toenails on the front stairs. She had figured it out, which was good, but I'd begun to wonder if this young stray had ever even been in a house before.

That night, we put an extra dog bed in our bedroom, but given how timid Bumble Bee was, we left the door open so she could roam, even though it was unclear if she was housebroken. We turned out the lights, not knowing where she was in our two-story house, sure that the next day she would look less worried.

In the morning, I awoke to her hot, sweet breath on my cheeks. I opened my eyes, and there was her little black nose up against my side of the bed, wiggling as she sniffed me. She whined softly, shifting from paw to paw. See, I thought, she's settling in. Then I realized that her excitement might have more to do with her full bladder than with being happy to see me. I clumsily grabbed my robe and rushed downstairs to let her out. While she was outside, I walked carefully through the house in my bare feet, examining rugs for dark, wet stains or worse, and found none. Rather, I found a slight, rounded depression atop the daybed in my office, where she had obviously slept. Along the edges of the divot lay a shell and a tennis ball, with other odds and ends Bumble Bee had collected from downstairs and brought upstairs to keep her company overnight. She had chewed on the corner of an orange velvet pillow. I picked up the pillow and stroked the frayed edge of the quarter-size hole. I was relieved she had had some fun, had acted like a puppy after all.

I turned to wake Scott and tell him the good news.

Penny Jane

2

FEARFUL DOGS

Scott and I stand stock-still like two statues in our living room's bay window. The tall panes cast the autumn night's darkness across us. I hear a lone car hum down the street. A foghorn drones in the distance. I fold my arms in front of me and sigh dramatically. Dixie Lou, a dirty tennis ball clutched in her teeth, dances around our feet. Her blond withers shimmy like a grass skirt. Her amber eyes beg us to play.

From where we stand, our backs to the window, we can see down the length of our long, old house. The living room, dining room, and kitchen are lined up one behind the other like railroad cars. This is a house for going back and forth, not for circling, which never seemed like a problem until we brought home Bumble Bee—or as we've come to call her, "she." Her shelter-given name does not suit her, and she doesn't know it anyhow. We want to change it but can't think to what. She is nameless for now, like some orphan in a Dickens novel, but she's not an orphan. She's ours. We are watching for our young, nameless dog, waiting for her to come into the house so we can all finally go to bed.

Since we brought her home two weeks ago, we have discovered that she is afraid of a long list of things. For starters, our new dog is afraid of us. Granted, we are tall and loom some. But the real monsters, the ones that scare her witless, are doorways, especially if we stand nearby. God forbid we hold a door open for her. She won't walk through that doorway for hours. To let her in from the backyard, we have to prop the kitchen door open. Then we have to vanish. Once she enters, if we make a move to close the door behind her, she will vamoose back outside. We have learned quickly that racing her, especially breathlessly lunging for the knob and then tripping en route, only scares her more, which is understandable. Still, I can't resist a run at the door sometimes, though she always beats me. Fear, this pup reminds me, is a greater motivator than frustration.

So we leave the back door open all day long so she can go in and out. The wind blows in brown, papery leaves, and endless seedpods from our neighbor's birch tree gather in the kitchen's corners. A squirrel or two has stood close to the entryway, eyes wide, paws set tentatively on the threshold. Rain splashed the maple floor one day. Though our city neighborhood by the bay is safe enough to leave the back door open all day, it is not safe enough to do so overnight, if only because I'm worried the dark may embolden those curious squirrels to come right in. One wild animal in the house is enough.

What should be a simple task—getting this dog to come in after one last piddle and closing the kitchen door behind her—has become a nightly test of our patience and intelligence. So far, though we have two graduate degrees between us, we are flunking. We could leash her and take her out and back in, which we try sometimes, but she often will not pee with us by her side. So, instead, we hash out a strategy over dinner—who will hide in the TV room, who will crouch behind the dining room table. Sometimes we even diagram it on paper napkins like a football play. I've become the door closer, because I scare her less than my tall, lean husband with his baritone. We need a new scheme nearly every night because she checks where we hid the evening before. Slowly it has dawned on us that this dog, unlike us, catches on quickly.

Tonight's plan is to stand as far from the kitchen door as possible, which is why we are in the bay window in the living room. Once she reaches the front staircase in our small foyer, I will stride from one end of the house, nearly twenty steps, to the other and close the door before she bolts. That sounds simple enough, but in this house there's next to no way to do so without passing her, which usually makes our pup turn on her pretty white paws and flee to our diminutive plot of grass and perennials. That is why I must keep to my post until she starts up those creaky stairs. Scott's job is simply to hold dead still so he doesn't scare her, which he can do by flexing a little finger, and to tell me when to go. I am prone to jumping the gun, which is why we have this dog to begin with.

"Do you see her?" Scott whispers.

I do, I think. I eye a small flash of movement among the chair legs. I hear the soft jingle of dog tags. Then I see her dainty white paws on our Oriental rug. She warily steps the length of the oak dining room table. Her tail is nervously draped between her legs. She slinks into the living room and rounds our large couch. When she spots us with her dark eyes we don't dare move. We look at the ceiling and banish thoughts of closing the kitchen door in case this dog can read our minds. She pauses. "Oh, there you are," her eyes say. She licks her lips and then turns her shiny head toward the foyer and the stairs, which lead to her bed upstairs, to a small oasis of safety. She walks to the bottom step.

"Should I go?" I whisper.

"Not yet," Scott whispers back.

But I do. I can't seem to stop myself. I step forward softly on tiptoe, my arms flat by my sides. I'm moving but doing my best to look as if I'm not, as if I'm being swept along in a stream. Dixie Lou follows on my heels, wiggling her bum excitedly. She bumps the tennis ball in her mouth against the back of my calf. I make it past our messy coffee table. In the foyer, our new dog has stopped just shy of the staircase, a paw set tentatively on the first step. She stares over her back at me, a question framed in her pinched brow. Scott shakes his head and frowns at me. I freeze. My nose begins to run. I don't dare raise a hand to rub it, so I sniffle as quietly as I can. Dixie Lou drops her tennis ball with a thump. She lets out an exasperated squeak.

All this stillness seems to restore our worried dog's courage. Ever so slowly, she returns her gaze to the stairs and starts up the steps. I'm off, though Scott has not given me the A-okay. I want to close that door with the full force of my being. I want life to be simple again, to rush along in all its familiarity. I hurry past our long dining table. I step on a squeaky toy that shrieks. As I near the kitchen, I hear her toenails scrape the wood floor behind me. I break into a sprint. She easily passes me on the right, a shot of black and white aiming for the safety of outdoors, of the shadowy damp grass, the breeze, and the moon.

This is what it is like to adopt a shelter dog, something thousands of people do every day, something that looks and mostly is relatively easy—that is, if you don't choose a frazzled, half-feral farm dog.

Our routines are shot. Our sleep is ruined. I've caught a cold. My husband has fallen behind at work and comes home grouchy each night. I'm behind on my book, and as my daily page count dwindles, I grow more frantic, even shrill. Overwhelmed, I quit walking dogs at the shelter. All my efforts to help homeless dogs are focused on this single, wild stray in my house.

She barks hysterically each time we tread up and down our creaky old steps. She goes upstairs if we are downstairs and downstairs if we are upstairs. Dixie Lou tags along with Scott to his newspaper's office while "she" spends her days parked on the landing outside my office door, not for my company but to keep a wary eye on me. Should I turn too fast in my swivel chair to grab a dictionary—*whoosh*. She flies down the steps to save her life, her long toenails skidding on the wood. To leash her, I have to walk quickly toward her, which sends her into a frozen crouch and makes me feel like an enormous heel. She purses her black lips as if to form the letter *O*—what we have begun calling "snake mouth." I quickly hook the leash on her droopy pink collar, worried she might snap my hand. I have to lift her into the car's backseat, which prompts another snake mouth. As I drive, she nervously paces. She's nearly escaped out the back passenger window— twice. The second time, I was rounding a highway entrance. I steered with one hand and reached back with the other and somehow grabbed her black bottom to yank her in. Breathless from the adrenaline burst, I pulled over on the highway shoulder, pressed my forehead to the cool steering wheel, and sobbed, my own version of snake mouth.

I knew there could be a few rough days, maybe weeks. I knew something about shy dogs. But this girl is beyond shy. Sunk deep into the couch of our TV room one night, with Dixie Lou, the only relaxed creature in the house, snoozing at my feet, I wondered out loud, "Why did we ruin our nice life?"

"I don't know," my husband answered.

One of the many nice things about puppies, in addition to their freshly baked muffin smell and their Buddha bellies, is their sponge-like brains. Those sweet, open faces say it all. From three weeks, when their eyes and ears start working, to about sixteen weeks, when they can eat hard food and shred an espadrille in seconds, the puppy brain is designed to soak up the world around it, even if that world includes another species, us clumsy, lumbering humans. Those few ounces of gray matter readily acclimate to the strange trappings of our busy, loud life: squawking car horns, flags that snap in the wind, and the rat-a-tat of marital squabbles. Puppies learn to ride in cars, sleep by themselves, and let toddlers pull their tails. This is why people raising puppies destined to be service dogs are handed a list of more than one hundred items to introduce them to during that early phase: screeching babies, skate-boarders, cheering crowds, tunnels, garbage cans with rumbling wheels, and people twisted into strange yoga poses. This is what is called socializing a dog.

Come week twelve or so, the pup's maturing brain begins to become far more suspect of novelty in all its forms, be it riding in an elevator or meeting a man in a ball cap. They won't readily accept a person trundling along with a walker. They will have to think about that walker. Is it a threat? For pups who've done a lot, seen a lot in those early weeks, the world becomes a familiar, comfortable place, which gives a youngster a lot of confidence for when it comes across some-thing new, such as a person pushing along a contraption with wheels. For the pups who haven't done or seen much, the world can become a nonstop rush of unnerving experiences.

What's "new" to dogs, who notice everything, often surprises people, who comparatively notice next to nothing. I once brought a shelter dog, a golden-colored, matronly mastiff mix named Bertha, home for a few nights of R&R. Bertha happily climbed into my car. Then she caught sight of the sunroof overhead and spent the ride with her head tilted skyward, anxiously staring at the changing images passing overhead. Once inside my condo, she fretted over her reflection in my hall mirror. Who was that dog? In fact, most of the shelter dogs I've brought home for overnights have barked at their reflections. Some have leapt when they've heard my finches fly in their cage. One climbed onto my desk to see what was making all that noise outside. It was sparrows singing. Another jumped out of his skin at the sound of my turning on the TV. Novelty, I always remind myself, is in the eye of the beholder.

This is how you undersocialize a dog: You isolate him somehow. You keep him in a crate through that key period, as puppy mills often do, or chained in a yard, as dogfighters often do. But you don't have to own a puppy mill or fight dogs to create an undersocialized dog. Even well-intentioned owners can create one by being overprotective, perhaps by scooping the dog up in their arms every time another dog approaches, or limiting their pets to the small world of their house and backyard. A puppy growing up in a shelter also leads a sterile life. He meets people and other dogs, but doesn't learn about televisions, mirrors, sunroofs, or birds tweeting at sunrise. A puppy who is born as a stray is sure to be anywhere from undersocialized to outright feral. If puppies live with their own canine family, like our pup, they will be at home with other dogs, which is at least one hurdle, but not with humans. That's exactly the predicament of our girl. Everything about being a pet is new and alarming to her. She will have to *learn* to live inside a house, to trust us, to be our dog. How long that will take or if she even can—who knows? Until then, she spends most of her days worried and afraid no matter what we do.

During this phase, our deeply undersocialized dog would easily have fit in at the ASPCA's Behavioral Rehabilitation Center in Madison, New Jersey. Here, all the dogs are scared. As I walk the length of their kennels, many take one look at me with wide eyes, turn on their paws, and flee quickly to their outside runs. When I step outdoors to see those runs, a row of tails flashes out of sight as many zip back through the passageways to their kennels. The braver dogs stay put, pinch their brows, and bark at me. Why won't this woman with long arms go away! One, a houndy-looking pittie named Philomena, with a blot of pink scar on her head, was found in a crate with a dead dog in an abandoned back-yard. White scars stipple an Akita's black muzzle. Cosmo, one of the few whose face relaxes into a wide, open-mouthed smile, is a white pittie who looks as if he dipped his nose into a coal bin. He was plucked from a dogfighting ring. A shaggy brown mutt named Leo ran loose for who knows how long in North Carolina. He played with the neighborhood dogs, even the cats, but wouldn't come near a soul. Nobody could catch him.

Finally, Leo, like a wild animal, had to be darted.

To call these dogs fearful doesn't do their emotions justice. Terrified is more like it, terrified as in you are swimming in the ocean and a shark fin slices the wave right in front of you. That's how these dogs feel if someone plops down by them or cinches a collar around their neck or a strange woman with a notebook quietly passes their kennel. At least that's how they feel when they first come to the center. Hooked to a leash, some dogs thrash like a swordfish caught on a hook. Others defecate and urinate when a trainer steps into a room with them. They scream. One dog shook so violently he looked as if he was having an epileptic seizure. A few zone out so much they look catatonic, like young Flynn, who came from a hoarding case of sixty-eight dogs in the South. When trainers first tried to work with the reddish-gold mutt, he sat upright on his haunches and leaned his back against the wall behind him. Though his eyes were open, his head drooped dramatically to one side as his sharp muzzle pointed to the floor. His back legs lazily splayed out like a drunk's.

The trainers here, all slender, calm women who drape leashes like sashes across their chests or coil them around their waists like belts, take none of this personally, not even when the dogs bite their leather-gloved hands. The center is run by Kristen Collins, a tall, athletic-looking woman with an aquiline nose and a theatrical manner, a holdover from her previous career as an actress in New York City. In her twenties she appeared in small productions, recorded voice-overs, and paid the bills for her stage habit by copyediting. Drama was, she thought, her calling until she fell hard for Juno, a three-week-old pittie puppy with an injured leg who needed a home. With her white and apricot markings, dark eyes, and coffee-colored nose, Juno, Collins says, resembled a little cow. Collins and the "wee cow" went to training class, where Collins fell hard again, this time for training dogs. The improvisational nature of the work reminded her of the stage. She apprenticed with that trainer, went on to have her own practice, worked with the Richmond SPCA, and returned to college in her thirties to study animal behavior, eventually earning a master's degree. Her best teacher, however, was good-natured, attentive Juno, whom she taught to fetch a bottle of beer from the fridge, though the pittie, like so many teenage boys, sometimes forgot to close the door. Unlike a teenage boy, Juno would go back and close it when Kirsten asked her to.

Juno had as perfect a puppyhood as the dogs at the center have not. Collins knows firsthand why they are in such a state. While she worked for the ASPCA's Anti-Cruelty Behavior Team, Collins says she inhaled the hideous smells and saw the severe isolation of hoarders' houses and puppy mills. Working on the team, she says, was addictive. The high came from plucking dogs out of the profound filth and chaos of a hoarder's house or from puppy mill cages stacked eight feet high. Typically, the team members would wait in the thin early-morning light while law enforcement officers arrested and removed the human offenders. Then they would head in for the dogs. Sometimes she and Pamela Reid, who leads the Anti-Cruelty Behavior Team and oversees the Behavioral Rehabilitation Center, would be dispatched to evaluate dogs whom other organizations had rescued, as they were for the animals saved from hoarders by the Young-Williams Animal Center in Knoxville, Tennessee. Collins shows me a photo of what the Young-Williams rescuers saw when they swung open the front door at a house in Knoxville: dozens of eyes glinting in a darkened hall. Inside, they found dead dogs and starving dogs. Excrement covered the floors and the furniture, even the hoarders' beds. The hoarders, an elderly brother and sister, slept on the kitchen table. Collins shows me another photo, this one of someone in blue scrubs holding up a card with the number sixteen written on it next to a surprised-looking dog caked with feces and dirt. The team found that the little gal had extra toes on her back feet, likely the result of rampant inbreeding among the dogs, none of which was fixed. Collins took her home and named her Toefu.

Collins worked with Pamela Reid, who still oversees the Anti-Behavior Cruelty Team as well as the rehab center in New Jersey. Reid has a PhD in psychology and is a crack agility competitor with Snafu, a devilishly speedy blend of whippet, border collie, and terrier. Running Snafu, Reid says, is like driving a Ferrari. Earlier in her career, she ran a large private practice in Toronto helping people solve their pets' behavior problems, which often was a frustrating endeavor. Dogs, she found, were often more teachable than their owners. She moved to the States in 2001 to join the ASPCA, where she planned to research how effective certain dog-training practices actually were without an owner around to muck them up. Then the ASPCA began investigating more and more cruelty cases across the country and needed people on the scene who could evaluate the rescued dogs' behavior. Reid tested the dogs pulled out of horrible circumstances to see who could become pets and which were beyond repair. Some dogs, she says, amazingly just needed a bath and a haircut. Some dogs improved with the training, walks, human contact, and order they received while in the rescue team's temporary housing. Many, however, needed intensive help, such as some of the dogs from a 2010 case in a country town in southern

Tennessee. An elderly man had taken in strays until he had far more than he could care for—eighty-five. It was a classic case of Good Samaritan gone wrong, as can happen with hoarding. The various German shepherds, Labradors, and hound-type dogs were found chained to posts, housed in pens, and wandering freely around the property. Most of the dogs were transferred to shelters in Atlanta and Nashville, but some of dogs couldn't be touched, never mind leashed. They were like wild raccoons, Reid tells me. No shelter would or could take them. Reid realized that dogs like these needed their own shelter, one where they could learn how to become pets and where Reid might learn how to loosen fear's grip on them so they could live in a home.

Fear, it is easy to forget, is a normal emotion. Without it, a species won't last long. Yet especially acute, chronic fear makes it impossible for one to relax or concentrate or think, for humans and for dogs. That is why this "normal" emotion lurks behind most of the behavior problems that plague dogs. A dog nips a child because he is scared of children. A dog frantically shreds the curtains because he is afraid to be alone. A dog growls when someone reaches for his food bowl because he's afraid of losing dinner. These are the reasons owners surrender their pets to shelters, and the reasons it can be hard to find a dog a home. Shelters are really in the business of treating fear, and if more dogs are going to find homes, shelters need to know how best to address it—but at this point they don't. How to treat fearful dogs in a shelter has been little studied. Shelters must rely on their best hunches in an environment that can unnerve even a happy-go-lucky pooch. Reid wants to change that.

In 2013 the ASPCA opened the first shelter devoted to rehabilitating and studying extremely fearful dogs. They built a white, boxy building on the back of St. Hubert's Animal Welfare Center, in Madison, a wealthy, leafy suburb about an hour's train ride west from New York City. There is room for thirty dogs, who mostly, but not exclusively, come from ASPCA cruelty cases. What they have in common is that they would be impossible, or nearly impossible, to find a home for in their current state. The dogs stay an average of twelve weeks, though some finish in half that time. As the dogs are treated, the trainers gather reams of data so they will, in the end, have scientific evidence of the practices that worked best. Then they will know how to treat not only these extreme cases, but also the more garden-variety fearful dogs, the ones found in many shelter kennels.

Fear, trainers tell me, is the most misunderstood emotion in dogs. People assume a scared or nervous dog just needs a cuddle. For dogs who are afraid of people, a pat, a hug, and especially a kiss—which is how people get bitten in the face—are the last things they need. Scared dogs would rather you didn't even look at them. Some people, who typically brag of their natural way with animals, mistake a worried dog for a disobedient one, who needs to be shown who is boss. They then proceed to frighten the dog more with rough handling and a loud, bossy voice. People, often men, pull them out from under tables, where they have hidden, which is a good way to get bitten on the hand. We think if something doesn't scare us, it shouldn't frighten a dog. It's only a ceiling fan! It's only linoleum! Humans hate fear. We harbor this religious-like belief in not only facing our fears, but conquering them in one fell swoop. If you are afraid of heights, go skydiving. If a dog's afraid of water, toss him off a dock. We want to snuff out this weakness in ourselves and our dogs.

Not only do we not understand fear in dogs, but we don't know it when we see it. A study found that almost everyone, trainers and pet owners alike, recognized a happy dog: that gaping mouth and turned-up corner of the lips. Yet nearly half of the dog owners surveyed could not identify the body language of a fearful dog: ears back, body rigid, head lowered, tail tucked, forehead rounded, panting, and what is called whale eye, when the whites of a dog's eyes look like crescent moons. Maybe we are blind to these signs because we believe dogs live in a blissful world beyond worry, beyond fear. Certainly the dogs of myth and fame are all brave hearts, from the greyhounds of the medieval knights up to our movie star dogs Rin Tin Tin, Lassie, and even Toto, who, despite his size, chomped the Wicked Witch of the West. But perhaps the terrier chomped her green hand not because he was courageous but because he was scared out of his wits.

Collins says the key lesson they have learned so far at the Behavioral Rehabilitation Center is that profoundly fearful dogs can learn to trust, to relax—even dogs such as Coconut. The little dog was rescued from JRT John's Jack Russell and Shiba Inu Kennel in Lake City, Michigan, a long name for a puppy mill that shorted the dogs at every turn. Authorities removed 150 animals from outdoor enclosures, where the dogs lived year-round and where most did not have clean water. When Coconut, a leggy, white Jack Russell mix, arrived at the center, nobody thought she would make it. In a video taken of her early days, the little dog twirls on her leash, bucks, and gnashes her teeth. Enclosed in a room with a trainer, who quietly sits on a couch, Coconut frantically tears around the room as if it's on fire. It's hard to watch, and Collins says that at one point she wondered if it was even humane to put

Coconut through the training. Yet the freaked-out dog turned out to be food motivated, which meant the trainers had something she wanted—treats. The trainers could use food to make frightening experiences less so, to slowly build positive associations between themselves and her, and to motivate Coconut to learn the basics of being a pet dog. In the video's closing images, Coconut walks on a leash like an old hand, twitching her short tail while she smiles for the camera. She lounges on a couch with a woman she's just met. When the stranger bends over to kiss Coconut on the head, the fluff of white happily pants. Coconut now lives with a retired couple on the Jersey Shore.

The short answer of how Collins and her team transformed Coconut and the other dogs who have "graduated" from the rehabilitation center is by going slowly, taking nothing for granted, and always, always considering the world from the fearful dog's point of view. During the new arrivals' first three days at the center, trainers leave them alone so the newcomers can settle in some. Then the trainers start sitting on their kennel floors at mealtime and, if they can, feeding the dogs by hand. Next the dogs are carefully introduced to the trappings of a pet's life: collars, leashes, couches, even TVs. The center has four drab rooms that could fit into some Eastern Bloc apartment high-rise. Each is outfitted like a living room or bedroom. Collins points out a teetering standing lamp in the corner of one that especially unnerves some dogs. Many also take note of the shiny black square of the TV. Two rooms have doggie doors, so if the lamp, the TV, or the trainer plopped on the couch is too much, the pup can escape outside and gather his nerve in the fresh air. Many of the dogs are most relaxed outdoors, Collins says, because few were ever inside a house before they were rescued. Most of the dogs also lived with other dogs, so as part of their cure, they attend play groups, where they can wrestle and sniff one another's bum. The dogs swim in a blue plastic kiddie pool or dig in a sandbox the shape of a giant green turtle. Doing what canines naturally do soothes them. That is why we pass some volunteers shaking aerosol cans labeled "squirrel scent" or "partridge scent." They squirt a few shots inside toilet paper tubes, which will be given to the dogs to dig their muzzles into. Who can worry with a nose full of weasel perfume?

Back at the kennels, which aren't exactly quiet, what with the barking, there is a kind of hospital hush because the trainers are so calm. They don't break into high, cartoon voices or squeal endearments as so many shelter workers do with dogs. Collins riffles through a wall of leashes looking for her favorite. She has become, she explains, as picky about them as most women are about shoes. She grabs a neon orange slip lead. I follow her to Kissy's kennel. The charcoal-black Akita steps lightly from paw to paw as we approach. Since arriving six weeks ago, Kissy has walked on leash with one or two trainers, but not with Collins. As Collins slides quietly through the kennel door, Kissy vamooses to her outside run. In the now-empty kennel, Collins slowly bends down on one knee with her back to the dog. She holds the orange slip lead aloft in one arm to her side, as an invitation for Kissy. The Akita pokes her head halfway through the doggie door. She springs back into the kennel, wags her tail then tucks it, play-bows, and then tucks her tail again—dog language for "I can't make up my mind." Collins, a new person in Kissy's kennel, is freaking her out, but the Akita would like to go for a walk. What to do? Kissy runs outside again and then swooshes right back in through the doggie door. Collins waits on one knee on the concrete floor, staring straight ahead. She lets the leash brush against Kissy's face as the dog nervously dances around, to show Kissy that she won't make a sudden move, that it is Kissy's call. After about five minutes, a look of resolve falls over the Akita's dark face. She steps to Collins's side and holds still. Collins softly slides the lead around her neck.

Each day at the center is one of such baby steps, and we head outside to take a few more. As Collins swings open a door, Kissy pauses.

Thresholds, Collins says, are a common problem. If the dogs used to live only inside, they don't like walking out through a doorway. If they lived outside, like my stray, they don't like walking in. Kissy looks doubtful, and then gingerly steps over the doorframe and into the sunshine, where a small group of trainers and other dogs await us on this breezy fall day. Leo, the stray who had to be darted, is close to graduating. He's been at the center for three months. Today he will practice walking with unfamiliar dogs and people, including me. Leo knows only one of the trainers well. One he doesn't know holds his leash. The mutt, who has the shaggy brown coat of a Chesapeake, does know the route and leads the way as we march along the grass that edges the boxy white building and then across the parking lot past windshields shimmering under the noon sun. Every dog's tail is up and all their gaits are loose, including Kissy's. Leo seems unbothered by so many new people. On the far side of the parking lot he starts up a rise with all of us parading behind. He turns left and pads along a grassy patch that edges the parking lot and then leads the way along a trail into some trees. The trainers pause to debate if they have time to keep going or need to head back. As they talk, Leo, now ankle deep in crinkly brown leaves, pinches his brow. His tail droops. The trainers don't usually stop here. It's just one too many new things for the former stray. Not wanting to push Leo too far, Collins turns small parade around and we head back in a loc single file toward the center. Leo's tail springs back up. His momentary nervousness seems like a small setback, but it's enough to make Collins think he's not quite ready to graduate.

To graduate, the dogs have to, among other things, wear a collar and walk on a leash. They have to let people approach them and come across something new without panicking. Being shy is okay. Also, ideally, they can walk up and down a small set of steps, but not doing so is not a deal breaker. The deal breaker is whether they have demonstrated that they can bond with a human. Once they demonstrate this, they are transferred to shelters and put up for adoption. The center has had so much success—graduating some two hundred dogs who have found homes—that it will not close in 2017 as planned, but will move to Asheville, North Carolina, to set up shop permanently. Photos of the graduates cover a wall near a small office in the middle of the kennels, a kind of command center of leashes, food, and harnesses. The dogs beam in birthday hats, curl up in laps, hang their heads happily out of car windows, their tongues flapping in the wind. Collins pulls me away from the cheery pictures because here, amid the not-so-cheery dogs, it is Zen time. Before the trainers go to lunch, they turn the lights low in the kennels and key up some classical music. The days are busy here and being afraid is hard work. The dogs, like kindergartners, settle in for a midday snooze.

Additional photos of smiling graduates adorn a roomy, sunny main office shared by several trainers. A quote is also tacked to a bulletin board: "Everything you want is on the other side of fear." Flynn, the once catatonic pooch, confidently pads around the room. He's turned out to be quite the affectionate goofball. He's "graduated," but Collins is keeping him on a few extra weeks to help other dogs such as Katie, a little coffee-colored number with droopy teats and a pointed, upturned snout. Katie was doing so poorly in the kennels—she'd poop and pee at just the sight of people—that they brought her into the office to live. That seems completely counterintuitive because here she is with people all day long, but they ignore her. She could get used to humans simply by watching them work at the computer or make a cup of coffee or gossip. In the office, she also met her boyfriend, Flynn. Anxiety is contagious, but so is confidence and happiness, which Flynn exudes. He's also an expert tumbler.

"Get a room!" someone calls as the two roll over and over each other down the length of the couch. Flynn is easily twice her size and can put Katie's head in his mouth, which she lets him do as they wrestle. The trainers shake their heads and turn back to their keyboards and let love, fun, and joy work their slow magic. When the two dogs grow weary and curl up tight together on the couch, Collins squats low and scratches Flynn's pricked ears. He leans into her fingertips and rolls on his side. Then Collins slowly moves her hand toward Katie, whom she's never petted before. Dogs take cues from other dogs, which is probably why Katie, having watched Flynn enjoy Collins's patting, doesn't flee or flinch as the trainer's hand nears. Katie does bury her face in the couch as if it's too scary to look, but also lets Collins softly nuzzle the top of her head. I want to cheer at this baby step, which is in fact a giant step, but know not to. I might scare little Katie.

It's exhausting being a fearful, unsocialized dog. It's exhausting living with one, especially when you don't know what you're doing, which I didn't when I adopted my farm girl. This was long before I went to the ASPCA's center, long before Kristen Collins explained doorways to me, long before I worked with fearful dogs, back when most adopters like me signed a form and got a "good luck" from any shelter. All I could think to do was tiptoe around my new dog. I could scare her just by pulling a can opener out of a kitchen drawer. Scott had only to raise his low voice a nano-decibel and she'd cringe. We, dog lovers, loved by dogs, had become dog bogeymen. We began to snap at each other. We growled, "She was fine until you opened the newspaper," or "If you'd only take smaller steps you wouldn't scare her so." Each of us heaved great sighs at the other's thoughtless ways as we waved our arms while telling a story or noisily emptied a trash can. When Scott suggested taking her back to the shelter, what I wanted to reply was "I'd like to take you to the shelter."

Then, of course, she went into her first heat. She stained the living room couch. "Is that what I think it is?" Scott asked. Her days of roaming the house were over. We lured her into our bedroom with treats and closed the door. I attempted to get her into a crate but accidentally closed the door on her bottom, which, of course, terrified her. So much for crate training. When I turned the light out, she stood in the middle of the room staring at me with her dark eyes. At about 5:00 a.m., I awoke to her pacing and soft whinnies. I lay there hoping against hope that she'd settle down before I finally threw back the blankets and staggered into the day. The next night, I tethered her to our bed so she couldn't pace. Once again, I woke at 5:00 a.m., this time to a mysterious grinding. She was nervously chewing a foot of our pine bed. I leapt up to save my furniture from ruin. I called our agility trainer. She suggested giving our new dog a bone to distract her from chewing the bed frame. I fell asleep with some knobby cow joint the size of a softball on my nightstand. When I heard the grinding of dog teeth on pine in the early-morning gloom, I clumsily reached for the wad of bone and pushed it into those busy jaws. That bought me about an hour before she began to gnaw on the furniture again.

"What is she doing now?" Scott rolled over and asked.

"Quiet, you'll scare her," I barked and got up.

The next night, I armed myself with two bones stuffed with peanut butter; and then the next night, a third bone. Finally, Scott and I began taking turns sleeping with her in the small guest room, which has a cast-iron bed. That way one person could sleep until a normal hour, and the pine bed would be safe. Taking turns in the guest room also afforded us some respite from our squabbles over snoring and blanket stealing. We'd quit kissing each other goodnight to avoid getting our fangs tangled.

Tonight is my turn with her. My eyes flash open at 4:00 a.m., though she is quiet. I've woken up because I'm so worried that she will wake me up. How stupid, I think. I lie frozen the way I did as a child so long ago, when I feared a monster was under my bed and that the tiniest movement might invite an attack. Now I am a middle-aged woman and the monster is this hapless dog. I fear she might hear the quickening of my waking breath or sense my mind whirring, and rouse. I loathe rising in the early-morning darkness. Sunrises, despite their beauty, make me feel out of sorts, even hopeless.

My throat is still dry and tight from the cold I can't shake. My mind races from one worried thought to another—how much I miss the shelter, my looming book deadline, my currently irksome husband—until it lands back on the young dog draped over the new canvas bed on the floor. She needs a name, I think. We have to name her so we can start to feel that this half-wild animal is truly ours. What little we know of her personality so far inspires names such as Scaredy Pants or Wild Thing or Hopeless, none of which will do. Stella Rondo is too showy. Bunny and Fancy too flip. Blackie, a classic dog name, is too generic, and possibly inappropriate these days, especially for someone with a bit of twang in her voice such as I. Whitey wouldn't be a problem, but the dog is mostly black. Lying there as still as a corpse, my mind wandering around in the dark, I ponder the vague, inadvertent racial overtones of dog names. I remember once, during a trip to Monhegan Island, a woman asking me what my Aussie's name was and her face clouding when I answered, "Dixie Lou." "Is she southern?" the woman asked me with a scowl. Then I think of that strange yet perfect island, how Dixie Lou found an open box of pizza on that trip. When I've distracted myself so much I begin to drift off, it pops into my head: Penny. She'll need a middle name, as Dixie Lou has, but I can think of that tomorrow. It's enough to have landed on her first name. Penny. It's just plain enough, winsome enough, for this spooked, slender dog, but more than that, it has an understated positive ring. I'm thinking "lucky penny," a bit of nearly worthless tarnished copper still worth bending over for. She hardly feels like a good-luck charm just now, but names alone can sway you. Maybe I can convince myself that bringing home this stray farm dog was a stroke of incredible good luck. Maybe, I think, like a child steeling herself against the monsters of the night, believing will make it so.

Maybe.

Boaz

3

THE BOND

Volunteering at a shelter, you get the impression that the whole world is moving or has allergies. Those are the two reasons most often given when dog after dog is surrendered to a shelter. I try, at least a little, to give people who have left their pets behind the benefit of the doubt, though I often suspect they aren't telling the truth, or at least the whole truth. What can you make of a young couple who hand back the chubby pug they adopted only the day before because, overnight, they decided to move to Singapore next week? And I find myself harrumphing when I see "new baby" listed as a reason on the obligatory intake form. "Then why'd you have a baby?" I'll mutter to myself, even though I know I'm hitting a new height of unreasonableness. When you are looking into a dog's confused eyes, it's hard to cut your fellow human one iota of slack. Though I have all the patience in the world for dogs, I often run short of it for my own species. I am not the only one. Up and down the shelter halls, we volunteers and staffers huff, "Can you believe?" over and over. We roll our eyes until they ache. We sigh until we are hoarse. The "us versus them" metaphor doesn't do justice to how we can feel.

So I cringe when Scott brings up returning our feral pup after Penny nearly jumps out of the car again. There have been one or two bright moments. She hasn't had one accident in the house. Once I've managed to get a leash on her, she walks like a show dog outside. She and Dixie Lou mostly ignore each other, but they get along. That doesn't make for much of an argument, but I argue with Scott nonetheless, because returning Penny will make me one of "them." True, she hasn't been our longtime pet. I wouldn't be like the people who deposit their incontinent dog they've had since puppyhood because they've installed new wall-to-wall carpeting for the holidays. We've had Penny for only a few weeks. Shelters expect that some adoptions aren't the right match. Still, for me, a shelter volunteer, if I return her I would be crossing a line I'd never get to step back over.

What Scott doesn't know is that my will is crumbling, which became clear when a few days ago, as offhandedly as I could, I offered Penny to our cleaning person. Granted, Lynn is one of the most reliable, loving people I know. She laughed. I played along as if I were joking, though I wasn't.

"I'd give you a hundred dollars," I said, faux-snickering to cover any desperation in my voice. "Ha, ha, ha," Lynn chortled her way out of the kitchen before I could up my offer. I slunk to the bathroom, sat down on the toilet, put my head in my hands, and sobbed as quietly as I could because Lynn hadn't taken Penny, because she might have taken her, because I'd asked her. What was I willing to do for a dog? I didn't know anymore. What I did know was that although my life had been turned inside out, I still didn't want to be "them."

Who are these people, the ones who give up dogs? Researchers have found that they are mostly nothing like me. They are younger, less educated. They are renters with lower incomes than mine. They are more likely to have misconceptions about housebreaking and to have gotten their dog for free. They tend to keep their dogs outside and not take them to the vet or to training classes. One study found they are less likely to have nicknames for their pets or to carry their dog's picture in their wallet. The researchers asked about the nicknames and the picture because each indicates how strong a bond you have with your dog.

This is what I may have in common with "them." I have neither nicknames nor photos. Even though I've given Penny my beloved grandmother's middle name, Jane, in the hope that it might make my heart swell with love for her, it has not. I mostly just feel sorry for Penny Jane, which never makes for real affection. The only thing that stands between this border collie mix and the shelter is my oversize pride—in other words, my humanness. When I consider packing her into the car, I worry about her future, which would not be bright. I foresee adopter after adopter returning her. Who wants a dog they can't pet, who whines before dawn breaks? Yet I worry as much about myself. How would I live with myself, having cast this hapless dog onto the open seas? If I become "them," I won't be me.

The story of dogs and people, though murky, reads like a fairy tale. Somehow the wolf transformed from a terrifying animal into a creature we couldn't keep our hands off. When and how this happened, if people domesticated dogs or dogs domesticated themselves, can work a roomful of evolutionary biologists and the like into quite a lather. We may never know if our woolly-haired ancestors bred early dogs to help them bring down mighty mastodons and protect their camps against the dangers of the night or if hungry wolves essentially tamed themselves while pigging out at village dumps. It may not matter to anyone other than those scientists, but what is obvious is that, as wolves evolved into dogs, they became animals perfectly designed to pull on our heartstrings.

What researchers can tell us is why *Canis lupus familiaris* has such a hold on us. Those big eyes in a small head, just like a child's, make humans want to protect and nurture them—what is called the "cute response." Puppies, those soft balls of fur, trigger the "supercute response," prompting excruciating squeals of baby talk from even the sternest women, but adult dogs pull on our parental heartstrings as well. This is how dogs, in a way, never grow up. They are always our "children," the Peter Pans among us. They are also our kindred spirits. We are each as social as social comes. Neither of us, human or dog, wants to be alone for long, and too much solitariness will undo us. We each like, even require, physical contact, far more than most other mammals. Our faces are each highly expressive, with even similar smiles, though most people keep their tongues in their mouths. Like us, most dogs play throughout their lives, though they keep to tennis balls and sticks while we graduate from blocks to tag to golf. We each like eye contact, a lot of it. For most of the animal kingdom, looking another creature directly in the eye almost always spells trouble, as in "I'm about to bite a leg or two off you." Not between humans and their pet dogs, though, at least not the socialized ones, for whom eye contact is necessary social glue. The beauty of dogs is that you can look into their eyes endlessly, something you can't do with another human, not even your lover.

This fairy-tale friendship is also the work of a magic potion, oxytocin. The hormone fills us with love for our children, our mates, and our dogs. When I run my hand down Dixie Lou's back, oxytocin crests in my bloodstream and love for her fills my heart, as does the blissful calm from feeling at one with the world. This may explain why working with shelter dogs always puts me in a good mood, even when I'm worried sick about one, or another has ripped my coat again. After laying my hands on so much fur, I happily overflow with oxytocin. The shelter dogs may, too. As evolution would have it, the magic potion works both ways. That is why dogs love being petted so much. When Dixie Lou holds still long enough for a back rub, oxytocin courses through her veins just as it does through mine.

Long before there was any science to explain why dogs blissed people out, and vice versa, Freud noticed that his Chinese chow, Jofi, not only calmed him during therapy sessions, but also did the same for his neurotic patients. Freud was a latecomer to dogs, getting his first in his seventies, and then never being without one again. Bushy, roly-poly Jofi followed him everywhere. As ever-regal chows go, she was rather comical looking, with her disheveled coat and open face. She sat by him at the dinner table, where Freud fed her the food from his plate that he could not chew because of his worsening jaw cancer. During therapy sessions, Jofi stretched out on the floor by Freud's supine patient on the tapestry-covered couch. As his patients described curious dreams and prattled on about old family resentments, Freud often responded through Jofi. If she scratched the door to go out while a patient divulged her hatred for her father, Freud would pronounce, "Jofi does not approve of what you are saying." If Jofi wanted back in, "She's giving you another chance." When one patient waved his arms as he let loose with some bottled-up emotions, Jofi hopped atop him. How Freud interpreted that is lost to history.

Nearly a century later, more people than ever believe, like Freud, that their dogs are family members. Much is made of this in jeering newspaper stories about the billions of dollars Americans lavish on their pets. Academics and researchers marvel at what a break with the past we've made in how we consider our pet dogs. Yet oxytocin didn't just bubble up in our spoiled twenty-first-century brains. We are tied to a long line of dog lovers, including the ancient Greeks, who carried Malteses with them everywhere; or the Aborigines, who kept dingoes as house pets. Beloved dogs pepper our history. Frederick the Great had his mausoleum designed with a view of the graves of his eleven dogs. Empress Josephine, risking Napoleon's sizable ire, refused to kick her pug Fortune out of their bed, even on their wedding night. Abraham Lincoln reportedly lumbered into a frozen river to save his dog.

Lord Byron, who was not known for his faithfulness, nursed his Newfoundland, Boatswain, as he died of rabies, risking contracting the deadly and cruel disease himself. Byron's epitaph on Boatswain's tombstone concludes, "To mark a friend's remains these stones arise; I never knew but one—and here he lies."

I found far humbler tributes at the Pine Ridge Cemetery, a graveyard owned by the Animal Rescue League of Boston, where pet dogs, cats, rabbits, and at least one mouse are buried. A bowling ball–size orb of pink granite blotted with black lichen reads, "Timothy Titmouse Brooks, 1916 to 1926." I, the only visitor that day, walked the looping road in the old section looking for dog graves under the awning of the old trees. Dried pine needles gathered around worn tombstones inscribed with upbeat names such as Prince, Flash, and Beau-Beau, whose stone was in the shape of a heart. The statue of a foxy little mutt sat atop one pocked stone. Mosses and time mottled the inscription. I had trouble reading many of the words carved into the stones, but that didn't take away from their meaning: that in 1898 or 1930, some family or lone soul had loved their pet so much that they paid for a grave and a block of marble or granite, which they then stood in front of, probably saying a few words and then weeping harder than perhaps they expected. The mourners covered their faces with their hands or pulled handkerchiefs from their pockets. Eventually, they turned to leave, in a car or maybe a horse and cart, and returned to a house that would be decidedly, unnervingly quiet without Prince or Flash or Beau-Beau.

I found the new section of the cemetery, with its treeless, clipped lawn gone yellow like straw in the late-summer heat, far less charming. The stones are mostly of one shape and set in straight rows as in a military graveyard, as if an army of pets had fallen there. The stones are bulkier, and so shiny you can see your reflection in them. Amid this harsher order, I found a black stone engraved with the likeness of a crooked-mouthed terrier named Sparky. The generic outline of a Lab was chiseled into another stone, along with the dog's name, Pudding. Most stones bore no likeness, only the dog's name and epitaph—for example, "Nappy, He loved Greatly and Was Greatly Loved." I thought about the dogs, but to my surprise, I thought more about the people. I stood amid those graves, filled with the sadness of death but also the comfort of being among my tribe, a tribe that not only bonds deeply with dogs but that does so even though they know what's coming. If dogs have a flaw, it is that their time on earth is so short, which is why when you give your heart to one, you can be sure it will be broken. That is the price of a dog's boundless love.

This is the mystery of Penny Jane. I so easily

throw my heart away to animals, even ones that aren't my own. I have cried my eyes out over shelter dogs I've walked once. On the spectrum of pet love, I'm at the far end, where most shelter people are. All I have to do to get a well-spoken shelter leader to tear up is to ask her about her pivotal dog. Mindy Naticchioni, at Cuyahoga, still gets weepy over her first foster dog, whom she had for just over a week. We shelter people are beyond soft touches. It's the people toward the other end of the spectrum, the ones who keep their dogs tied up in the backyard, who tend to surrender their pets. Not us, not me. Yet even if I could give Penny Jane my heart, I doubt she'd take it. I doubt she would miss me. She might even be relieved to be free of me. Perhaps, I realize, I have been a fickle lover all this time, needing a dog's love first before I could return it. Certainly I've taken dogs' easy affection for granted—until now.

One morning, Scott says, "It would be easier to return Penny Jane than to get a divorce." He doesn't laugh; nor do I. I'm bleary-eyed. She woke me up at 4:00 a.m. again.

Two syllables fall out of my mouth. "Okay." I will be "them" after all.

"Good," he says and leaves for work with Dixie Lou. I am relieved. I am numb. I trudge up the back steps to my office. Penny Jane follows at a safe distance.

• • •

If a weak, broken, or nonexistent bond can make a dog like Penny Jane homeless, then shelters need to understand how this age-old friendship works or doesn't. Yet how much can we know in the end? How do you scientifically explain why some people toughed out the mayhem of Hurricane Katrina to stay with their pets? We can examine the biology and survey legions of dog lovers, but there is something mystical to this cross-species love affair that seems beyond science's easy reach. Patricia McConnell, one of my heroes, agrees. She has pondered this unlikely friendship between humans and dogs for decades. McConnell gives all late bloomers hope. After an early marriage, children, and all kinds of jobs, including one night as a go-go dancer, she enrolled as a freshman at the University of Wisconsin in Madison when she was thirty. She earned her PhD in animal behavior ten years later, in 1988 (when most scientists were convinced canines were soulless fur robots), by studying how the sound of words, such as long, slow ones, affect communication between dogs and their trainers. McConnell hasn't run a study since. Instead, she has devoted her life to teaching Americans how to get along with their dogs. She's done this with her books, her website, and her lectures around the country. Along the way, she has puzzled over why some people will put up with their dogs biting them while others will surrender a pet who needs only a refresher in housebreaking.

When I ask McConnell what keeps a bond from blossoming or breaks it, she has a one word answer—fear, that old monster again. Fear will quickly put a stop to all those warm feelings, for the person or the dog. A dog snaps at you because you've scared him by accidentally cornering him or by showing him who's in charge and pulling him roughly off the couch. Now you are afraid of your dog. He's afraid of you. A vicious cycle ensues. This is one of the many reasons McConnell beats the drum for positive-reinforcement training methods. Most of the behavior problems she saw as a consultant were the result of people using old-school punishment: nose swats, collar jerks, and so on, techniques that often scare dogs. What creates a bond, she tells me, is trust, trust that nothing bad will happen to human or dog. Most dogs naturally trust humans. We simply need not to squander that trust. But those are socialized dogs, unlike my Penny Jane. I couldn't squander her trust if I wanted to, because she came with no ready supply. Undersocialized dogs like Penny Jane have to learn to trust humans, and that can take months, maybe years. Until then, these dogs aren't likely to bond with anyone. Humans may have trouble bonding with such a dog, too, especially if they can't pet him. No petting, no oxytocin.

McConnell lives on a farm in the hills of southern Wisconsin with a flock of sheep, a Cavalier King Charles spaniel named Tootsie, and two border collies, Willie and Maggie, the most recent addition to the pack, whom McConnell declares herself gobsmacked over. She's just so damn cute with that one ear flipped up. Maggie loves to work sheep during the day and then worm her way onto the sofa for a belly rub at night. The thing about love, McConnell says, is that it comes in so many different flavors. She loved Cool Hand Luke, the heroic border collie she's written about in a number of her books, because he always had her back. He even once saved her from a charging ewe. She loves fearful yet goofy Willie, the perpetual, somewhat problematic teenager, because she has his back. His need for her fires that bond. Tootsie spent seven years in an Amish puppy mill. When a rescue took her in, she was as fat as a tick, had an infection in her mouth and ears, and needed tooth after tooth pulled. McConnell wanted a lapdog, what she calls an "oxytocin pump." Quiet, good-natured Tootsie has been happy to oblige. In exchange, McConnell is happy to smother her with all the love she's always deserved.

As bad as McConnell has it for her dogs, she knows they have it worse for her. Dogs always do.

They are the more ardent lovers in this unbalanced relationship, a relationship that happens to be essential to a dog's happiness. We have a long list of expectations for this friendship: that the dog make us look important or protect us or fend off our loneliness. Dogs don't care if we live in a trailer or have a lisp. They just want, need, to be with us. A dog without a human bond is always somewhat at sea, always looking for an anchor. I've seen this at the shelter, where most of the dogs throw themselves at me as if asking, "Are you the one?" That explains the tidal wave of unqualified love that rolls out of the kennels. Even the shy pups have trouble keeping their affection in check. I once took out Boaz, a little terrier mix with a snub nose and snaggletoothed underbite. He sat for me to leash him but nervously turned his head away. When I walked Boaz into a roomful of trainers for a demonstration, he glommed on to me as if I were his long-lost friend. When I handed his leash to people for training exercises, he trembled and stared at me with worried eyes that cried, "Help!" He climbed into my lap every chance he got. We had met only fifteen minutes earlier. The first time I walked Luke, a long drink of beauty like any Weimaraner, he couldn't really be bothered with me. Then I annoyed him by clumsily trying to loosen his tight collar. He bumped my forearm hard with his nose, which is dogspeak for "Cut it out." I did. I returned him to his kennel sure that I hadn't made a very good impression. Yet the next time Luke saw me, he forgot he was a Weimaraner and carried on like a Labrador, twitching his stump of a tail and loudly whining at me through a play yard fence to come closer. Surprised, I fell to my knees and pushed the side of my face against the fence so he could lick my cheek. It took me a few years of volunteering before Luke, Boaz, and countless other shelter dogs made me realize they are not so much homeless as humanless, and that that was worse.

In his book *Dog*, Raymond Coppinger, a biologist who has studied canines longer than most scientists have, writes that if our species were to disappear, dogs would vanish with us. Yet it wouldn't work the other way around. Should *Canis lupus familiaris* disappear, we *Homo sapiens* would hardly blink. He's right, though I think we would be lonelier, even lesser. Who exactly would we be without dogs? Our creation stories and myths are riddled with them. In one of my favorites, the ancient, unpronounceable Indian epic poem the *Mahabharata*, five brothers make a long, arduous journey to the gates of heaven in the Himalayas. Along the way, a stray dog joins the group. Brother after brother dies along the route, until only one and the dog are left. As the twosome climbs the mountains, a god driving a chariot appears. The god begs the brother, but not the dog, to step aboard and he will shepherd him to heaven. The stray must stay behind, the god says. The brother refuses. The stray has been his loyal companion. He won't abandon him now. Hearing that, the dog reveals himself to be the god of righteousness, and our hero, having returned the dog's loyalty, steps through the gates and into heaven.

The hours pass. As has become her habit, Penny Jane lies on the landing just outside my office. I lose myself in my writing. I walk Penny Jane at lunch and return to my desk. Scott comes home with Dixie Lou. We make dinner. We watch TV. If Scott had expected me to take Penny Jane back by the time he got home, he doesn't mention it. In fact, neither of us mentions taking her back to the shelter. Again. Ever. Maybe this one day, when she didn't seem like "ours," let us catch our breath. Maybe knowing that we could return her if it came to that, we can soldier on. Maybe we can turn our lives inside out for a dog, for this dog, for Miss Penny Jane. As dogs well know, the human heart is a mystery.

Jasmine

4

BOSTON

The Animal Rescue League of Boston hugs the border of one of the city's most fashionable neighborhoods, the South End. On one side of the shelter, a southwestern restaurant plates upscale tacos, and on the other a boutique hotel draws a steady parade of roller suitcases. Across the street, people duck into and out of a chain drugstore, a pizza parlor, and a neighborhood hardware store all day long. Though the Animal Rescue League of Boston has a large play yard, with an A-frame and a teeter-totter for agility training, both painted bright red and yellow, none of the people walking by all day seems to notice the shelter. Whenever I tell people I volunteer at the ARL, they always ask, "It's right in the city? Right in the South End?" Yes, it's right under your nose, I want to say. I wonder if people don't see the shelter because they don't want to. Most shelters are set far out of the way, in industrial parks or next to a municipal dump, and dream of a location like the ARL's, but maybe a highly visible spot doesn't make that much of a difference. Animal shelters make most people so sad and uncomfortable that they can look right past them wherever they are.

In Maine, I walked shelter dogs in the quiet of the woods. Now I ply city streets full of high-end strollers and big-ticket haircuts with a homeless mutt by my side. I steer brawny pitties through the neighborhood's red glow from all the brick, across lines of cheery theatergoers, down rows of polished row houses, and past young girls with tight buns and long necks hurrying into and out of the Boston Ballet's headquarters. I take the dogs to the Boston Public Garden to loop the pond, relax on one of the many wooden benches, and watch the ducks preen, the squirrels bounce about, or a white swan or two glide by on the pond's mud-colored waters. I also like to loiter on a stoop near one of Boston's best restaurants, where I will stroke a dog's back while we people-watch. Granted, walking dogs who aren't keen on other dogs through a neighborhood filled with people parading their mostly purebred pets makes for some adventures, but I've found plenty of quiet alleyways and narrow streets. My favorite is a shaded, sunken alley edged with weeds and shaggy, forgotten gardens that the dogs love to push their noses into. I've also learned to quickly pull my charges between parked cars, even Simba the ninety-pound boxer, so they cannot see another dog promenading down the sidewalk. The pet owners find this very curious and often call to me, "Mine is friendly." "Mine is not," I call back.

At the ARL, I can do more than walk the dogs.

On Wednesdays a group of volunteers alternately bathes the dogs or trains them. On bath night, we run the dogs across the street to a grooming business that lets us use their two standing metal tubs and stacks of thin white towels. We plop little terriers into the elbow-deep tubs and heave the heavyweights in for a lather. Lacking a crane, a small team of us hoists a Saint Bernard into a tub. After we lift the dripping giant out, we have to dry ourselves off. We wash only the dogs the shelter's trainers think will abide it, which surprisingly is most of them, maybe because we shovel treats into their mouth as we hose the grime of kennel life out of their coats. We do have to choreograph who comes when, keeping in mind who doesn't like whom. Some dogs hate other specific dogs so violently that it can be a challenge just getting them past each other in the street. The ones who growl and lunge at any dog usually get the last shampoo of the evening, when the floor is covered with soggy towels, we are nearly as wet as the dogs, and the room is perfumed with the scent of freshly washed fur.

A clean dog has a better shot at getting adopted, as does a dog who puts his bottom on the floor on command. When people looking for a pet visit the kennels, first they exclaim, "Look how cute he is!" and then the chant starts: "Sit, sit, sit, sit, sit, sit." Even when I tell people that the Yorkie they have been droning on to does not know how to sit, they are undeterred. "Sit, sit, sit, sit." People obviously want dogs who sit. That is the first thing we work on during training classes on Wednesdays, when about a half dozen or so volunteers stand in a circle, each clutching the leash of a dog in the glare of an auditorium. Using slippery chunks of hot dogs, we can quickly teach most dogs to drop their bottoms to the floor. However, the dogs in the shelter are not "most dogs." Some are so aggravated by the sight of other dogs that they have to work behind a table flipped on its side. Some are so nervous that they sit and stare, won't even glance at your handful of hot dog chunks. There's a lot of arranging of who can stand next to whom. The staff trainer often has to yell to be heard over the barking. Some of the volunteers have never trained a dog, never mind lived with one, and look as confused as the dogs. Amid this chaos, we manage to teach our four-legged pupils not only to sit, but also to lie down, to look in our eyes, to walk on a leash, to offer up a paw, as best we can. This is why dogs who stay with us for months end up knowing a lot of cues. When visitors begin the chant with our longtime residents, typically the pitties, before the second "Sit," the dogs' butts are on the kennel floor.

When we moved from Portland to Boston so Scott could take a job, we left behind our roomy house and the nearby bayside park for a small condo on the narrow streets of Charlestown, within walking distance of Boston Harbor. The "girls" then became city dogs, a role that surprisingly fit Penny Jane, who in her first two years with us had morphed from a fearful dog to a shy yet content dog. Like most undersocialized dogs, Penny Jane still did not enjoy being petted and next to never solicited it, though, oddly, she liked being dried off with a towel. What she liked was activity: riding in cars, staying in hotels, and going for long city walks. In some ways she had become utterly fearless. She could ride in elevators. In Boston we took her on the T. When I went swimsuit shopping at Lord and Taylor, I brought her along for moral support. She, whom I once considered one of the worst mistakes of my life, quietly lay on the dressing room floor while I wrestled two-pieces on and off.

This great transformation was the result, mostly, of our simply ignoring her. In her early, difficult months with us, I finally, in my sleepless, frazzled haze, thought to type the phrase "fearful dog into the Internet, and like an oracle, my computer screen provided me with answers. The oracle told me that I should pay Penny Jane as little attention as possible and stop looking at her, especially in the eye. If we hadn't been so desperate, I'm not sure we could have done what seemed so unnatural for any dog lover, but at that point we would have tried anything. We began to treat Penny Jane as a kind of stray dog in our house, one for whom we set out food and water and then left alone. When friends came for dinner, we'd tell them to forget that Penny Jane was even there, and not to call to her or stare at her. Some could do it, and some could not resist trilling, "Oh, come here, sweetie," at which point Penny Jane would tuck her tail and slip away into the house. "Oh, I'm sorry, honey. Come back!" they'd yell as I bit my lip.

We also gave Penny Jane a safe haven. We doubled down on her crate training. We started from the beginning, feeding her breakfast and dinner in the darkened shell of her "den," tossing in treats and chews, building up good association after good association with that plastic box until Penny Jane willingly entered and let us close the crate door behind her, and we all began to sleep through the night. She spent most of her first year with us in her crate. The moment we unleashed her from a walk, she'd bolt for its comfort upstairs. She'd stay there until we hollered her name for dinner. Having noisily inhaled a bowl of kibble, she'd then dash back upstairs to her crate. We took none of this personally. In fact, it was a relief not to have a nervous dog underfoot. We all began to relax. Sometimes, when Scott, Dixie, and I watched TV in the evenings, we'd hear the funny patter of Penny Jane's toenails coming down the steps. She'd come to the TV room's open french doors, stand quietly, and peer at the three of us, sometimes even wagging her upright tail. We knew not to remark on this small burst of friendliness. Instead, we quietly faced the TV screen while, out of the corners of our eyes, we'd see Penny Jane briefly wag her curled tail and then, as if frightened by her own boldness, turn on her ballerina paws and flee back upstairs.

This was good enough for us. We could live with the nonsense around the doors. We got used to her barking at us when we walked up and down our old, creaky steps. While we were busy ignoring her we missed the slow magic our small expectations were working. All we knew was that we had quite a list of nicknames for Penny Jane: PeeWee, Pretty Pants, and Poocheena, which became Cheena, which became, inexplicably, African Wild Cheena. Outdoors, she was almost a normal dog. She was so food-driven (once, she even sucked an earthworm out of the ground) that we were quickly able to train her to come to her name and run off leash. We discovered she was an expert hiker, unlike Dixie Lou, who insisted we throw tennis balls, sticks, or pinecones as we trod along. Penny Jane, meanwhile, explored the world, snuffling through leaves, looking up old trees at squirrels, and poking her nose into woodchuck holes. She rarely kept to the trail with us. We'd see her off to our side a good twenty feet away, weaving through the birches and maples. Scott joked that he would train her to find truffles.

By the time we moved to Boston, we were deeply attached to our Penny Jane. As corny as it sounds, we loved her for her. That was, in a way, an accomplishment. For the first time, I loved a dog who showed no great love for me back. Occasionally she would bump the back of our calves with her moist nose, which we took as some kind of affection. On the beach, she'd burrow into the sand like a badger next to my towel, kicking heaps of sand on my sunblock-slicked back. She also, I realized, kept an eye on me. One day, the girls and I ducked out of a drenching rain and into a grove of evergreens in a favorite park. Amid the cover and dark of the trees, I tossed Dixie Lou's tennis ball far down a path and then, as both girls ran ahead of me down the trail, I bent over to hitch their leashes around me like sashes. Suddenly I heard a noise like a gust of wind right behind me. As I stood up, I saw Penny Jane racing up the trail, her eyes fixed just past me. I turned. There was a middle-aged man in a hooded raincoat surprisingly close to me, close enough to grab me. He was balanced on the balls of his feet as if he'd been running and had come to a quick stop. His dark, worried eyes were not on me but on Penny Jane. He turned and ran so hard that his large coat noisily flapped. I let Penny Jane chase the dark-eyed man until he was nearly out of the trees, and then I hollered until she came back. Dixie Lou, a tennis ball in her mouth, finally came up the trail to see what was keeping me from playing fetch.

Still, Penny Jane was no Dixie Lou, who shadowed our every step, who erupted with toothy joy whenever we returned home, who showered us with endless, obvious affection. We were half-drunk on oxytocin most of the time thanks to our smiley Aussie. Penny Jane, our spare, so to speak, would have big shoes to fill, and sooner than we expected. A year after we adopted Penny Jane we learned that Dixie Lou had only one working kidney, which was slowly failing. She was only five. All we could do, really, was buy her special food and hope that her remaining kidney took its time konking out. Dixie Lou made it easy for us to forget we had her on borrowed time. For another three years she fetched maniacally, watched TV with us each evening, and flashed that nutty Aussie grin whenever we walked in the door. Then the fireworks show that was Dixie Lou came to a close. She was nearly nine. She chased sticks on her last morning, though she could hardly see. By the end of the day, she was fidgety, almost delirious. We had arranged for a vet to come the next morning to put her down at home, but we couldn't wait. When we asked Dixie Lou if she wanted to go for a car ride, she excitedly ran to the back door. Scott carried her into the emergency clinic. Near midnight, we walked back out empty-handed into a sharp January night. Waiting in the car for us was Penny Jane. She had lost her ambassador dog. So had we.

By the time I began volunteering at the ARL I had walked shelter dogs, worked with a high-energy Aussie, adopted a near-feral stray, basically run my own fearful-dog center, and gone to countless training classes. I had also written a book about the top school for exotic animal trainers. For over a year, I followed students at Moorpark College, in the hinterlands northwest of Los Angeles, as they learned to walk cougars or trained baboons to skateboard. I talked with professional elephant trainers, dolphin trainers, and lion trainers. I became a student myself, learning the finer points of what is called positive training, or training with positive reinforcement, or clicker training. What-ever you call it, it helped me earn a much deeper understanding of animal behavior and how training worked. I wouldn't trust myself to teach a baboon to give me a high-five, but I did have some training chops. I wanted to put this know-how to work for homeless dogs.

Boston has two private nonprofit shelters, the Animal Rescue League and the Massachusetts Society for the Prevention of Cruelty to Animals.

The city of Boston's animal control office has an adoption center as well, but it never dawned on me that I could volunteer there. Back then, I didn't understand the exact difference between a private nonprofit such as the ARL and a city facility. Had I, I might have gone to the latter. As it was, I picked the ARL simply because it was the closest shelter to Charlestown. I could take the subway there, which turned out to be especially handy during the city's many messy snowstorms, when the roads became nightmarish. I could even walk the 2.5 miles across town, which, oddly, I tended to do after especially disheartening days or even ones when everything went just right. At the volunteer orientation, I found out that the ARL had an arm that was researching how best to help shelter dogs. They had trainers and a veterinarian behaviorist. In addition to the training classes and bath nights, volunteers could take dogs to the Real Life Room, which was fitted out like a threadbare living room with a couch and rug, both well stained. Then I began to meet the dogs. I had inadvertently picked the right shelter for me.

Most of the dogs at the ARL are adult mutts, many of whom have a medical problem or some kind of behavioral quirk. Some of the ARL's dogs are ready to move right into your house, what we call "plug-and-play dogs," such as Biko, the one-year-old stray with the untraceable chip. He loved to play fetch, was a crack at training, and found a new home in a week. A lot of the dogs are overenergetic adolescents who swat at you with their paws, and maybe grab the hood on your jacket. Some are uneasy with other dogs. Some growl if you reach toward their food bowl or peer at them through the kennel door. Some piddle on the floor when they see a man. The pitties are problems unto themselves, even if they are the best-adjusted dogs in the shelter. In a city full of renters, many landlords won't allow them. Even if you are one of the 34 percent of Boston residents who own their home, home insurance may not allow the dogs, either. That largely explains why Sidney, a young lunk with a melon-size head who lived for belly rubs, spent eighteen months at the ARL.

The ARL's wards—mostly adult mutts—are pretty typical of the dogs you'll find now in many big-city shelters. Boston, like any city with a high spay/neuter rate, has few unwanted puppies, so few you'll find few dogs under six months old at the ARL. Breed-specific rescue groups pull nearly all the purebreds from shelters, which explains why the ARL has mostly mutts. These adult mutts who are abandoned or surrendered often don't get an ideal start in life. They might be hyper-active from spending long days in a crate or they were never housebroken. These problems are not uncommon among pet dogs, but shelter dogs have no devoted owner, no advocate, no one to say, "We love him like he is." If Penny Jane were to go into a shelter, even in her improved state, she would be a challenge to find a home for because not many people want a dog who doesn't like to be petted. In my home, she's just Penny Jane.

If it seems as if there are more dogs with behavior problems in shelters now, that's because there are. Not long ago, these dogs, even the ones with the slightest issues, never made it to the adoption floor. They were put down. When Sharon Harmon applied to become operations manager at the Oregon Humane Society in 1989, the local newspaper was running headlines above the fold that went something like this: "Thousands of Animals Killed at Humane Society." Her father mailed her the clippings, hoping they would discourage her from taking the job. Harmon read the headlines and thought, "Why is this news? It happens everywhere." This was when shelters were still flooded with a constant river of rejected animals, a river far deeper and wider than the relative trickle of adopters coming through their doors. When Harmon took the job at Oregon Humane in Portland, the shelter was putting down dogs for barking, leaping on people, destructive chewing—in other words, normal dog behavior. They had like many shelters then, she says, an "if-it-sneezed-it-died" philosophy," which sounds exaggerated but isn't. When there weren't enough adopters for the healthy dogs, one with kennel cough had to go.

Then that river of dogs began to ebb most everywhere, thanks to the spay/neuter movement, thanks to increasing pet ownership, and thanks to the no-kill movement. Without the constant deluge of animals, shelters had the space and resources to reconsider who could find a home. Oregon Humane, like most shelters, began lowering the bar for who was adoptable beyond puppies. Maybe people would take home adult dogs, big dogs, even old, big dogs. They did. Then the shelter reconsidered dogs with garden-variety foibles, dogs with mange or ringworm, dogs like Scabie Ben. Scabie Ben was a five-year-old retriever of some kind with no fur on the front half of his body. Harmon remembers that you could smell him before you saw him. She expected Scabie Ben would be euthanized. Then a volunteer begged to foster him. The staff indulged her. At home with the volunteer, Scabie Ben grew his fur back. Then the volunteer found him a home. "I thought, if we could save a dog like Scabie Ben, who else could we save?" Harmon's next "ah-ha" moment came when an adopter handed her a photo of his Jack Russell atop the Thanksgiving table, baring his teeth over the turkey. She was mortified. The adopter laughed. He was proud. Harmon realized that what one owner finds unbearable in a dog, another may find funny, even desirable. Might there be homes for the "lost causes," the snappers, the growlers, even the biters?

Now Oregon Humane has no time limit on how long animals can stay, and it finds homes for nearly all of them—98 percent, one of the highest adoption rates in the country. That takes a lot of staff, time, and money because half the dogs who come to the shelter need some kind of help. Torn ACLs, heartworm, and skin infections are pretty straightforward fixes, especially in an age when most major shelters have a vet on staff; Oregon even has a hospital. Behavior, however, is far trickier. No pill will make a dog stop growling at men. That's why Oregon Humane has a staff of six trainers. It also has an animal communicator. "She tells us things like 'He doesn't like the slippery floor.' I don't know if she's right, but it makes everyone feel better," Harmon says.

There isn't an animal communicator at the ARL, if only because this is flinty old Boston, where just smiling at someone can be taken as suspiciously New Age. The ARL is also far smaller than Oregon Humane, which has room for 180 dogs. The Boston shelter is the largest of the ARL's three locations, but there are only 20 kennels, each with a raised bed, usually toys, maybe something to chew on. With their chain-link-covered doors, the actual kennels are nothing special. In fact, they resemble those at some of the city animal control facilities I've seen. They are just as loud, too. Barks echo off the painted cinder-block walls and cement floor. The ARL, however, is not a city pound. A private nonprofit, the ARL can pick and choose which animals it takes in, but the shelter is not all that choosy. Ragtag animals that other private shelters or rescue groups might reject often come here and then stay until they are adopted. The ARL does not euthanize for space, but it will put down an animal with severe health problems or ones it believes are too dangerous for a home. Of course, even with medical tests and behavior evaluations, these are judgment calls, often painful ones. Shelter work is not for the fainthearted.

I arrived my first day in my gray T-shirt with the word *volunteer* emblazoned in red across the back. A young, willowy staff member led me back and forth across the shiny rectangular building, showing me door lock codes, where the leashes were, and how to put a chest harness on a dog who's bouncing around. (You drop a handful of treats on the floor and then get busy while he's munching away.) I followed her down the long, narrow hallway that slices through the first floor, squeezing past staff members in red hoodies hurriedly toting cats in cardboard boxes or bowls of dog kibble. We ducked into various rooms. In one, parakeets fluttered and bunnies busily pushed hay around their enclosures. I hadn't thought of people giving up bunnies, but they do. They also give up iguanas, ferrets, even gerbils. People carry their pets into the intake office, a cramped, glum room at the far end of the building. At the other end of the building, in the roomier and more cheerful lobby, smiling adopters whisk their animals out the front door and to a new life.

The willowy staff member and I stepped into a small room with dimly lit kennels for lapdogs and the like. Little faces turned up to watch us pass. We pushed another heavy door open into the bright light of the back run, where larger dogs bunk in far roomier digs. The dogs woofed when they saw us. Some chuffed. Some let it rip. The range of styles and pitches made for an orchestra of sorts, as if each dog knew his part. These dogs were not ready for the adoption floor. Some had just arrived. Others needed training or to be spayed or neutered. The staff member pointed to the colored dots on their kennel boards. A green one, she said, meant the dog was as easy as pie to walk. Any volunteer could take out a green dog. A blue dot signaled one who wasn't so easy to handle. Maybe he pulled hard on his leash or would bite at the harness as you tried to put it on. Only the staff could walk dogs with a red dot.

Those dogs tended to be big and hyperactive. Some were so scared that they might snap. As a new volunteer, I was supposed to stick with green dogs, but when I mentioned to the willowy staff member that I had had an Aussie, she handed me the leash of a blue dog.

Most of that first year was a blur of dogs coming and going as I learned the ins and outs of how the shelter ran. As it is now, I remember only the few I worked with a lot, such as Hawthorn, a puppy with elephant-size ears, or those who stood who out for some reason, such as the ink-black German shepherd named Bishop. Her coat was long and lush. She was young, about two years old. I would have noticed her alone for her looks, but she also had curious letters written on her kennel board: "LE."

LE stands for law enforcement. An LE dog is, unfortunately, caught up in a court case. This can be because the dogs were confiscated from their owners who mistreated them. They were used in dogfights or were starved or beaten. I've seen an LE dog whose snout had been closed with a garbage bag plastic twist tie, another who'd had his face broken, another who was thinner than a runway model. When he wagged his tail, he nearly toppled over. LE dogs are confiscated from cruel owners, derelict petting zoos, incompetent rescues, and dogfighting rings.

Football player Michael Vick's fighting dogs are the most famous LE dogs.

All these dogs become material evidence to the crime that was committed against them. As such, they must be held in a shelter while the criminal case inches its way through court. Until there is a plea agreement or a verdict or some kind of a resolution, the dog cannot be put up for adoption and remains in a shelter kennel. This is how a crime can be visited twice on an animal, first by the abuser and then by the legal system, which sends the dog into a limbo for months or, in extreme cases, years. That is bad for dogs and for shelters. LE animals can take up much-needed kennel space and funds. When I talked to Harmon in the fall, she had eight LE dogs, Akitas from a puppy mill. The court case against their owner was scheduled for June. In the end, the case took twenty-three months to be resolved. Only then could the Akitas be put up for adoption.

A dog can also fall into legal limbo if his ownership is contested, such as in Bishop's case. Her owner had been sent to jail but had refused to relinquish her. He wanted a family member to pick her up, but Bishop had been found dirty, kept outside with a too-tight collar on a short chain. The shelter was not going to return her to the same sad situation. However, the ARL did not legally own Bishop, so it could not put her up for adoption. It could sue for ownership and/or prosecute her owner for negligence. Either way, Bishop was stuck in the shelter indefinitely. That usually spells trouble for German shepherds, who, with their high-energy and sensitive natures, often do not fare well in the chaos and noise, and they make it obvious. Many take to spinning in their kennels. They pinch their brows. Their eyes become frantic. Other dogs can look confused in the kennels. A German shepherd can look as if he understands exactly what has happened to him.

Bishop, luckily, was relatively easygoing for the breed, and she had a light touch. She danced around her kennel, tossing off tufts of fur every-where. Her kennel often looked as if a pillow of black fur had exploded. I took her out every time I went in, including one Christmas Day. Scott came with me that time, and we walked Bishop through the lovely quiet that had descended on Boston's South End. We called out "Merry Christmas" to the few people we passed. Whether it was the holiday or Bishop's beauty, people beamed at us. I kneeled on a snowy sidewalk and hugged her while Scott took my picture with my first LE dog. As was the case with so many of the shelter dogs I have loved, one day I came in and Bishop was gone. Arrangements had been made to move her to a private rescue in New Hampshire. I asked about her now and again, but no one seemed to know anything. Finally, I heard that the couple who had adopted her had contacted the shelter looking for her vet records. They had renamed her Calypso.

I walked dogs that I thought other volunteers might not take out much, typically bruisers such as the hippo-size Skye, who was as good-natured as she was huge. One summer night Skye and I joined a half-dozen shelter dogs and volunteers for a walk through the Boston Public Garden. We were a motley crew among the foreign tourists and topiary. Skye and I pulled up the rear of the single-file line that wound its way past the boxwoods and roses. As we lumbered past a large nonworking fountain, she dove for a dirty puddle that had collected in its bottom. As one hundred pounds lurched into the fancy fountain under a classic Boston pink dusk, I dug my feet in and hollered, "Oh, shit," through the soft early evening. With that, Skye turned her great head, looked back with a bit of surprise, and took mercy on the middle-aged woman in an ill-fitting shelter T-shirt. In Maine, the dogs had sometimes made a fool of me, such as when I slipped on the ice with Baxter, but in the privacy of the woods. In Boston, I often played the clown in plain sight, clinging for dear life to a charging mutt as we passed a buzzing restaurant patio or tangling with some youngster biting the leash as we crossed the nutty intersection by the Boston Public Library. In a city of cool customers, I could look like a real doofus. My "Volunteer" T-shirt didn't help.

I also got in the habit of taking out the dogs I'd walked before. That way, we could get to know each other, and I hoped it would give the dogs some small bit of routine amid the chaos, and a bit of friendship. Among the swirl of faces, they would know mine, and I would know theirs. Sharyn, an adult pit bull mix, was surrendered because the landlord said she had to go. She arrived in July, as svelte, smiley, and stylish as Skye was massive. Her face was black on one side and white on the other, like Cruella De Vil's. Sharyn didn't care much for other female dogs, and she once bit a puppy through the play yard fence, but she loved people. She was never anything other than perfect with me.

Sharyn and I walked long loops through the South End that summer, past the community garden, where giant sunflowers rose overhead throughout the summer and into the fall, when the sparrows mobbed their dried blooms for seeds. Despite her beauty and bright eyes, no one adopted Sharyn. Next to no one even asked to meet her. As the months passed, Sharyn and I became better and better friends. All the dogs were excited to go for a walk with me, but Sharyn was excited just to see me, and I her. What I didn't know about my friend was that the stress of the shelter had given her colitis. A trainer had seen her jumping repeatedly off the back wall of her kennel, another worrisome sign. What I did see was a small bald patch on her lovely face. She had ringworm. She was moved off the adoption floor. Nobody will die from ringworm, a misnamed fungal infection, but it's highly contagious to other dogs and humans. The last time I'd seen ringworm was on the arm of my overly athletic teenage brother when we were in high school. I wouldn't even sit on the same couch with him, but for Sharyn, I pulled on rubber gloves and off we went among the Christmas lights. After I'd closed her back in her kennel, I scrubbed my hands and arms long and hard up to my elbows. As I was leaving after one such scrubbing, a staff member told me there was some question as to whether Sharyn was adoptable. I was surprised, so surprised by what she was telling me that it didn't sink in. As I walked to the T, I wondered what more I could do for Sharyn. I couldn't foster her. With her dog aggression and now ringworm, I couldn't bring her home to Penny Jane. On the train, I pondered how I could help Sharyn until, not having come up with any answers, my mind drifted off to thoughts of dinner and the relaxing aimlessness of the evening ahead.

The next time I went to the shelter, I found her kennel empty. I went looking for someone to ask, thinking, as I walked, No, not her. Yes, her. She'd been euthanized. The staff had decided that her dog aggression plus the ringworm had made her next to impossible to adopt. Life in the kennels was so miserable for her that it was inhumane to keep her there anymore. I understood and I didn't. My friend was gone. I walked back to the kennels and grabbed a small Lab mix with bright eyes, one that would be sure to find a home before I had half a chance to become attached to him. I didn't even read his name or sex on his kennel board. I just called him "Puppy" as we walked. Without thinking, I led us on one of Sharyn's favorite paths, past the sunflowers, now toppled and broken, as I pined for my friend. She was all I thought about on the subway ride home. My mind never drifted away from her sweet black-and-white face. I wished I had walked Sharyn more, done something, anything. Next time, I promised myself, I would.

When the shelter asked me if I wanted to learn how to walk and train the "red dogs," the ones only the staff could walk, I said yes. When they asked me if I wanted to learn how to help with play group and later help with adoptions, I said yes.

Brody
(courtesy of Robert Denton)

141

5

THE STORY OF SIDO

Brody showed up in the back kennels the June after I said good-bye to Sharyn. The juvenile German shepherd leapt up on his kennel door with a bang and whined to say hello. He looked at me with his almond-shaped eyes lined with black. Brody's owner had dropped him with a dog sitter for a weekend and then never returned for the pup. After two months, the sitter brought him to the ARL.

Brody had a short, fawn-colored coat stippled with black. The black dipped to a sharp point between his eyes, like a widow's peak. When he wasn't smiling, he often furrowed his brow as if working out a math equation in his head. He looked to be eighty pounds, and was. He would have been intimidating except that the tip of his pricked left ear flopped forward. German shepherds don't show up at the ARL often, probably because they aren't a popular breed in Boston, city of Labs, doodles, and Frenchies. There had been maybe one other at the ARL since Bishop, the law enforcement dog, the year before. When Brody arrived, I could hardly find a leash and a harness fast enough to take him out.

I stepped into his kennel slowly, tossing treats ahead of me as always, as a goodwill offering, but also to keep the young bruiser from rushing the door or pouncing on me. As Brody turned excited, I managed to snap a harness on his thick chest. Off we went. That became the summer of Brody. I always walked the young shepherd first, and then maybe a second time before I left. I went extra days just to see him. If I arrived and another volunteer had him out, I felt miffed. I stood by the adoption desk tapping my foot, waiting for that volunteer to return with *my dog*. I liked all the pups I walked, even the ones who peed on my shoe when I wasn't looking or pulled me down the brick sidewalks like chariot horses, but I was bonkers for Brody. I really let my heart go with him because his future looked so bright, even if Boston was ho-hum on the heirs of Rin Tin Tin. Brody was handsome as well as nicely behaved. He was energetic, no doubt, like any juvenile, but he got along with most dogs and adored people. He was a little goofy on a leash, grabbing and tugging on it for fun, but he wasn't hard for me to walk. He got the runs, probably from stress, but otherwise, he was holding up pretty well in the shelter.

How could I fall in love with a dog and not take him home? I can't explain it, except to say that when you volunteer with shelter dogs, you become accustomed to saying good-bye, like a traveler making friends or having affairs along the road. It becomes a habit, a way of thinking. I found I could bond over and over knowing full well I would never see these dogs again, which was both curious and liberating. I often thought of myself as a kind of guardian angel to accompany them through the limbo of their shelter stay. "I'll watch out for you," I told Brody each time I returned him to his kennel.

I came in one night in late July, as the summer light was just beginning to fade but the heat was not, and Brody was gone. He'd been adopted. I had been right. I was so happy for him, but missed him. The usual bittersweetness washed over me. I shook it off by grabbing a leash, pushing open a kennel door, and scattering goodies on the floor. One thing is certain in a shelter. There are always more dogs to walk.

Summer rushed along. The beach called my name. Penny Jane had holes to dig. I had novels to read. I threw myself into the Atlantic's chill while Penny Jane watched from her burrow. With Brody gone, I didn't go to the shelter as often, but religiously attended the joyful mayhem of Wednesday-evening training classes. I dropped slippery chunks of hot dog into the maws of dogs who sat, who stayed, who shook my hand. Many dogs, once they figure out the ridiculous thing you are asking when you say, "Shake," get this look like "If you say so" and then plonk their paws hard in your hand. As nonplussed as they are, feeling their rough pads against my palm makes me inexplicably want to kiss them, though I don't. My rule is if a shelter dog wants to kiss me, fine, but I never take the initiative, because I like my nose where it is—on my face.

The first Wednesday in September, I checked the class list that the auburn-haired trainer had posted in the shelter's long hallway, scanning it quickly to see whom I wanted to work with most. I typically preferred the more challenging dogs, such as Hercules, a young pittie with a Buddha potbelly and the markings of a Boston terrier. His former owner had kicked him so badly in the head he'd broken Hercules's sweet face. Hercules was no worse for it. Life, despite its deep disappointments, was too much fun for him. Barking and jumping were his hobbies, which made him my kind of dog. As I hustled past the small kennels filled with little, fuzzy things to get Hercules, I noticed a German shepherd tucked in one. Written in alarming red marker on his kennel board was the message "Staff Only." There was no name. That dog looks kind of like Brody, I thought, as I rushed by. After class, as I passed the shepherd again, he pressed his front paws on the kennel door, which I took for general overexcitement. But he swished his tail at me, even woofed. After bidding a hasty goodnight to Hercules in his kennel, I went to look at the shepherd. It was Brody. I put my fingers through his door so he could lick them. I leaned my cheek against the gate so he could lick that, too. I cooed, "Hello, baby." I was so happy to see him, yet crushed. He'd been returned, and for a reason that made him off-limits to the volunteers.

I went looking for a staff member. The first one I found told me that Brody, sweet Brody, had been returned for biting his owner. The adopter reported that Brody had repeatedly snapped at him, had even attacked him in a pet store. The staffer didn't have to say anything. I knew what that meant. The shelter would not adopt out a dog who bit people. He would probably be euthanized. I returned to his kennel and got down on my knees as if praying, so he could lap my face once more. When I began to blubber, I said a hasty last good-bye and left the shelter and Brody behind.

I was up half the night. I was as confused as I was upset. This wasn't the dog I knew at all. I was certain Brody wasn't aggressive. How could I prove that? At some point, I began to think of Sharyn. I slept in bits and pieces until the dark shaded to gray. I got up, rousing Penny Jane, who followed me into my office. I called the shelter. At the buzz of the recorder, I said, "I'm willing to foster Brody." I hung up, went back to bed, and fell into a deep, dreamless, untroubled sleep.

· · ·

When I tell people I volunteer at a shelter, the first question they ask me is if it is a no-kill one. The term grates on me if only because there is no easy answer. I ought to just say yes, because technically it is. But the ARL doesn't call itself that, for complicated reasons. I also know what the person is asking. What they want to know is if the ARL euthanizes, or "kills," any animals. They are thinking in black-and-white. The ARL, like so many shelters, exists in deep shades of gray, where *no-kill* does not mean exactly what it sounds like. The term rings with the clarity of a gong, but *no-kill* is no absolute.

I explain that the ARL euthanizes animals who are too sick or too dangerous to adopt. Most people nod understandingly. If they nod enough, I continue with my stump speech. I explain that some no-kill shelters or rescue organizations accept only animals that will be easy to place, or they transfer their dangerous and sick dogs to another facility that will do the right thing and euthanize them. That way, the first rescue keeps its angelic halo nice and shiny. The ARL accepts animals other shelters might not, which means it has to make some tough choices sometimes. When people's eyes begin to glaze over or my own voice sounds a little "blah, blah, blah" even to me, I stop. But if these people had more time, I'd tell them a story about a dog named Sido and a man named Rich Avanzino.

Sido was an eleven-year-old sheltie/collie mix with long, peach-colored fur that fell to her knees like a skirt. She lived in San Francisco's Mission District with Mary Murphy, an elderly, reclusive widow. Murphy told her neighbors that if they ever saw she'd left her blinds down, they should check on her. One morning, a few days before Christmas in 1979, the neighbors looked at her windows. The blinds were down. They knocked on her door. Murphy didn't answer. They called the police, who found Murphy dead from an overdose of sleeping pills. When the coroner came for her body, he found a petite female dog nervously hovering near Murphy. He followed protocol and called the San Francisco Society for the Prevention of Cruelty to Animals to come for the dog.

The next day, the lawyer for Murphy's estate rang the SPCA to say she was coming to collect Sido and to have her put down, as Murphy's will dictated. The elderly recluse had added those instructions just a few days before her suicide because she feared Sido would not be well cared for in her absence. The shelter manager told Avanzino, the shelter's director, about the lawyer's call. Avanzino walked back to the kennels to see Sido. She trembled in her kennel. He took her to his office, where she calmed down and settled at his feet. He drove her home that night, where Sido acted as if she'd always lived with his wife, two kids, and dog. There was nothing wrong with Sido other than that she was old and now homeless. When Murphy's estate lawyer arrived the next day, Avanzino told her that he would not hand over Sido to be put down. He suggested they go before a judge and together ask for the will to be changed. The lawyer said no way, that if he didn't give her the dog, she'd sue the San Francisco SPCA. She'd sue him, too.

Rich Avanzino loved nothing more than to be sued. By 1979 he had run the SF SPCA for five years. He was relatively young, thirty-eight, and had an epic appetite for work and no fear of controversy. Like so many people in the shelter world, he had wanted to become a veterinarian and had started down that path. But an anatomy class convinced him otherwise. He couldn't stomach dissecting a live frog or the invertebrates. Moreover, in the 1960s, some vet schools still took animals from city shelters who were destined to be euthanized and used them as teaching tools. Students would practice surgeries on these dogs and cats before eventually putting them down. Avanzino wanted to *help* animals, and that didn't seem like helping. He switched his major and earned a doctor's of pharmacology and then went on to law school. He spent five years as a lobbyist in Sacramento hammering out the finer points of health care policy. He earned a reputation for turning around nonprofits, which is why the SF SPCA recruited him for the director's post. The organization was close to bankrupt, and that was only one of its problems.

"I ran the biggest cathouse in San Francisco and never got arrested," Avanzino tells me over lunch, his face scrunching up with glee. Avanzino can look rather stern, with his heavy brow, thin lips, and sharp eyes, but not when he smiles. He has a deep, gravelly baritone worthy of the pulpit, and like a lot of tall, lean men, he hunches his shoulders forward, which can make him look as if he's in a rush. In a way he has been in a rush his whole life, working eighteen-hour days, going to work as early as 2:00 a.m., which is why he got to know the night maintenance man so well. When we run into the man on the street, Avanzino wraps his long arms around him as if he is a lost brother.

Avanzino has a number of lines he uses regularly, and the "cathouse" remark is one of his favorites, but though it's a good one, it might not work on people under fifty. Another favorite is to begin a sentence with "When the dinosaurs ruled . . ." When Avanzino became director of the SF SPCA, the dinosaurs did rule. The private animal shelter found homes for only 10 percent of its animals. His predecessor believed that the primary way to control pet overpopulation was to kill homeless animals, Avanzino says. All the adult female cats and dogs were euthanized automatically, along with old dogs, sick dogs, large dogs, and black dogs. Some thirty-five thousand animals a year were led to the Euthanair machine, an oxygen-less chamber in which the animals were suffocated. The machine, the largest in California, ran from 11:00 a.m. to 7:00 p.m. every day. If Avanzino had known how many animals met their end at the SF SPCA, he tells me, he would never have taken the job.

The dinosaurs ruled pretty much everywhere then, and most shelters across the country had numbers as bad as the SF SPCA's. The no-kill movement was tiny, grassroots, just private rescues run mostly out of people's homes. Like the SF SPCA director Avanzino replaced, many shelter leaders, overwhelmed by the number of homeless animals, felt they had no choice other than to euthanize them in the most humane way possible. Avanzino was no Pollyanna, but it struck him as insane that animal welfare societies "would be the main executioners of our family members on four feet." There had to be a better solution.

His first day on the job, he showed up an hour early at the SF SPCA's then-aging art deco building in an industrial corner of the city. Semis lumbered down the streets. Workers from a printing plant and a clothing sweatshop came and went. The neighborhood's residents were mostly

152

homeless people, some of whom camped in the shelter's arched entryway at night. The society's assistant director, who'd been passed over for the director's job, kept Avanzino waiting for three hours in the lobby before showing him around. She pointed out his parking space, a temporary one. Nobody expected him to last longer than a month, she explained. His office had no furniture other than a folding chair, and no supplies. He asked for paper and pencils, but none were delivered until late in the afternoon. Avanzino was undeterred. In his early weeks, he got rid of the Euthanair machine. Animals would be put down one by one by injection. That was more humane, and slowed the parade of animals to their end because it took more time. It also made it more personal, because someone had to hold the animal and give it the final shot. He made other changes quickly, including starting a volunteer program. The staff was not happy about this, and signed a petition saying so. They feared that volunteers would take their jobs.

By the time Sido appeared, the SF SPCA adoption rate had soared from 10 to 60 percent, and Avanzino had racked up a list of firsts for shelters, including running a grooming college at the SF SPCA. The students practiced lathering fur and trimming toenails on the shelter dogs, making them sleek enough for the show ring. Yet Avanzino wanted to do more than just change the SF SPCA. In an industry inclined to think small, he thought big. He wanted to change the world for homeless animals. He'd try anything, even if it meant going to court—especially if it meant going to court. His goal was to get sued or to sue every six weeks. Court cases meant media coverage. Media coverage brought in donations and adopters but also put the issue of homeless animals right in the public eye. One of his favorite ploys was "Bucks for Balls." The SF SPCA offered to pay senior citizens to kidnap unfixed male cats, bring them in to be neutered, and then return the animals to where they'd found them. The SF SPCA paid a ten-dollar bounty for every set of "balls." The elderly of San Francisco rounded up three thousand cats, mostly other people's, and brought them in to be snipped. Still Avanzino was disappointed. He considered "Bucks for Balls" a failure because even though the SF SPCA had flagrantly broken the law, no one sued the society or him over it. However, his male staff members made their displeasure known. They signed a petition complaining that Avanzino was gender insensitive.

At first Avanzino had no grand plan for Sido other than to save her life. He already had a Great Dane, a stray he had adopted from the SF SPCA. Sido got along with Toby, but could hardly be bothered with her. She had eyes only for Avanzino. He took her everywhere with him. Each morning, she rode to work with him, laying her head in his lap as he navigated the rush-hour traffic. She accompanied him on his daily rounds of the shelter. She settled down in his corner office, nuzzling staff members who came in. The dog who had led a rather shut-in life with her late owner had quickly morphed into a social butterfly. When a *San Francisco Chronicle* reporter came to interview Avanzino about the court case, Sido laid her dainty paw on the newspaperman's knee and licked his hand as\ he took notes. Adding to her charms, Sido was crazy photogenic, with her squint-eyed smile and luxurious ruff. When she posed for the SF SPCA's magazine sitting atop a hill in her old neighborhood, with San Francisco's skyscrapers in the background, her fur blowing back, her eyes on the camera, she looked like a movie star.

After the *Chronicle* broke Sido's story, three thousand people wrote to the shelter to say they wanted Sido, a dog so ancient most shelters back then would have assumed no one wanted her. Avanzino crammed the letters into his file cabinet. If the SF SPCA could save her life, clearly Sido would have a home. The society's lawyers, how-ever, warned Avanzino that this was a long shot. Not only would they have to break the terms of a last will and testament, but they would be bucking a legal system that considered pets property, like a couch or a car. They would have to prove that Sido, a living, breathing creature, was not the same as a pearl necklace. They would have to prove that Sido, an animal, had rights. That's exactly what Avanzino wanted them to prove. If the lawyers pulled that off, it would save thousands of animals who were put down because their owners had stipulated so in a will, or as one newspaper story put it, who were "condemned to death by a hand from the grave." If Avanzino's lawyers were successful, they would set an incredible legal precedent—that animals had rights.

Avanzino took Sido to each hearing, but not to the final ruling, on June 17, 1980. If the SF SPCA lost, as his lawyers told Avanzino was likely, the judge would order him to turn the sheltie over right then. No way was Avanzino doing that, even if he was held in contempt of court. When he left the house that morning, he told his wife and kids that he might not be home that night. He might go to jail. On his way into the city, he dropped Sido at a staff member's home and then drove on to City Hall. According to the plan, if the judge's ruling went against Sido and Avanzino went to jail, the staffer would ferry Sido to a secret foster home. At City Hall, Avanzino marched up the imposing stone steps to the second-floor courtroom, where he found TV cameramen from the major networks. They crammed into the back of the wood-paneled courtroom while Sido's supporters filled the long benches. Avanzino joined the attorneys at a large table before the judge's bench. Not far into the proceedings, the clerk of the court interrupted the judge to say that Governor Jerry Brown was on the phone. The governor had called to tell the judge that he had just signed a bill specifically sparing Sido. The dog would live regardless of the judge's ruling. Yet the governor's last-minute move would have no effect on all the other dogs condemned from their owners' graves. The judge took care of them. He ruled that the right of a deceased person to dispose of his or her property does not extend to a living thing. That set the precedent Avanzino had hoped for. The buoyant courtroom looked around for the dog who had inspired this monumental ruling, whose life had been spared. "Where is Sido?" they echoed. Avanzino rushed into the hallway to a pay phone.

The staffer with Sido, parked about a block from City Hall, leashed her up, and headed with her over to the courthouse. Her jubilant supporters awaited her on City Hall's wide stone steps. Cars streamed past the front of the grand building. A traffic cop stood amid the current of vehicles. The crowd on the steps cheered when they spotted Sido across the street. Sido looked at the noisy crowd and saw Avanzino. She ripped her leash out of the staffer's hand and dashed into the road. The City Hall crowd gasped as a flash of peach shot through the moving cars. Would Sido now die before their eyes? The traffic cop never saw her. Some cars luckily did and braked for her as she raced across the broad street, cheating death one more time, and ran into Avanzino's embrace.

Avanzino had never planned to keep Sido, but in the end he did. She remained his constant companion for the next five years. She also inspired him to think even bigger for homeless animals. If so many people, from average pet owners to a governor, had cared about this old dog's fate, there must be homes for all animals: the old ones, the ones with one eye, the unstoppable barkers. What if the entire city of San Francisco were no-kill? The small shepherd who escaped death twice made Avanzino think that anything was possible.

By the time Avanzino left the SF SPCA in 1999, he had accomplished what once had seemed impossible and become a father, if not *the* father, of the no-kill movement. In a city overrun with social causes, one out of three households donated time or money to the SF SPCA, making it one of the richest shelters in the country. Membership, which was once a few thousand, was closing in on one hundred thousand. He had built a $7 million, one-of-a-kind shelter, with kennels on the adoption floor that resembled rooms in houses, complete with futons, TVs, new throw rugs, and art on the walls. He offered to let homeless people stay the night in the kennels, which made homeless advocates and animal protectors alike furious. Nobody sued him, unfortunately. More than any-thing, Avanzino had pushed San Francisco to become the first no-kill city in the United States. No homeless animal who was deemed adoptable was put to death, not even at the city dog pound. That wasn't enough for Avanzino. He wanted to make America no-kill, to make it a country where putting down an adoptable animal was unaccept-able. So did software magnate Dave Duffield, a billionaire and, like Avanzino, a profound animal lover. To memorialize his family's beloved miniature schnauzer, Duffield created Maddie's Fund, endowed it with $200 million, and hired Avanzino to work toward a goal that was almost as audacious as the moon launches—to make every shelter in the country no-kill in ten years, by 2009.

I went to San Francisco to meet Avanzino and to see the city on the hill, a city where 93 percent of the animals who went into shelters in 2015 found homes. I met Avanzino at a small, mostly empty café not far from the SF SPCA. He rattled off numbers easily over his green salad—such as seventeen million people get a pet each year. If shelters got 25 to 30 percent of that market, homelessness would be solved. "It's doable," he intoned, and then apologized once or twice for slipping into a stump speech. After lunch we walked the few blocks to the SF SPCA. The neighborhood is one of hard lines and few trees. Boxy, low-rise warehouses still dominate the streets, which are short on pedestrians. Some sidewalks crack and tilt. Homeless people have built a small camp out of tents and cardboard just across the street from the SF SPCA. It's been there on and off for decades, Avanzino tells me.

The out-of-the-way, less-than-ideal location is typical for most shelters, but the SF SPCA's size, nearly two city blocks, is not. The wonders inside include a veterinary hospital, a biosecure unit for puppies with parvo, nine-meter-square kennels for cats, and a spay/neuter clinic that fixes more than ten thousand animals a year. The shelter has room for one hundred dogs. What knocked me out, though, was the adoption area, as shiny and airy as an Apple store, and quiet enough to hold conversations. Gone were the kennels Avanzino once suited out like living rooms. Now dogs lounged amid toys in large rooms with glass doors and windows. I tapped a computerized screen on a dog's kennel and his details materialized. In a small play area in the middle of the kennels, two mutts circled a white bench shaped like a dog bone. Yet even the Taj Mahal has an off day. The smell of pee bit the air. The drain in the play yard was malfunctioning. The dogs were also the same motley crew you'd find at most places, including a terrier named Pumpkin who charged his door if you looked at him for too long. The terrier, who had bitten a volunteer, had been there for months.

The SF SPCA copresidents Jennifer Scarlett, a veterinarian, and Jason Walthall, who spent decades in retail, led us through the byzantine building. They were very friendly with Avanzino, but also deferential. "We stand on the shoulders of giants," Walthall said at one point while looking at Avanzino. In return, Avanzino was friendly and respectful. He did not reminisce or tell war stories as he toured his old haunt, as most people would have. Afterward, when I asked him over coffee what he thought of how the adoption area had been revamped, he said diplomatically that it served the new leadership's purposes, and then let slip that they preferred a more "show-offy space." Then he explained why "show-offy" could be a good thing. Avanzino can always see the good points in positions, even those he doesn't agree with, or at least why someone would think that way. The only thing he can't stand is timidity, in any form, a trait that has haunted the animal welfare world, in his opinion. This was just a month shy of his newest

161

goal for a no-kill nation, 2015. I asked him if he still thought that goal was reachable, and he heartily answered yes. Though I knew that was impossible, I nodded in agreement. Optimism is contagious, and sitting there with Avanzino, sipping a dark roast, I was filled with hope. A no-kill nation would mean not only that more dogs had homes, but that every dog who needed a home would have one. Well, nearly every dog.

There is wiggle room in "no-kill." The philosophy accepts that some animals must be euthanized: ones that are profoundly ill or are too dangerous, what are called the "untreatables." The guesstimate is the too-ill and too-dangerous make up 10 percent of animals in shelters. But that's an average. There may be shelters where they make up more than 10 percent or far less, but if 90 percent of a shelter's animals leave it alive by being adopted or transferred to another facility that will find them a home, it can call itself no-kill. There is also wiggle room in who makes up the untreatable 10 percent. Medical cases are much more straightforward, especially now that there are veterinarians who specialize in shelter medicine. Much of what was once considered untreatable in a shelter (distemper, heartworm, even mange) now is treatable, and under the definition of no-kill, only animals with life-threatening illnesses should be euthanized for health reasons. Behavior, which makes a dog adoptable or not, is far murkier territory. Most shelters use some kind of behavior evaluation to judge if a dog is adoptable, but there are many kinds of such tests, and each is only as good as the person giving it. Add to that the fact that shelters have conflicting ideas of what makes a dog unadoptable. For example, some shelters think that ones who snarl when someone reaches for their dinner are too dangerous to send home, while others put them on the adoption floor. And how treatable a dog is also depends on a shelter's resources, whether there are trainers to help soothe a fearful dog or get a jumpy dog to settle down. In other words, how "treatable" a dog is can depend on which shelter he ends up in. There is no all-encompassing standard, and there probably never will be, for which dogs are behaviorally sound enough to go to a home. Somebody makes a subjective and irrevocable call with dogs like Sharyn or Brody.

I told Avanzino that I agreed with the philosophy of "no-kill," but the term bothered me. It is so widely misunderstood by the public. It's so polarizing, and has pitted shelters against one another because if you aren't "no-kill," that makes you a "kill" shelter. In fact, the ARL, like other humane societies, goes out of its way not to call itself "no-kill," though less than 10 percent of its animals are euthanized. It doesn't want to offend shelters that don't or can't hit that mark.

Then there are the municipal shelters that are obliged by law to accept every stray who comes their way, and who are therefore overwhelmed with more animals than they can care for. Is it fair to call them "kill" shelters? I asked Avanzino. This was nothing he hadn't heard before. This is just semantics, he told me, which to a writer is kind of everything. To Avanzino, what matters is that the shelter world has an ideal, a goal to strive for. What matters is that killing adoptable animals becomes completely unthinkable. If you believe that, you can work eighteen-hour days, get criticized, go to court, take chances, and maybe change a city, maybe a country, maybe the world.

Despite what his owner said, I was convinced that Brody was adoptable. The only way to prove that was to bring him home. When the shelter called me back to make sure I truly wanted to foster him, I said yes. It was decided that Brody would go home with the shelter's veterinarian behaviorist for a week and then, if he did okay there, come to us. Between her and us, we would see if what the adopter who'd returned him had reported was true, including whether Brody was aggressive toward men. We would foster the German shepherd like detectives trying to solve a mystery. It was his only hope. Fortunately, Scott, whom I'd never consulted before offering to foster Brody, who'd never even met him, was game, despite the fact we'd just splurged on a new leather couch. Then I showed him Brody's intake form, which included a lengthy description of his biting his adopter's arm in the middle of a Petco.

"I don't know about having a dog like this in our home," Scott said. I swore up and down that there was something off about the adopter's story, that maybe he'd exaggerated or even lied. I pointed to the sections in the form where the adopter described Brody not accepting him as his alpha. "He's a Cesar Milan guy." Neither of us is a fan of dominance training, if only because it can backfire so badly, especially for someone who doesn't understand its finer points. Then I put my finger on the very last line where the adopter wrote that he was moving to Texas.

"See," I said. "I bet that's the real reason he brought Brody back."

Still, I was deeply puzzled that my experience with Brody was so different from that of his adopter. Back then, I still thought a dog was the same dog with everyone. This was before I realized they are like humans, always adjusting themselves to the company and the circumstances they are in. Social creatures, like us and dogs, are by nature shape-shifters. Brody had been one dog with me and obviously another dog with his adopter. We had to find out why.

Brody made the grade at the vet behaviorist's.

He didn't bite anyone. He didn't growl. She found Brody to be just another active adolescent goofball. Now it was our turn. We met him in the Real Life Room. Scott and I sat on the stained couch while one of the trainers gave us pointers on Brody as he happily traced large circles around the room. We ran our hands down his back as he flashed by. Brody smiled and smiled. When Scott took hold of his leash to take him downstairs, he bolted into the hall, nearly pulling my tall husband down.

On the car ride home, Brody lived up to my description. He sat calmly in the rear of our station wagon. He faced backward and watched the cars behind us. His great head blotted out half the rearview mirror. When some drivers behind us waved at him, Brody cocked his head. Once at home, we brought Penny Jane outside to the back-yard to meet him. She seemed somewhat confused, maybe even mortified, but also resigned. She could never predict what we thought up. Brody sniffed Penny Jane here and there but really couldn't be bothered with her, to her relief. The four of us, a total of twelve feet, clambered up our back wooden staircase. I swung open the condo door for our very first foster dog. Brody, eyes bright, mouth open, shot down our long hallway, sprang atop our coffee table, and launched himself, front paws out as if he were diving, onto the couch. Then he eyed the toy basket on the floor and pounced on that. He grabbed toy after toy as he ricocheted around our living room. We both tried to keep out of his way, but our condo seemed to shrink and Brody to grow in size. We might as well have let in a mastodon. Penny Jane took one look at this commotion and retired to the bedroom.

"He's excited," I explained to Scott, who looked worried. I sat down on our couch, which we had covered with a throw to protect it. Brody dove into my lap, pulling the cover half off, exposing all the leather we had paid so much for. He danced around, smashing his wagging tail into my face, and then hurdled off to push a toy into Scott's hand. Scott's face tightened. He remained standing.

"I've never seen him like this," I said to Scott, which wasn't exactly reassuring.

I called Brody and handed him a stuffed banana I had brought from the shelter. He tossed the slip of yellow high and then rose up on his back legs and caught it in his teeth, which is what he did over and over for the next three hours.

Walter Joe Jr.

6

JUMPY-MOUTHIES

When we were ready to go to bed that first night, both filled with dread about how sleepless the coming hours might be, we opened the door of the oversize crate we'd squeezed into our bedroom, and Brody magically stepped inside. We all fell into deep sleep. A plushy banana rose and dropped over and over in my dreams. I woke once to hear Brody lightly snoring and then fell back asleep to his breathing's rhythmic swells. He didn't rouse until our alarm buzzed in the morning, and then quietly sat in his crate until I opened the door. After breakfast, the four of us walked out into the dry warmth of a September day. Summer had yet to let go, so we left our jackets behind. We took our routine path, down to the flat, blue harbor, past the crowded marina where the white boats rise up and down on the tide, and then looped back into the shadows of Charlestown's brownstones. Penny Jane padded along as usual, her tail held high in a neat curl. Brody sauntered like a king. He tugged hard on Scott's arm, but I could see my husband succumbing to the magic of leading a German shepherd, a dog everyone notices. When we reached the grassy rise around the Bunker Hill Monument, where tourists with backpacks had already gathered, Scott asked me to take his picture with Brody in front of that great spike of granite. Brody sprawled on the cool concrete steps and panted softly. Scott draped his arm over Brody's shoulders and smiled that daft smile of someone falling hard for a dog. And he did fall hard. Both of us did.

Within a day we had nicknames for him (Monster Mash, Moustafa, Beast), a sure sign we were goners. We fell in love even though Brody jumped on Scott's head on weekend mornings as he tried to sleep in. Even though he would grab my underpants out of my hands as I, balanced on one foot, was about to pull them on. In fact, holding up anything to look at it (a newspaper, a letter from the IRS) was an invitation for Brody to snatch said thing. He grabbed sheets of paper as they emerged from my printer, then danced merrily around the room with my copy in his mouth. He was a punk, but a happy punk. To help vent his punkness, I would call my friend around the corner and ask if Pip, her over-energetic young mutt, could come over for some "Greco-Roman wrestling." Brody and Pip would rise up on their back legs, swing their front legs, and thump chests so hard you could hear it. Then they would chase each other around a few rhododendrons I had planted in our building's very small garden, kicking up mulch, running in tighter and tighter circles until they rose up again. *Thump!*

During the workday, Brody quietly lounged on the couch in my office, laying his head on the armrest to watch birds fly by the window. When he spotted red-tailed hawks circling high in the sky, he raised his eyebrows. He mostly left Penny Jane alone, though when he lay on the office couch next to her, he sometimes brushed his substantial tail or haunch against my shy gal. Penny Jane would inch away. Sometimes she'd have to leave the room.

Penny Jane might have disagreed, but we found Brody easy to have around, even given his bulk. Though he liked to take things out of our hands, he never picked up anything in the house, not a throw pillow or a sandal. Brody was friendly to other dogs, even the ones who broke free in the park and charged us. He calmly rode in the car. Sitting erect, he solemnly studied the traffic trailing us. I reported to the shelter that Brody had shown no signs whatsoever of aggression.

We could not let him off leash other than in our small fenced-in backyard, so we walked him at length all over Boston, on bridges over the breezy Charles River, down the bumpy brick sidewalks of Beacon Hill, and under Boston Common's old, towering trees. Like any German shepherd, Brody seemed to walk on air despite his size. He didn't have the steep slope to his back of a purebred, and his coat was probably too short, but he had all the breed's aplomb. As we led him down the city streets, the world divided into two before us. Half the world went all moony in the face when they saw Brody. They'd walk by murmuring, "Gorgeous, so gorgeous." The other half passed us with knitted brows and worried eyes. Some people even held their hands up by their shoulders or hurriedly crossed the street. One young woman who'd been intently talking to her companion as we strolled by shrieked when she looked down and suddenly noticed Brody in all his regal wolfishness beside her. I'd never walked a dog who could inspire such polarized reactions. Pitties come close, though I've found people will sometimes scowl at you, not the dog. Yet, more and more, as the myths surrounding their "violent nature" are debunked, people will smile at a pittie, and some young African American men stop me on the street to rave about the one I'm walking. No young black men stopped me to fawn over Brody, though, or, for that matter, any other German shepherd, the breed of choice for the police, the breed set loose on civil rights protesters in the 1960s. A dog has no idea of the history that trails it. We had to learn how other people might see our foster dog. To us, Brody was just Brody—though we had to admit that such a majestic dog at our side did give us a sense of power, especially when we knew that this dog, who could inspire fear and awe, liked nothing more than to run around with my underpants in his mouth. He—we—had everyone fooled.

Some shelter dogs take a week or so to relax in a new home, and when they do, their true personalities may emerge, and you may find you brought home a different dog from the one you expected. Suddenly the quiet hound bays all morning or the laid-back puppy laps the house. That's why shelters warn adopters that they may see a change in their dog once he settles in. The same goes for a foster dog. About a week after Brody moved in, I was leading him and Penny Jane to the marina when he playfully bit the leash. He'd done that before, but he hadn't done what came next. He cocked his eye at me as if he'd just thought of the funniest prank. Then he bit his way up the leash, threw his paws on me, and mouthed my forearms. He jumped and grabbed, jumped and grabbed, a clumsier version of Greco-Roman wrestling. His mouthing didn't hurt, but his teeth were on my skin, which the human brain does not like. I could not think at first. Cars flashed by on the street. I worried I'd trip. I had a leash in either hand. Penny Jane stood quietly by my side. A car slowed and the driver yelled out the window, "Do you need help?" I called back, "No," though I probably did. I dropped Penny Jane's leash and stood on it, which freed one hand but occupied one foot. I reached in my pocket, pulled out a handful of treats, and sprinkled them onto the sidewalk. Brody paused. I could see him debating cookies or wrestling. Cookies! He released my arm and turned his nose to the pavement. The mystery of the biting and the aggression was solved: Brody was what trainers and shelter people call a jumpy-mouthy.

There are a few ways to make a dog into a jumpy-mouthy. You can start by taking a puppy from his litter too early, before he is eight weeks old. A wrestling match of puppies is not pretty. Littermates chew on heads, tug ears, and yank tails. The fur scramble may look like mayhem, but there are rules. If a puppy chomps down on another's small snout as if it's a sandwich, the chomped pup will screech holy hell and might stop playing. The chomper realizes that maybe he overdid it. If a pup wants to play, he has to develop what is called bite inhibition, or a soft mouth. A puppy wants to play almost more than he wants to eat, so he learns to use his mouth nicely, but one that is taken from his litter too early won't have learned this crucial social skill. He may go into the world a mini-shark, ready to rake dogs or humans in the name of a good time. One such youngster, a snub-nosed girl the color of tea, arrived at the ARL one summer. Her idea of playing was a cage fight. One night, as I was shoving toys into her mouth to keep her teeth off me, she suddenly latched on to my thigh like a bear trap. I thought I was on my way to the emergency room. When I sprung her jaw off my leg, I saw that she had miraculously torn only my shorts. Through the rip, I eyed the purple of a bruise bloom. Her face said, "Ha, ha!"

A young dog with a soft mouth can still be made into a jumpy-mouthy. Lots of people encourage their puppies to nibble their toes, chew on their hands, or jump on them, forgetting that the puppy will become a full-size dog, and soon. Most breeds are close to their adult size by six months. What was funny with a puppy is a pain with a juvenile with a mouthful of adult teeth and paws that reach your waist. The actor and profound dog lover Jimmy Stewart said he never discouraged his pups from leaping on him, because, he felt, they were trying to kiss him and were just being dogs. He had a point, but Jimmy Stewart was a tall guy with a sense of humor, so even if his golden retrievers knocked him down, he probably had a good laugh over it. Most people don't feel that way about getting pasted to the floor by two paws. A lot of people might drive such dogs to the local humane society.

A shelter can easily make jumpy-mouthies out of dogs who were anything but when they arrived. Shelters don't do this on purpose, but that is what can happen when you shut young, exuberant pooches in a kennel for most of the day. There they don't get enough exercise or human contact or mental stimulation or play. They become bored, often anxious, too. When somebody shows up with a leash, these pent-up dogs explode with excitement, which is why as you step into their kennel all you see is a blur of paws and fur. Before I step in with a jumpy-mouthy, I take off my scarf or tuck in my hoodie strings so a wired dog can't latch on to them. I pull down my sleeves so he won't accidentally rake my arms. I remain calm, throw choice treats onto the concrete floor, ask for sits, or turn my back to the bouncing dog. The trick is to do nothing that will make him wilder. Sometimes all I can do is step back out of the kennel for my sake and the dog's. Should a twirling, grabby pooch accidentally scratch someone with a toenail or tooth hard enough to draw blood, he must go into a state-ordered quarantine of ten days. During that stretch, no volunteers can take him out, which means less of everything, which typically makes the jumpy-mouthy jump and mouth more.

I see lots of these dogs at the ARL. Most shelters across the country do. It's one of the most common behavior challenges. These dogs are typically between six and eighteen months old. These teenagers, like human teenagers, are as high on energy as they are low on self-control. They are mostly large dogs, such as Lab mixes or pitties. Not that there aren't little dogs who leap on people, but they can't hurt you by accident the way the lugs can. One jumpy-mouthy gave me a fat lip. Another, a slender, nervous shepherd mix with a long nose, bounded at me and scratched my arms with her humongous dewclaws nearly every time I stepped into her kennel. Another, Greg the stray, ripped my coat, broke my watchband, and stretched a sweater sleeve to twice its length when he took hold of the cuff and ran. He also would pull off my gloves if I wasn't careful. A leggy black number named Ciera ripped a clipboard out of my hands as I was showing her to potential adopters. I was glad the skinny mutt had because I wanted the young couple to see what they were in for. "I love her," the guy said as I tried to wrestle the clipboard back. One person's jumpy-mouthy is another's soul mate.

The tragedy of jumpy-mouthies is that though their conduct is nonaggressive and treatable, and often just goes away in a home, they are frequently labeled too wild—or, worse, too dangerous, as in Brody's case—for adoption. That's often why Mike Kaviani finds young, large dogs on the "euth" list at the city of Austin's animal control facility. Kaviani runs the behavior department at Austin Pets Alive!—a large private nonprofit shelter in Texas's capital. Austin saves 90 percent or more of its homeless animals. The whole city, not just an individual shelter or two, has been no-kill since 2011. So far it's the largest city in the country to pull that off. In 2012, Kaviani was hired to help Austin reach for the stars, so to speak, to see how close it could get to 100 percent. To help save that last 10 percent, Kaviani specifically plucks dogs from the city shelter's euthanasia list who've landed there because they've been deemed unmanageable—dogs such as Jake. The young pittie was reportedly slamming up against his gate and was so mouthy that volunteers held out towels tied with knots for the stray to grab instead of their arms when they went into his kennel. Jake was a classic jumpy-mouthy. Kaviani transferred him to Austin Pets Alive! and sent the youngster to his version of finishing school—play group.

Play group is exactly what it sounds like: chasing, tumbling, cutting up, dogs getting to be dogs. Each morning, some sixty to one hundred dogs kick up their heels over the course of three and a half hours at Austin Pets Alive! Another forty or so rumble during the afternoon session. The dogs run loose in what resembles a fenced-in, beat-up suburban backyard with some old tires, a pink kiddie pool, and a desk chair on rollers. Ten to twenty dogs come out at a time, and they are grouped according to play styles, from the acrobats to the wallflowers. Some stay for only twenty minutes. Some romp the morning away. These are Kaviani's rock stars, the unflappable dogs who get along with everyone and don't tire of the party. Like the ambassador dogs at the ASPCA's rehabilitation center, the rock stars often mentor newcomers to play group, help take the rough edges off some of the nuttier ones, and enforce some decorum. Jake turned out to be a rock star, if a sleepy one. The once overexcitable boy became famous for curling up in a plastic lawn chair and napping during the hijinks.

Kaviani began his shelter career as a teenager cleaning kennels and walking dogs at the city shelter in his hometown of Irvine, California. While there, he began a program to save dogs from Southern California's overcrowded municipal facilities. He learned so much about dog behavior working at the Irvine shelter that he gave up his plans to study psychology, becoming the only member of his family not to have an advanced degree. Though Kaviani is still young, he's already put in long years working with home-less dogs, and all that time has taught him that play group is a near cure-all for jumpy-mouthies. More than that, he says, he wouldn't even attempt to save rowdier dogs without play groups. That is why he started one his first day in Austin. If the exercise, social contact, and mental stimu-lation of the daily romps don't purge a dog's rambunctiousness, play group dials it down to a tolerable level. Some still need training but only the basics, such as sitting to greet people, Kaviani says. They don't need heavy behavior modification, just a chance to be themselves: young, crazy dogs. Given his chance, Jake proved that he was very adoptable. After four months at Pets Alive!, the black pittie went home with a youngish couple who reported back to Kaviani that they loved him.

Kaviani learned the finer points of running a play group from the master, Aimee Sadler. Sadler pioneered play groups in a city pound in East Quogue in 1998. The Long Island facility was dark and dank, she says, with two long rows of facing kennels. The dogs carried on at one another most of the day. Sadler, a private trainer, had been hired to work with the shelter's wards for three hours once a week. That first day, she stood amid the twenty or so barking, whining, bouncing dogs and pondered an impossible task: How could she make a difference for all of them with so little time? She went out to the pound's fenced yard and told a staff member her plan—to let the dogs play together.

Though dogs are some of the most gregarious of social animals, nearly everything about shelters and how they are run is designed to isolate them, especially from one another. That's done for safety reasons but also because of a that's-the-way-it's-always-been-done attitude. Sadler, however, was not of the shelter world. Her ideas about animals came from years of working with a long list of species. At Magic Mountain, an amusement park north of Los Angeles, she pulled on a wet suit, picked up a bucket of silvery mackerel, and taught dolphins to flip and sea lions to bark on cue. She worked as a movie animal trainer and then a horse trainer. She liked training marine mammals the most, never quite jibed with big cats, and didn't enjoy working with monkeys. She dreamed of training elephants but never got the chance.

Like any exotic animal trainer, Sadler always took into account a species' natural behaviors, the behaviors for which evolution has hardwired it. For example, parrots are designed to forage. Tigers are born to stalk. Animals need to express these behaviors. If they can't, they become bored, depressed, or neurotic, start pacing or plucking or swaying. We so easily forget that dogs are a *species* with their own natural behaviors. *Canis lupus familiaris* is hard-wired to run, smell, play, and socialize. If a dog can't express those behaviors, it may bark, growl, jump, or mouth. It may become "unmanageable."

Sadler could never quite pay the bills working with exotics or horses, but she could with the far less sexy job of working with dogs. When she moved to New York State in 1998, she opened a training and boarding business out of her farmhouse. She'd bunk as many as twenty dogs in her house at a time. One Thanksgiving she had thirty-two. Sadler didn't use kennels or crates.

181

Her kids watched TV surrounded by paws and tails. Sadler fell asleep to the soft symphony of dogs snoring in her bedroom. For Sadler, living with large groups of dogs was second nature. Still, standing in the fenced yard of the East Quogue pound that afternoon, she was nervous. The shelter dogs were understandably edgier than pets, and so much was at stake. If this first session became an epic dogfight, that would quickly be the end of play groups. Sadler put on her best game face. She had the dogs drag leashes hooked to their collars. That way she could quickly get hold of one if she had to. Their kennels opened onto the fenced yard. She and a staff member began letting the dogs out one by one. They began to play.

Since then, Sadler has essentially traveled the country spreading the gospel to shelters. As with any gospel, some aren't ready to hear it. Sometimes an obvious, simple answer unsettles people. Others are inspired. The ARL is one of about 150 shelters that have taken play groups to heart. A year or so after Sadler trained the ARL staff, they trained me. I learned how to watch the body language of multiple dogs at once, to note whose tail was stiff, whose was wagging. I learned the rules of play group: no toys, no treats, no petting. We don't want to give them anything to compete over. I learned that should a fight start and two dogs latch on to each other, not to pull them apart, because as you do, their clenched teeth will tear flesh, causing more harm.

Early on Saturday mornings, all these dos and don'ts swirl in my mind as I watch the dogs mill around. A few usually just wander among the group nosing the ground or surveying the nearby street. Shy dogs untuck their tails and wiggle. There is always a surprise or two. A grumpy Chihuahua happily runs back and forth under the tall legs of a hound mix. A posse of youngsters will dash up and over the agility A-frame like rodeo dogs, then screech to a halt and look at one another as if to say, "Whose idea was that?" Amid the dogs noodling and cavorting, I will momentarily let my guard down and just watch them play. For that one hour, they get to be fundamentally themselves, *Canis lupus familiaris*. They get to be dogs. And we humans get to express one of *our* species' natural behaviors—watching dogs have fun.

I spotted Alfred immediately. The Goldendoodle rested his chin atop the five-foot-high kennel wall. He cocked his head of blond fuzzy kinks and smiled. The eighty-eight-pound boy was standing on his back legs to look out over the Animal Humane Society of Minnesota's vast and airy dog adoption floor. From his vantage, he could also watch people coming and going in the lobby, which is where I was. Our eyes met. I burst out laughing.

I was looking for Alfred because Paula Zukoff, the society's behavior director, had told me all about him, about how incorrigible he was and that she'd basically given up training him—which sounds worse than it was. Nine-month-old Alfred had been transferred to the private, nonprofit society, one of the largest in the upper Midwest, six weeks earlier from a facility in Missouri. He was likely given up for his youthful exuberance plus his size. Alfred's back rose easily to Zukoff's hip, but he was still a crazed puppy. Despite someone's adopting him soon after he arrived in suburban Minneapolis, probably seduced by his blond good looks, the Goldendoodle was back four days later because he was "too much responsibility"—code for "he's like having an orangutan in the house." When Zukoff got word that Alfred was bounding on volunteers, placing his paws atop their shoulders, looking them right in the face, she pulled him off the adoption floor and into her department before he accidentally coldcocked someone.

Goldendoodles are golden retrievers crossed with miniature or standard poodles. Breeders began crossing the two back in the 1990s to create a hypoallergenic seeing-eye dog. There is no such thing as a truly hypoallergenic pooch (all dogs shed at least a little) but that hasn't kept

184

Goldendoodles from becoming one of the most popular "designer" breeds, one you next to never see in shelters. My neighborhood is overrun with the fluffy hybrids. They are part of the standard package for the wealthy, young families of Charlestown: a stroller tough enough you could push it up Mount Everest and forty pounds of crimped golden fur. Alfred, though, is no poof. He is a Yeti of a Goldendoodle. Still, he's crazy cute like all doodles, with their button eyes in a fop of soft hair, like a stuffed animal sprung to life. Those doll-like faces, though, often belie a nuttiness within. Somehow, crossing two smart, energetic breeds results in a kook with legs going in four different directions. Goldendoodles can seem overcome with the joy of being alive. Alfred certainly was.

Zukoff has been working with dogs for more than twenty years, from when she got her first one as an adult, a well-mannered collie named Dante, whom she could train to do anything. Dante never, ever pulled on his leash and once earned 198.5 points out of 200 in an obedience competition. Early in her career, Zukoff wrote off dogs such as Alfred as obnoxious brats. Over time, she came to believe that their poor manners were an expression of anxiety. Zukoff says that this was the case with Alfred, who flailed at people in his kennel. Like Kaviani, Zukoff uses play groups to take the edge off jumpy-mouthies, but she puts equal emphasis on teaching them manners and how to calm down. The staff do not play fetch or tug or do anything that would rile these dogs, who are experts at going bonkers. Instead, they bring them into their offices to lounge quietly, to practice relaxing, at which they are amateurs. Each morning, Alfred would play with his best buddy, a twenty-pound irascible terrier known for head-butting the trainers when they leaned over to leash him. Afterward Zukoff would bring Alfred to her office. He'd take a while to settle down, and then would sprawl like a throw rug in the middle of the floor, the only place in her office where he had enough room to stretch out. One of the trainers taught Alfred to sit, but he never entirely gave up leaping on them.

There's more than one way to work with jumpy-mouthies, but all trainers agree that what most need is a home. Sometimes that's the only way to remedy a behavior, but it means admitting a certain degree of defeat, and taking a chance. You can't make an obedience champ out of a young dog who is cooped up twenty-two, twenty-three hours a day, which is why I found Alfred on the adoption floor. At first Zukoff listed him as a "hidden gem." Potential adopters had to make an appointment to see the Goldendoodle. All the people who did were overwhelmed by Alfred's size, except for one middle-aged man, who lived with his elderly mother. He took the

Goldendoodle home—where Alfred knocked his mother to the ground. When Alfred came back, Zukoff put him on the adoption floor so people could see how enormous he was, but locked his kennel so only staff could take him out. When I saw him, he'd been there a week. He put his paws on his door, wagged his head, let his tongue droop out to one side. Despite the vagaries of his young life, he looked happy. That was a Monday. The next weekend, he was adopted. Other than a name and phone number, Zukoff had no details about who'd been brave enough to take home this zany dog big enough to polka with. Months later, Alfred still had not come back. Zukoff had left a message on the adopter's voice mail, asking if all was well, but never heard back. Sometimes no news, she says, is good news.

Brody acted up only when he was on leash, never in our condo. At least we had that going for us. We also quickly learned that taking different routes on our strolls seemed to distract him from all his shenanigans. We always watched for the telltale sign that he was about to let it rip—that cock of his head, that glint in his eye. Seeing that, we'd quickly throw treats on the ground to make him forget about the wrestling match he had in mind. Yet if he turned one of his gorgeous eyes up at me as we were walking across an inter-section, I could not stop to toss cookies. I'd take hold of his collar as calmly as I could and silently walk on while he clacked at my arm. Once I had stumbled my way to the sidewalk, I'd start with the treats. If those morsels didn't do the trick, I'd push him to the ground and firmly hold him there. There we would stay, despite the curious looks of passersby, until Brody had relaxed and started looking around. As a preventive measure, I doubled the Greco-Roman wrestling to burn down his juvenile flame. Sometimes my friend simply opened her back gate and sent her dog down the alley to my yard on his own. I'd drink a gin and tonic on the back steps while they chased and thumped.

What Scott and I didn't do was as important as what we did. We never grabbed Brody roughly, kneed him, or smacked him on the nose, which some trainers and manuals advise. We didn't even yell at him. Most jumpy-mouthies interpret rough handling as fun, especially a confident dog, and they only party harder. I suspected this was what happened between Brody and his former adopter, but, honestly, just pushing a jumpy-mouthy off you, which would be most people's natural instinct, can make him go bananas. That's how we get into trouble with dogs—that our natural instincts can be the exact opposite of theirs. One species is pushing the other to stop the playing. The other species thinks the pushing means "game on." Neither Scott nor I ever got Brody to stop his spells entirely, but we learned how to manage them. That is a real credit to Scott, because men generally have less tolerance for looking like fools than women do, and Brody could make you look as if you'd never walked a dog in your life.

Despite his "aggressive" nature, the longer Brody stayed, the more we wanted to keep him. Around week three, Scott began combing real estate listings for a larger condo. By week four, we even went to look at a house nearby. We were under immense peer pressure. When you foster a dog, everyone, even the most casual of acquaintances, asks, "Really, you aren't going to keep him?" "How could you not keep him?" Even friends without dogs, who could easily adopt the dog, will question you. Even the shelter staffers. The job of a foster is to help a dog find a home, not give him a home, but everyone forgets that. Everyone also forgets that you already have a dog. Penny Jane was not as happy with Brody as we were. If we were in the living room, she'd go to the bedroom. She quit coming into my office. She was withdrawing into the loner she'd once been. For me, the resident dog always comes first. That is why, in the end, we did not keep Brody—not because our condo wasn't big enough, not because he kept running off with our underwear, not because he mouthed our arms so that people stopped and stared on the street. He felt like our dog enough for us to put up with all that. If we had thought Brody would have a terrible time getting adopted, we might have decided otherwise, but we were convinced he had a good shot. After five weeks, we had more than proved that he was not aggressive. He was gorgeous, quirky, and lovely.

That is how we came, essentially, to return a dog to a shelter, which is about as wrenching as you would guess, even with a foster dog you are supposed to return. Returning your first foster is the worst, though I've since had dogs for one night whom I could barely put back in their kennels. On the drive across town to the ARL, Brody rode in the rear of our station wagon. As always, he turned backward to watch the cars behind us. We had packed some of his favorite toys. In the parking lot, he leapt out when Scott opened the hatchback, but once we got inside the building and approached the door to the kennels, he dug in his paws. Treats, happy voices did not persuade him. Scott and I had to pull him together. When we closed his kennel door, Brody looked at us with confused eyes. We each welled up, said a quick good-bye, and bolted for the car, where, bereft and guilty, we drove across town without a shepherd in the back. When we got home, the condo felt so big—too big. We took the cover off our leather couch, sat down, and told stories about Brody.

Five days later we heard he'd been adopted. A young woman who worked at a dog kennel was going to take him home. Brody could go with her to work each day. He could Greco-Roman wrestle to his heart's content with the dogs kenneled there. It was, in fact, a far better life than the one we could have given him. We still missed him, but a mountain's worth of guilt was lifted from our shoulders. I went to the ARL the next night to walk Brody one last time before he left for his new life. We traced one of my favorite loops in the South End. He sniffed as I savored his company, my eyes welling here and there. The sorrow was simpler now. This German shepherd I took into my home, who watched birds out my office window, who got into bed with Scott each morning, was going home with someone else. He'd been ours but not. We passed the community garden where a platter-size sunflower had plummeted to the ground and cracked in half. We slipped down my favorite alleyway and then headed up busy Tremont Street, in the soft twilight of a balmy October night. Just as we passed a full restaurant patio, Brody cocked an eye. "Oh no," I said with a sigh as his paws landed on my shoulders. I had forgotten to bring treats. Out of the corner of my eye, I saw a woman step out of a furniture store and start running my way. "It's all right," I called. She stopped, looking unconvinced. The patio of people hoisting wedges of pizza and wineglasses turned in their seats toward us. With all eyes on us, Brody and I danced one last time.

A couple of months later the shelter's vet behaviorist asked me to foster a Jack Russell mix, an extremely fearful guy from an animal hoarding case. This terrier was so upset when he arrived at the shelter that he was all bared teeth. A staffer whom I considered fearless confided in me that Walter had scared her worse than any dog she had ever handled. This did not deter me. In fact, he seemed like the perfect foster dog for us. I had never wanted a Jack Russell, with all their energy. I was not a "small dog" person, whatever that meant. I preferred female dogs. This dog, unlike Brody, would be so easy to give back. Sure, I told the vet behaviorist, we'll foster Walter.

Hash Brown

7

PITTIES I HAVE LOVED

For the first year or so of volunteering at the ARL, I made my way across town to the shelter once a week, typically to the Wednesday training class. The trainer raised her naturally loud voice over the barking to boom things such as "Don't let your dog just bark." Then I started going twice a week, especially after I realized how adopters glutted the place on Saturdays, keeping the staff so busy that the dogs didn't get their usual midday walk unless a volunteer took them out. Then, some weeks, I went three times, if only to ease my own worries. I'd picture the dogs in their kennels, bored or frantic, and I'd chuck my plans for a shopping trip. I'd dig my dreadful gray volunteer T-shirt out of my dresser, pull on a worn pair of jeans, grab my oily bait bag, and go. The more I volunteered with shelter dogs, the better I understood the bottomless depth of their needs and how little difference I could truly make. That realization can drive some volunteers away. It made me want to do more.

The "red" dogs have the most powerful draw on me. Only staff members and a small group of volunteers can take these dogs out. At a minimum, the red ones, like all the dogs, get out three times a day with staff, on ten-minute walks or longer stints in play group, but that leaves them in their kennels for as long as twenty-three hours a day. The red dogs are typically jumpy-mouthies like Brody, or they are so fearful they might snap if you barged into their kennel and reached too quickly for their collar. Many of the skittish and snappy ones are the miniaturized dogs, nervous Chihuahuas, terriers, and Pomeranians. Being so small in such a big world understandably fills them with dread or ire or both. There is also a smattering of huge dogs, so huge (such as Titan, the imposing Airedale with a greasy coat) that they could, even with two harnesses, pull you down if they sprinted for a squirrel. Scott once asked me what I would do in that case. "Drop to the ground, make myself dead weight, and hang on with all my might" was the best answer I could give him, which made my husband sigh. No dog has ever put me to that test, not even Titan. In fact, the more Titan got to know me, the more he, with his great girth, behaved like a perfect gentleman. Dogs, like people, relax with their friends.

I like a challenge, and the red dogs are always that. Puppies are sweet but too easy, as are most of the small dogs, except the ones who are petrified or hostile, such as Princess, the plump rat terrier mix with a spade-shaped head topped with a pair of kangaroo-like ears. Her bottom rounded so she looked like she had a bustle. She also had, like most terriers, an attitude. For weeks, every time I walked past her small kennel, she'd be wound in a tight, glowering circle on her bed. Her kennel was marked "Staff Only." I'd toss some treats in there and call hello without breaking my stride. Then, one day, a red dot appeared on Princess's kennel, which meant I could take her out. I opened her door and held up a leash. A deep rumble arose from the knot of fur. I calmly but quickly bid her adieu. A staff member whose shoes Princess had bitten told me that if the terrier remained on her bed when I opened her door, I should leave her alone. If she came off her bed, that meant she was ready to go out. So, for weeks, I'd crack Princess's kennel door and offer the leash invitingly. She'd grumble and bare her spiky canines, and I'd chirp, "Well, okay," as I retreated, relieved. I don't like that hard a challenge. Truth be told, I hadn't exactly warmed to Princess, even though I knew she was threatening me only because I frightened her. Still, out of a sense of duty, I continued inviting her out. One day, Princess quietly stepped off her bed with her dainty white feet and scampered over to me. At first, I was too flabbergasted to be scared. She sat calmly (not even a lip curl) while I leashed her. Nervously, I led the terrier outside for an uneventful tour of Boston's South End.

From that day on, I was one of the kangaroo-eared terrier's best friends. Once Princess saw me walk through the kennels, she would wait by her door until I came to her. I was one of the few volunteers who could easily walk her. When I kneeled down to pet her, she would put her small paws on my knees to lick my face. I confess that the first time she did that, I cringed, braced to say good-bye to my nose. Another time, she hopped into my lap for a picture. Clowning around, I held her pointy ears together. "I can't believe she didn't take your hand off," one volunteer said when she saw the photo. That she didn't, that she chose me to be her friend, was all pretty heady stuff. I fell for Princess—as did the man who adopted her even though she bit him, twice, during their introduction.

Now I have a red dog in my house, at this moment on top of my ancient drying machine. Walter lays his little sausage body out flat. He rests his tiny head near the dryer's edge and moves his dark eyes back and forth to follow us as we pass. His stillness is that of a coiled snake, so we give him a wide berth. He wears his leash constantly because we can't touch him. He sleeps in a crate at night and, as soon as we let him out in the morning, he, with his stubby legs, hops on top of his crate and leaps from there to the dryer—and there he stays until I pull him down by his leash for a walk. Outside, he steps down the sidewalk hesitantly. The second we return home and I drop his leash, he climbs back onto the dryer. There he spends his day warily eyeing me while I work at my desk, though he has neither growled nor snapped at me. As I did with the Queen of Fearful dogs, Penny Jane, I ignore him.

"He's on your dryer?" my mother asks when I call her. "Why can't you touch him?"

"Because he might bite us," I say.

I cut Walter a lot of slack. First he got stuck with an animal hoarder and lived in the chaos of sixteen other terriers for who knows how long. The hoarder, I was told, called animal control to come get the crowd. She'd been served eviction papers. Some of the dogs, including Walter, ended up at the ARL. He was so terrified by this change of scenery, and all the strangers, that he became little more than a set of gnashing teeth. He tried to bite anyone who got near him. The staff had to cinch a catchpole around his small neck to move him into and out of a crate. He raged so that he bit his own mouth and tongue, bloodying them. The ARL was thinking it would have to euthanize him because he was too dangerous. But the vet behaviorist, who was taking some of the terriers home to foster, took Walter, too. She let them loose in her fenced-in backyard with an outdoor kennel, where they could be on their own and calm down. All of them pretty quickly did, and even became friendly—except for Walter, who kept his distance. About a week after the vet behaviorist had brought the terriers home, she looked out her window and saw Walter lying on his side in the grass. The terrier was still. His best friend, Shorty, was cuddled up beside him in the chill of an October morning. Walter was in shock and so cold that the vet behaviorist's husband was able to lift him and carry him into their house. Walter's haunches were punctured and bruised. Dirt was ground into the wounds. The other terriers must have attacked him overnight. The vet behaviorist and her husband cleaned his wounds on the dining room table.

Walter can sit on my dryer all he wants.

Many of the ARL's red dogs, as you would guess, are not terriers. They are pitties. So are our blue dogs, and our green dogs. It's simply a matter of numbers. Pitties fill a quarter of the kennels typically. They also can take the longest to be adopted, often waiting months for a home. We do what we can. We tie bandanas on them. We sit in the lobby with them so they can cover visitors with kisses. We name them after celebrities, which explains why a little caramel-colored puppy became Val Kilmer. We've had a Beckham, Claire Danes, Ryan Gosling, Halle Berry, Carrie Underwood, and Tom Hanks. I suggested naming one Boz Scaggs, but the young staff had no idea whom I was talking about, though they had heard of Dolly Parton. For my part, I had to ask whom Gronk was named for, which provoked much hilarity—the idea that I, a Boston resident, did not know the name of the New England Patriots' tight end.

Now I stand, a tennis ball in each hand, in front of Gwen Stefani, a young sweetie who has the alertness and work drive of a border collie. As pitties go, she's leggy, with the svelte, fit figure of an Olympic swimmer. Also, she has neither the typical broad chest nor the chunky head of most pit bulls. In fact, her "pittiness" is only in the roundness of her forehead, the jut of her muzzle, and the shortness of her coffee bean–colored coat. There is nothing intimidating-looking about Gwen, who, in fact, with her pricked black ears and expectant smile, usually looks as if she's just arrived at a party.

Gwen was found tied to a pole in Saugus, a town northwest of Boston, in the last weeks of the winter. She was transferred from an animal control facility there to the ARL. Since then, she's been spayed, evaluated, and trained. She gets along with other dogs, and is as beautiful as a thoroughbred racehorse. Beyond being a pittie in Boston, where there is still plenty of stigma, her only flaw, if you think of it as a flaw, is that she buzzes with energy. She doesn't want to hang out with you and has no time for petting. She wants to play fetch—constantly. One afternoon, I took

Gwen to the play yard to work on the agility equipment, to teach her to run up and over the wooden A-frame, maybe try the teeter-totter. But when I unhooked her leash, she quickly tracked down a scuffed tennis ball. She brought the ball to me, which was her way of saying, "There will be no agility training today."

Gwen loves to fetch so much that she's kind of mixed up about it. She wants me to throw the ball, but she won't give it to me, not even for a piece of hot dog. I doubt she'd give me the ball for a cheeseburger, either. There's only one thing I can do. Find another tennis ball. I crisscross the yard methodically, like a police officer searching a crime scene. With Gwen by my side as I scan the grass, I wonder how many hours of my adult life I've spent looking for tennis balls and throwing them. Hundreds, maybe thousands. I see the balls in my mind falling like rain, which is why I, in my reverie, don't see the one I nearly trip over. It's ancient and gored. It's been forgotten under the tallest of the play yard's trees, trees that bear the markings of thousands of homeless dogs. "Yay!" I cheer, but before I get the one syllable out, Gwen drops the slobbery ball in her mouth and pounces on the gored one.

Gwen is kind of grabby, which, for me, has made fetch a game of strategy and finger preservation. If I'm not careful, when I pick up the ball, she'll latch on to it and my hand. I have to get the ball safely away from her before I reach for it, so I push along the one she's dropped with the toe of my shoe. The ball's foamy white slobber collects dirt as I do. Taut, almost trembling, Gwen cocks her head and peers at this mess as I roll it along, until it's a yard or so away from her. I scoop up the ball in a flash and raise it high over my head like a trophy. Gwen drops the one in her mouth as if in awe and bounces toward me. I briefly feel the ball's wetness and the grit in my palm before launching the wad almost the length of the play yard. As Gwen rockets after the whoosh of yellow, I snatch up the ball she's left behind. For the next hour, we play this tricky game of trade until at least I'm tired. When she pauses to noisily lap up some water, I hide both balls in my pockets and toss a harness onto her. Balls out of sight, she lets me lead her inside to the Real Life Room to lounge. I scan the floor before we step through the door, making sure there are no wayward balls. Seeing a clear coast, I unleash her and sink into the stained couch, hoping she will join me. Instead, she presses her head hard under the couch, even moving the furniture some with her shoulders. I lean over to see what all the fuss is about. She has found a tennis ball.

Since I started volunteering at the ARL, I seem always to be worried about a pittie. Now it's

Gwen. Before her, there were China, Neena, Brownie, Precious, Hercules, and of course Sharyn, among many others. There are sure to be more after Gwen. Pitties come into the ARL steadily, as they do at almost every shelter. A shelter that doesn't have one probably doesn't accept them for some reason. I have found them at every facility I've visited. A few trickle into the shelter where my mother volunteers, in the rural outskirts of Greater Cincinnati, where shopping malls have yet to devour all the farms. I find plenty more in the many noisy kennels of the SPCA Cincinnati, where so long ago I pointed at the profoundly mutty Tang and said, "That one." When I walked down the long row in the mid-1970s, I don't recall the dogs yipping and yodeling on either side of me tending toward one look or type. Now most of them resemble pitties.

Pitties are the type of dog most commonly found in shelters, followed by Chihuahuas (yes, Chihuahuas), and in third place, Labrador mixes. Shelter directors tell me they noticed an increase in the blocky-headed, slick-coated dogs by the 1990s, if not earlier, as they began to outnumber the Lab mixes and shepherd mixes. The number of pitties has swelled ever since. No one is sure exactly why. The dogs tend to come from urban neighborhoods, but not exclusively. They tend to be unfixed, which could mean they have more of a chance to breed. The human love of labels alone may be to blame.

I never thought to ask what kind of dog Tang was. Between his nose and tail, he had three different kinds of fur. He was obviously what they used to call a Heinz 57. He was simply a mutt, which is a true dog, after all. Now he would be listed as maybe a cairn terrier mix, which would be quite a stretch, given his log-shaped body and short legs. But a shelter has to list a primary breed for a given dog. Computerized records and rabies vaccine certificates require it. Signs of a distant purebred must be found in a mongrel. Never mind that Mother Nature, who likes her mysteries, does not cut and paste these breeds together—add a Rhodesian ridgeback's long cowlick here or the drooping jowls of a coonhound there—but blends their traits into something new and often unexpected, which can leave shelter staffers scratching their heads. Still, they have to come up with something. So they consider a splotchy coat, floppy ears, or a pointy nose; maybe get out a book on dog breeds; and make a wild guess. This deeply inexact science has produced some nutty labels at the ARL, one of my favorites being Dogue de Bordeaux mix. Oh, if I could only get back the hours I spent explaining that to adopters.

This guessing game is mostly harmless, except when it comes to the pitties. Once the word *pit bull* is scribbled in marker on a kennel door—what with the stigma, the landlords who won't allow them in their buildings, and the home insurance policies that forbid them—the dog within can have a harder time finding a home. Some of these dogs may be related to American pit bull terriers, American Staffordshire terriers, or Staffordshire bull terriers, three closely related purebreds, but many are likely not. Only a DNA test can say for sure what is in a breed's mix—not eyeballs, not even experienced eyeballs. For a 2012 study at the University of Florida, more than five thousand "dog experts" (trainers, shelter workers, and veterinarians) guessed at the mix in 119 mutts by examining their photos. If the dog had only 25 percent of a breed, the guess was considered right. The experts were wrong 75 percent of the time. They saw Australian cattle dog, Dalmatian, and Belgian Malinois in dogs who didn't have one lick of those breeds. They saw Sharpei where there was beagle, Catahoula leopard dog where there was Labrador. The study demonstrated that you cannot judge a mutt's lineage by its looks, especially when it comes to pitties. The experts "saw" thirty pitties. In fact, only twelve of those dogs had 25 percent of their genes from American Staffordshire terrier or American pit bull terrier. The others had a quarter or less or none. Instead, they had the genes of boxers, mastiffs, Irish water dogs, Malamutes, golden retrievers, and the rare Entlebucher mountain dog, a purebred that, to some eyes today, might look like a pit bull mix.

Gwen has been at the ARL for three months, and it has begun to show. When we play ball, she leaps up on me, barks in my face, swings her paws around while twitching her tail back and forth. I ask her to sit before I throw the ball to calm her, but that has little effect. In seconds she's at me again, pleading, demanding a toss. I am no tennis ball gun, which is what she needs. Fetching is her equivalent of pacing or biting her nails. It relieves her stress but also makes clear how anxious she has grown. Her obsession does little for my own stress. I take her for long promenades through the neighborhood, but I suspect she's thinking of tennis balls the whole time. I think about when an adopter might show up for her. Each of us worried in our own way, she and I make our way through the city streets.

Come June, the vet behaviorist takes Gwen home for a few weeks to see if she can relax away from the shelter, if she can become more a pet dog and less a neurotic athlete. I get reports that Gwen has warmed to the vet behaviorist's dog, even tussles with him. She has miraculously lost most of her interest in fetching, and even wanders past balls on the floor. The vet behaviorist brings back a far calmer Gwen, which we all hope will help her get adopted soon, before life in the kennels makes her a nervous wreck again. I think it's best if I don't throw a ball for her, so I take her to the Real Life Room instead of the playground. The moment we step into the room, Gwen sits and stares at a basket of toys on a bookshelf. She whines. Of course, there's a ball in the basket, but I grab a rope toy instead. When I hold the knotted cord out, Gwen gamely grabs it, and we tug back and forth. I want to teach her to let go of the rope on the cue of "give." While I clutch my end with one hand, I hold a treat under her nose with the other. This makes most dogs let go of the rope. Not Gwen. I pause and push the treat under her nose a second time. Forget it. This is when a smarter person would give up, but as with most humans, there is something in me that drives me *toward* my fears. I reach into the toy basket with my free hand and grab the tennis ball. I'm sure she'll give me the rope for that. I'm right. She's sees the ball, drops the rope, and springs at me. "Ow," I yelp. The ball and my hand are in her mouth. "Drop, drop, drop," I chant. Her teeth bear down on my thumb joint. If I pull, she's likely to bite harder, so I stand still as my thumb seems to disintegrate in her jaws. Gwen stares at me with those bright eyes, confused, wondering why I won't give her the ball. I wonder how close the nearest hospital is. Then she cocks her head slightly and loosens her grip just enough to free my hand.

"Are you okay?" a shelter trainer calls from her office down the hall.

"Yes," I call back as brightly as I can, though I guess I'm not. I hear the trainer heading down the hall to the Real Life Room. Miraculously, my thumb is attached and blood does not gush from my hand, but sometimes a cut takes a few moments before it bleeds. If Gwen has broken my skin and a staff member sees that, she will be put on a ten-day quarantine during which no volunteer can take her out. That's the last thing Gwen needs. As the trainer leans in the door, I hide my mashed hand behind my back and explain that Gwen got me "just a little." I hold out my good hand. "See." As soon as the trainer returns to her office, I examine my crushed thumb and wonder how such pain produced so little damage, only a swollen, bluish knuckle. I shake my head over how my good intentions nearly backfired. I almost made Gwen's shelter stay longer, which would have made her crazy again, which would have made it harder for her to find a home. For her, for me, I swear off fetch, tug, any game, no matter how much Gwen begs me.

I never have to test my will. The very next day, a couple adopts Gwen. The epic fetcher has found a home after nearly five months. Suddenly I need a new project. There is a smallish pittie (what we like to call a pocket pit) named Lovie who has a bum leg and likes to cuddle. She'll do just fine.

If I had my way, this is what I would write on all the pitties' kennels: "Classic American Dog." That's what I see when I look at Gwen and her kind. Yes, they have distant roots in the British Isles, where in the mid-nineteenth century, people crossed terriers with bulldogs. Immigrants brought those dogs to these shores, where they were likely crossed, on purpose and not, with other purebreds and mutts. The resulting dogs were often called bulldogs, but the term was used broadly. These "bulldogs" fought in the pits but also worked on farms and guarded homes. Many were companions. Helen Keller had one named Phiz. As a kid, James Thurber had one named Rex. (Thurber dreamed of Rex for decades after the dog died.) Budd, a stocky white pittie, rode along on the first cross-country drive in 1911. Driver Horatio Nelson Jackson made Budd goggles to keep the dust out of his eyes while he was riding in the roofless car. Jackson reported that Budd was the only one on the drive who "did not use profanity."

I found an archive's worth of historic photos of these dogs online. A turn-of-the-century women's basketball team, the players' hair swept high into buns, gathered around a pittie with a patch of black around one eye. A couple in 1920s wedding finery stands beside their black dog, who has clipped, spiky ears and a furl of tulle on his back like angel wings. A woman in early swimming regalia (hat, suit, stockings) pulls her smiley, panting pittie into her lap for the camera. The blur of white in the corner of a worn tintype of a logging operation turns out to be not a small cow but a "bulldog." These dogs were once everywhere. Scanning these faded images made me finally realize that there was probably one in my family tree. In the 1930s, my grandparents had a dog named Timothy Doleful, who by all descriptions could have been one of these "bulldogs." When I was a kid, Timothy Doleful loomed large in my imagination, as my grandmother told tales of him stealing my grandfather's hat and absconding with it into the basement, where he would pummel it into a pillow for a nap. I asked my grandmother over and over to tell me about Timothy Doleful. She claimed that when my businessman grandfather came home from work, Timothy would run in circles around the front yard. These gleeful loops grew wider and wider until Timothy, lost in happiness, would zip right into the side of the house. "BANG!" my grandmother would exclaim.

We've collectively forgotten these dogs that were everywhere in the nineteenth and early twentieth centuries. We've forgotten the ones who were pets and the ones who were heroes, such as Sallie, a sculpture of whom I tracked down along a ridge in Gettysburg National Military

Park. The diminutive brindle-coated bulldog was the mascot of the Eleventh Pennsylvania Infantry as the regiment plunged into the mayhem of the Civil War. Sallie was shot in the neck once, had many litters of puppies during the regiment's many campaigns, and reportedly knew the drumroll. She sat by injured company members on the battlefield. She accompanied the men into the three days of madness at Gettysburg. As hard as I tried, I couldn't picture that madness as Scott and I drove to the northern edge of the once enormous battlefield looking for Sallie on a late December afternoon. The high fields and rail fences were too beautiful for imagining cannon fire and corpses, the day too sunny to feel solemn. I scanned the monuments we passed, granite eagles with wings spread and solemn obelisks, and then spotted a single gun-toting infantryman standing at attention atop a marble column. I thought I saw a knot of bronze at the statue's base. We parked, and in a chill wind I ran across thick grass gone to gold to the soldier. There was a bronze of Sallie curled at the very base. She lounged the way only a dog can, relaxed yet alert. Her sharp eyes looked southwest, toward the enemy, for eternity. I wasn't the first to run across the field. Someone had left a dog biscuit by her nose. I couldn't help patting her smooth, cold head. Sallie survived Gettysburg and later led her regiment as they and other troops marched past President Lincoln near the Rappahannock River in Virginia. The president reportedly watched the parade impassively, somberly, until he saw Sallie, at which point he raised one large hand and doffed his towering stovepipe hat. In 1865, Sallie was shot through the head at the Battle of Hatcher's Run in Virginia.

Pitties were the war dogs of choice into the First World War, when Stubby became the first dog ever to be given a rank: sergeant in the U.S. Armed Forces. While training at Yale University in 1917, a private found a puppy with next to no tail, thus Stubby's name. Stubby became the mascot of the 102nd Infantry, 26th Yankee Division. He reportedly learned the bugle calls, the drills, and how to salute. He'd raise his right paw to his right eyebrow, or so the story goes. When the young soldiers shipped out to France, and the uncertainties ahead, they refused to leave their mascot behind as ordered, hiding Stubby in a coal bin aboard the ship until the vessel was safely out at sea. Stubby followed the company to the front lines. He barked when he smelled gas, running through the trenches and warning the men to pull on their masks. He found wounded men from his company in German trenches and barked until the medics arrived. He barked when he found a German soldier mapping the Allied trenches. Stubby bit him on the leg, tripping the intruder, who was then captured.

You can find Stubby in Washington, DC, in the Smithsonian's National Museum of American History, in a glass case on the second floor with a hodgepodge of World War I memorabilia, such as a crutch with a prosthetic arm attached to it. For some reason the stuffed brindle does not wear his vest of medals, but his studded collar rings his neck. His muzzle has the droop of a bulldog's, his mouth drawn down in a forever frown, yet his expression in eternity is one of calm vigilance. The museum's short label describing Stubby's role in the war doesn't do him justice. As I was rewriting it in my head, a man and his posse of children suddenly pressed in around me. "Hey, look at that mean dog!" Dad cried, and they galloped on through the museum as I, standing by the case alone again, said to no one, "That's Stubby!" The dog who survived the war, including being gassed and shot full of shrapnel. The dog who saw seventeen battles in all. The dog who met President Coolidge and then President Harding. Stubby died in 1926, at the age of nine, which explains his white face, which makes his dark eyes all the more moving. In front of the case, I found that if I stood just| so, his devoted eyes, which saw the wounded men, the German spy, and two presidents, looked right into mine.

• • •

In January, when a sheet of ice lacquers half the play yard, I find Gwen in a kennel. Gwen. The couple who adopted her last summer has returned her because she is so afraid of the man. She hid from him under the dining table, ran off from him when they took walks, and sometimes even urinated when she saw him. This started soon after the couple took her home, when the man had a bunch of his buddies over. The gathering was loud, raucous. Gwen cowered in a closet. She was scared of him from then on. They hoped she would improve, but she didn't, so they called the shelter to ask what to do. Hearing how poorly Gwen was faring, the vet behaviorist encouraged them to return her. Who would have guessed that within that ball of fire lived such a gentle soul? Gwen still has her party face, but she is slightly wide-eyed. She is given Prozac for her frayed nerves and spends her days lounging in the trainers' office so that she is in the kennels as little as possible. I always stop by to plant a kiss on top of her coffee-colored head. Last summer she was a pittie who loved fetch too much. Now she is a pittie with a history of growling at men. Who will want such a dog? Who will see Gwen for Gwen, a sensitive, smart girl who's had one bad break after another? In a city that seems ambivalent about pitties, who will see her just as a dog who needs a home?

Not long ago in Boston, any dog who looked the least bit like a pit bull such as Gwen had to be muzzled in public. During that unfortunate phase, I went to a low-cost rabies vaccine clinic in the city's Italian North End. Just as I held a quivering Penny Jane between my legs for her injection, a heavyset man showed up at the auditorium with his two brawny mutts. When I stepped to the counter to pay, two animal control officers, out of earshot of the man, debated if one of his dogs was a pit bull mix and, if they thought so, whether they should ticket him for no muzzle. As I left, they were still trying to make up their minds—was it or wasn't it?—while off to the side, the man was doing the right thing, getting his dogs vaccinated. That muzzle law was essentially repealed in 2012, but not because the Boston City Council had a progressive change of heart. Rather, Massachusetts joined a growing list of states that ban any kind of legislation that targets specific dog breeds. The state law nullified the Boston ordinance.

Boston's muzzle law is one reason Stacey Coleman doesn't think much of the city. Coleman directs the Animal Farm Foundation, a leading national voice for the equal rights of pit bull–type dogs. She has been fighting for their rights since 2001, when she opened her car door to one. Coleman was working at a publishing company in Indianapolis while studying to become an

American Sign Language interpreter. One day, as she drove out of the parking lot on her way to lunch, she spotted a colleague kicking at a black dog. The dog was trying to grab his bag of fast food. Coleman didn't want her colleague to hurt the dog, but she didn't want to embarrass him by asking him to stop kicking her. Instead, she braked, pushed open her car door, and trilled, "Little dog, little dog." The "little dog" ran full steam into Coleman's car, landed on the passenger seat, hopped onto the backseat, sat down, and smiled. She was all black except for a white bib, two white feet, and a splotch like spilled milk on the end of her nose. She was cute, but looking at her boxy muzzle and slick coat, Coleman realized, "Oh, my God, she's a pit bull." The most dangerous of dogs was panting on her backseat. Coleman got out of the car and closed the door. She called the local humane society to come get the dog.

This was at the height of the hysteria over the dogs that once kept Helen Keller and James Thurber company. They had gone from well-loved pets and war heroes to emblems of the violence and chaos in America's urban ghettos. Newspapers wrote of a mythic beast with locking jaws and bloodlust. Cities banned them. Many shelters routinely put them down. It was a very dangerous time for any dog who resembled a pit bull even in the slightest. The hype had gotten to

Coleman, but she couldn't quit thinking about that dog smiling on her backseat. She hadn't seemed dangerous, really. The next day, Coleman called the society to tell them that she'd pay for whatever medical treatment the dog needed, total carte blanche. No bother, Coleman was told. The nameless, unspayed stray pit bull would be euthanized. That was the society's policy. Shocked, and thinking on her feet, Coleman lied and said the dog was hers. She wanted her back. At first the society refused. Then Coleman hired a lawyer and signed a raft of release forms, and the little dog was hers, albeit with a severe case of mange she'd picked up in the shelter. Coleman named her Gertie, and lived with the happy-go-lucky charmer for the next fifteen years. During those years, Coleman's life and then her career changed. She got involved with her local humane society and devoted more and more of her free time to pit bulls, including fighting a proposed citywide ban in Indianapolis and starting the Indy Pit Bull Crew, a nonprofit that champions pitties. That eventually led the Indiana native east to the hamlet of Bangall, New York, to her job at Animal Farm Foundation.

Life slowly changed for pit bulls, too, as cooler heads began to prevail and the stigma against pit bull–type dogs began to wane. By 2012, Coleman felt the balance finally tip in the dogs' favor. More laws banning pit bulls were being repealed than were going on the books. Pitties had even become popular. A list of the top ten breeds based on 2.3 million dogs reads in descending order of popularity: Labrador retrievers, Chihuahuas, Yorkshire terriers, Shih Tzus, and then, at number five, a dog that isn't a breed at all, "pit bull." The dogs might be even more popular if so many landlords didn't bar them. When I talk to people about adopting a pittie at the ARL, I always ask them, "Do you own or rent?" because if they rent, there's a good chance their landlord will not allow them to keep the dog they have started to fall in love with. Even if they own their condo, their homeowner's insurance may forbid pit bull–type dogs. Coleman believes these housing battles will be won "by the almighty American dollar" as more homeowners and landlords take their business to insurance companies such as State Farm, which will cover the dogs. Until then, I will continue to ask potential adopters, "Do you own or rent?"

I asked Coleman what else shelters could do to find homes for more pitties. Her answer, in a way, was—nothing. Shelters need to treat them like dogs, any dogs, she told me. They should quit singling them out. Shelters make it harder for pitties to get adopted by insisting on home visits or not allowing families with children to adopt them. Shelters shouldn't hold pitties to a higher standard of behavior, adopting out only "ambassadors." Coleman tells me to call the people at the Washington Humane Society in DC, a large private nonprofit shelter. They know how to adopt out pitties. Like a lot of shelters around the country, Washington Humane joined the chorus against pits bulls. They considered them dangerous enough that they put down any dog who resembled one. A new director changed that in 2007. Suddenly Washington Humane had all these dogs on the adoption floor whom it had once declared vicious. They debated how to find them homes—as one top staffer put it to me, "What was the secret sauce?" They tried calling the dogs Staffordshire terriers, but found that didn't make any noticeable difference. They held pit bull–only special promotions, but then realized by spotlighting the dogs, they were implying there was something wrong with them. While they searched and searched for the magic charm, one of the adoption counselors asked what all the fuss was about. People were taking pitties home. Hundreds were being adopted each year. The secret to the sauce was that there was none. As Coleman says, if the shelters treat them as they do any other dog, people think of them like any other dog, just like their grand-parents and great-grandparents did.

At the ARL we can't treat Gwen like any other dog. The kennels on the adoption floor make her too nervous. Yet in the trainer's office all day she is out of sight. No adopter can happen upon her and notice her beauty and aplomb. The only way to find her is by coming across her photo on the Internet. I'm so worried about her that I stop worrying—if that makes any sense. We are out of to-do items and action plans. All we can do is hope and wait. We have no special sauce for Gwen.

In March, two months after she was returned to the ARL, a youngish couple comes to see her, just her. The dark-haired woman spotted Gwen's photo online (head cocked, pink tongue out) and fell in love. She and her partner have driven nearly an hour to the ARL to meet her. Gwen brings a ball to the woman, who feeds her a piece of apple. The woman wants Gwen even after hearing that she is on antianxiety meds and that her last owner said she growled at men. Just over a year after this beautiful girl was found tied to a pole in Saugus, she leaps into the couple's car and drives up the coast and out of our lives for good, we hope. A few weeks later the couple reports that Gwen is perfect. She is super snuggly. They call her Button Bee, Boo, B, and Snuggle Bee Q.

A DNA test was run on Gwen just before she was adopted. She is half bulldog and bullmastiff; the other half is a mishmash. In other words, Gwen isn't a pit bull at all.

Harmony

8

LIFE IN THE KENNELS

I pull steadily on Walter's leash to get him off the dryer. It's noon, time to go out, though he doesn't see it that way. He digs in his white feet, raises his rounded haunches, and lowers his little anvil of a head. This tug-of-war we have several times a day is something like reeling in a fish on a hook. I hear my father's voice in my head, coaching me long ago on how to land what turned out to be a raging catfish. "Slow, steady," I hear him say. There is something fishlike about Walter, with his long, stout body and pointy muzzle. I have quickly learned that the trick is to increase the pressure on his leash ever so slowly until he gives up and drops lightly to the floor. But Walter is not inclined to give up easily, at anything. I make a point of not generalizing about breeds, but terriers want what they want, and Walter doesn't want to come off his perch on the dryer. I crouch some to shift my angle. I tighten my grip. "Slow, steady." His collar pushes up against his black ears, crowds his face into a scowl. Suddenly the leash goes slack in my hand. Walter's collar has popped off. A victor at last, he takes a seat on the dryer, his sanctuary, triumphant but wary of my next move. I swear softly to myself so as not to frighten him. Now I have a dog I can't handle loose in my condo. I do not dare try to put his collar back on. Penny Jane, who's watched this whole curious scene, looks at me as if to say, "Now what?" I e-mail the only person in the world who can touch Walter, the vet behaviorist who fostered him. The vet behaviorist e-mails back that she can stop by our condo on her way home from work. As house calls go, this should be an easy one.

Sheila D'Arpino was the first in the country to complete a one-of a-kind program: a three-year postgraduate combined study of shelter medicine and animal behavior at the University of California–Davis's well-regarded veterinary school. She had wanted to be a veterinarian since she was a child, but once the California native became one, she found it wasn't enough. With so many shelter dogs euthanized for their behavior, Sheila believed that to truly help those animals she had to treat their minds as well as their bodies. At UC Davis she became the equivalent of a psychiatrist. She studied shelter dog behavior and learned how to treat their problems with training or, in some cases, with drugs. The biggest lesson she learned in the end, however, was philosophical: Every dog is an individual. There is no one kind of fearful dog, for example. Behind the crouches and tail tucks, a unique personality exists. That's a long way from the thinking of the seventeenth-century French philosopher René Descartes, which stymied our understanding of animals for more than three centuries and still holds sway in some quarters. Descartes argued that animals were not only soulless but lacked any kind of reasoning. They had no more intelligence or interior life, he believed, than that of a well-oiled clock. He called animals "beast machines." Even in the seventeenth century, many pet owners must have disagreed.

Now canines are the darlings of scientific cognition studies, and "every dog is an individual" has become *the* buzz phrase of the shelter world. It is, however, one of those simple proclamations that are easy to agree with but surprisingly difficult to apply, especially in an institutional setting, where labels and generalities come easily. It is especially hard to apply to growling, biting dogs such as Walter, who are often dubbed inherently "bad" or "dangerous" and are put down as a public service, as one shoots a marauding grizzly bear. Granted, a dog such as Walter, who behaved like a terrier from hell his first day at the ARL, poses a practical problem: If no one could handle him, there was no safe way to keep him in the shelter. Luckily, a veterinarian with special training and an enlightened outlook happened to work for the shelter just then. Even more luckily, D'Arpino had a yard and an enclosure where Walter would, she hoped, calm down. Only then would she see who this dog was behind the flashing teeth and growling, if he was, in fact, a "dangerous" dog or one who snapped when he was scared out of his wits. Slowly she got some answers. Once Walter moved into her house, he kept his distance for about a month. Then he began to follow Sheila around. He would playfully run around on his short, squat legs, mouth open in a smile, his long, narrow tongue flapping. Then he climbed into her lap.

When Walter sees D'Arpino, he leaps off the dryer and runs to her. When she sits cross-legged on our hallway floor, he plops into her lap. He puts his front paws on her chest so he can look into her eyes while she strokes his back. His glassy eyes brighten. He doesn't flinch when she clicks on his collar. We glimpse who a happy, relaxed Walter might be. I sink to the hallway floor next to her, hoping that some of her charm will wear off on me. After about ten minutes of chitchatting with Scott and me while she pets Walter, she has to go home to her family and her multiple dogs. I hold Walter's reattached leash so he won't follow his only friend in the world as D'Arpino leaves.

"Sorry, Walter," I say as I close the door.

The night returns to normal, kind of. I have to pull Walter down our front steps in the chill of a wintry evening to go for an overdue walk. He shivers as we head up and down the icy sidewalks. I wish I could put a jacket on him. Back inside, he hurries down our long hallway to the safety and warmth of the dryer. Then, for some reason, maybe because we're tired, Scott and I do something we never do. We lie down on the floor to watch TV. Not long after we have stretched out on our sides and arranged throw pillows just so, we notice Walter's small silhouette in the hallway. He pads tentatively toward us and then stops. He lets his head droop.

"Look," we whisper to each other, meaning "Look out of the corner of your eye."

Walter takes a few more steps toward us. When he has almost reached the living room's light, he pauses again. He seems to be thinking. Maybe he's thinking he'll have to make do with the two knuckleheads on the floor. Maybe he's thinking about the nice massage he just got from his only friend in the world. A look of resolve comes over his pointed face. He suddenly races at Scott and snuggles up against my husband's chest. We quietly raise our eyebrows at each other.

Walter slept with us from that night on, often putting his head on our pillows or worming his way under the blankets. He hopped into our laps whenever we sat down. He began to play, dashing up and down our long hallway while we yelled, "Mad dog, mad dog!" Walter was so crazy to ride in the car that we had to spell the word to each other, otherwise he'd bolt for the front door and start squeaking pathetically. He shadowed me, even sat in the bathroom while I took a shower. He also followed Penny Jane, who, in her aloof way, seemed to like him. Eventually we could take the terrier's leash off and put it on, and then his collar. He did nip me once, as I tried to brush road salt off a back foot. I knew I shouldn't have, but he was limping. Luckily I had a thick glove on, and he only bruised my hand. He had become a pet dog again, though one whose feet you'd best leave alone.

We sent him to the shelter with a good report card: loving, housebroken, funny. The dog who'd once been a gnashing mongoose clearly had a future as a family pet. Yet almost the moment the kennel door closed behind him, his eyes went black and glassy again. He growled at staffers when they looked into his kennel. For fear he would nip someone, only D'Arpino or I took him out. When he saw either of us, he exploded with happiness. When we left, he shut back down. I got word that the shelter was thinking of putting him down. How could they put a dog up for adoption whom they couldn't handle? I had never wanted a terrier, especially a Jack Russell. I had never wanted a male dog, or a little dog.

When we brought Walter home for good we

goofed up his name some to put our official stamp on him. He became Walter Joe Jr. We started calling him Waltie-Bear or Joey or Junior or Dub-yuh or Mister or Champ or Bubbles—all names he learned. Though he showed no signs of it in the shelter, he was completely capable of living in a home, not to mention riding in canoes, staying in hotels, and lounging on the beach. He was, as they say, "homeable" but not "shelterable." To be the former, as it turns out, does not mean a dog can be the latter.

These dogs are such conundrums. Shelter staff have to decide if a dog can be safely adopted based on his behavior in a stressful environment that in no way resembles a home. The equivalent would be judging a person while he is in the hospital, bedridden, stuck with IVs, anxious, bored, and with no family to comfort him. Would you see that person's true character? Or would you see the equivalent of Walter in the shelter? Luckily I haven't seen many Walters since I began volunteering. Most dogs manage okay enough in the enervating tedium, at least at first. Some even improve with regular meals and walks. But even the dogs who seem to thrive can, over weeks, months, appear to deteriorate. They bark more, jump more, maybe start to lunge at strangers or other dogs. They become obsessed with balls, as happened with Gwen Stefani. These dogs can begin to seem less and less adoptable, which makes it harder to find them a home, which means they stay in the shelter longer and longer. A vicious cycle begins. It's not always enough to find a dog a home. You have to find one *quickly*.

When Bridget showed up at the ARL one fall, she immediately claimed the title of the best-looking pooch in the shelter. The young, long-legged shepherd mix had a milky blond coat with smudges of brown just over her friendly, amber eyes. There was something Hollywood about her. She even liked to stretch out on a couch like a diva, with her front legs dangling over the side. Her owner had surrendered the ten-month-old just before Thanksgiving. He had adopted her on an impulse from a rescue that was going to put her down. Then he realized he had no time for a dog, especially such a sizable pup. Bridget came up to my mid-thigh, which at least made it easy for me to stroke her long back.

Bridget was affectionate and playful and gorgeous, which is why, despite her size, I thought the beauty would be adopted within a couple of weeks, tops. Though I walked her and always stopped by her kennel to say hello, I didn't dwell on her. A few of the red dogs occupied my mind: the ironically named Happy, a liver-spotted mutt with a wide smile who'd been at the shelter for four months, and Harmony, a young slip of a shepherd mix with bum elbows. Harmony was so afraid of people she'd pee when you looked in her kennel. Bridget did not need me to fuss over her, but Happy and Harmony did. Those two wouldn't be going anywhere soon.

Not long ago a dog wouldn't have stayed in most shelters for more than a week. Now many stay until they are adopted, which can take weeks, months, years. Some can end up spending their entire lives at a shelter, as Connor has at the League for Animal Welfare in Ohio, where my mother, now in her eighties, volunteers. Whenever I go there with her, I stop by Connor's kennel. A favorite toy, a blue plastic ball raked with tooth marks, rests in a bucket on his kennel door. When I visit Connor, I stand sideways, avoid looking at his white face, and talk to him in a low, calm voice, then toss him some goodies. He stands on bowed, twiggy legs, assessing me. I don't tarry. That way, Connor won't work himself into a barky lather. Only a few volunteers can walk Connor, my mother not being one of them. His walkers will also drive him to McDonald's for hamburgers. Whenever he leaves his kennel, Connor wears a jacket that reads "Don't Pet Me" on both sides.

This is how a dog ends up living in a shelter. Connor was surrendered as a puppy because he had trouble walking and would inexplicably tip over. The vet cinched a brace around his small neck and told the staff to keep him away from dogs. His convalescence didn't improve his legs, but isolating him from his own kind in those formative early months did make him dog aggressive. He liked humans just fine until he was five or six, when he started to snarl at people, especially strangers. He hated for anyone to surprise him or, worse, wake him up. A couple wanted to adopt him despite his crankiness. They visited him many times. They fenced in their yard just for him. They took Connor home for a trial afternoon. He inspected the newly fenced-in yard and then lay down for a nap. The couple didn't know that Connor didn't like to be roused. When they woke him, he snapped at them. They drove him back to the shelter.

The last time I saw Connor he was almost twelve. MRIs, blood tests—nothing has ever found out what is wrong with his skinny legs or his brain. One vet thought he might have suffered nerve damage during his birth but who knows? Sometimes when Connor lies on his side, his legs stiffen and cross so that he can't get up. "Connor is stuck," someone will tell the shelter manager. Then she finds one of Connor's people to go help him off his bed. He also sometimes barks at the ceiling as if there is something worrisome overhead. The shelter manager says he's the best weather forecaster ever. The sun can blaze, but if Connor shakes on his bed and refuses to eat, you'd better cancel your cookout—unless you don't mind grilling burgers in a thunderstorm.

In theory, Connor is still up for adoption, but the shelter manager thinks it would be best for him to stay put. Not all her staff agree. Some think it's inhumane to keep a dog in a shelter his whole life. A dog needs a home. At this point, the shelter manager thinks "a home" would be more inhumane for Connor. It would be like the reverse of sending a pet to a shelter. This life, with his blue ball, his favorite volunteers, his trips to McDonald's, is all he's ever known, she says. It *is* his home.

Most of the shelters across the country were designed to hold animals for brief stints. They weren't built to keep animals for the weeks or months it sometimes takes for them to get adopted. The facilities were built for cleanliness and safety first. The overall well-being of the animals came in a distant third. Dog kennels were placed close to cat kennels, though barking unhinges cats, not to mention the dogs. The concrete kennel walls and floors can easily be hosed, but the hard surfaces amplify the discordant woofs. A dog typically snoozes half the day or more, as Penny Jane and Walter Joe demonstrate regularly. That's not possible in a noisy shelter, which explains why, when I bring some dogs home overnight, the first thing many do is konk out. A mastiff mix who came to my condo several times would walk through the front door and straight down the hall to our bedroom, where she would sink her copper-colored bulk onto our queen-size bed for a four-hour snooze. As if the noise of the shelter weren't enervating enough, the dogs are isolated from one another yet can always smell and hear one another. As they are led out for walks, they can see one another. That riles the ones who don't like dogs, and it riles the ones who like dogs and would love a good wrestle. When the kennels are calm, I almost hate to take a dog out, because that sets everyone off.

None of this seemed to bother Happy when he arrived during the summer. He was a stray, a six-month-old kid. In the early weeks, he was such a charmer, crazy in his youth but so joyful and confident and curious. He thought the pigeons flapping in the trees in the play yard were funny. Women with big purses walking by the fence were so interesting. He essentially taught himself the agility equipment. He rocketed over the A-frame, then shot up and down the high walk. Given that, I tried him on the teeter-totter and, unlike most dogs, he didn't blink as he walked over the moving plank and it *ka-thunked* loudly on the ground. I assumed he'd go home as soon as he moved to the adoption floor, and he might have, except that once there, he began to yodel like a hyena. He even looked like one, ricocheting around his kennel. His charms returned the moment you took him out, but next to no one asked to see the dog who appeared to be crying his heart out. The weeks began to pass. In September, Happy went home with a family. A few weeks later they returned him for a long list of reasons, including a spot of dermatitis on his face.

After that, Happy became a red dog. He mouthed our hands and arms so that we couldn't get a harness on him. Instead we had to loop the leash around his chest in what's called a field harness. Then he pounced on and growled at a staff member. He let it rip at a few men as he passed them on the sidewalk. I wanted to bring him home for a much-needed overnight, but when Happy met Scott, he nipped my husband's hand hard enough to break the skin. That put Happy on a ten-day quarantine. Now when I kneel by his kennel, he smashes his side against the door so I can scratch him, but in his desperation to be petted, he often accidentally bends my fingers backward, which hurts. He clearly is no longer shelterable, and it's become harder and harder to tell if he is homeable.

With Happy on quarantine, I pour all my energies into Harmony. Not many volunteers walk her, because she's so afraid of everyone. Yet beneath all that worry I find something of a

Lucille Ball in this dog, equal parts looker and goofus. She's nearly as lovely as Bridget but has stick legs and a Pinocchio nose. She usually has a bit of poop worked into her lush blond coat, too, not to mention some smeared here and there in her kennel. Once, she had some stuck to her collar like a corsage. Another time, she had something I couldn't even identify caked on the end of her long nose. Harmony knows me well, so at least she does not piddle on the floor when I step into her kennel. Instead, this fearful dog morphs into Miss Jumpy-Mouthy. She comes at me all swinging limbs. I turn my back as she thumps me with her paws, which, because it's her, makes me laugh. I scatter treats on the cement floor to get her off me. While she eats, I harness her quickly as I scan the floor for poop. Sometimes I make it out of her kennel without a scratch or poop on my shoe, but not often. Still, I love her.

I'll spend an hour or so with Harmony and then walk some other dog with the time I have left, including Bridget, whom, week after week, I'm surprised to find still here. There's often a "HOLD" sign on her kennel, meaning someone is planning to adopt her, but then these adopters, one after the other, change their minds about our gorgeous girl. When Santa comes to pose for holiday photos with the dogs, Bridget has been there six weeks. I start to worry about her.

As one shelter leader put it to me, it's not a question of *if* a shelter dog will deteriorate. It's a question of *when*. There's some debate as to whether the dogs are deteriorating or, rather, displaying what is normal behavior under trying circumstances. That "normal" won't help dogs get adopted. That's why the current thinking on remedying kennel stress is to find a dog a home pronto. In the meantime, shelters such as the ARL do what they can to relieve a dog's duress with walks, play groups, snuggling, toy puzzles, all of which is referred to as "enrichment." Other shelters have constructed larger, better buildings with training arenas and soundproof kennels. Rich Avanzino, of course, has the most radical answer to kennel stress: get rid of the shelters.

Avanzino didn't always think this way. As director of the well-endowed, trailblazing Maddie's Fund, he was going to construct an Emerald City for homeless pets. In 2012 the foundation ponied up $20 million for an ample office park in a suburb due east of the Bay Area. Another $2 million went toward the design. The dogs were going to lounge in apartment-like settings at the shelter during the day and then sleep overnight in the comfort of foster homes. The apartment-like rooms were designed by an acoustical engineer to minimize the loudest barking. The dogs would be treated with aroma-therapy and water therapy. They would dine on the best of foods. While lavishing all this on the dogs, Maddie's Fund would find out what it took to keep animals healthy and happy in a shelter.

Then Avanzino had an epiphany. Even if he built the Emerald City of animal shelters, it would still be a shelter. The model was the central problem. Pets do best in homes, not institutions, he tells me. "The future of animal welfare is 'non-shelter-centric.'" Avanzino and Maddie's Fund shelved the architectural drawings and began developing a model foster network instead. They would demonstrate how to solve homelessness without a building at all. Maddie's Fund was not the first to think of using foster homes, which many shelters already use and is the model for most private rescue networks. Yet Avanzino is maybe the first person to see foster homes as *the* solution and shelters themselves as the problem. He believes that foster homes not only will be better for the animals but will draw more and more people to the cause. According to him, some 180 million people have cats and dogs, but fewer than 20 million donate to or volunteer for shelters or rescues. Avanzino believes that the way to involve more of those pet owners is to make them foster parents. In theory, fostering makes perfect sense on several fronts. In practice, though, it means mustering a vast army that is willing to take animals into their homes and into their hearts temporarily. That might not be so hard with puppies or adult cutie-pies, but most animal lovers aren't prepared to take a truly fearful dog such as Penny Jane or a snapper such as Walter Joe or a skittish dog such as Harmony into their homes.

Harmony desperately needs a foster now. The shelter is willing to fix her bad elbows, to shave them so they fit just so, but that would mean months of recovery. The staff doesn't want to put her through that in the shelter, where she's clearly a nervous wreck. I would take her if I could, but she doesn't get along with other dogs and is scared of men. If the ARL can't find somewhere for her to go, my kooky friend may have to be put down.

Harmony is a question mark. I still have hope for her. I don't for Happy. He has raged more and more at men, including one of the shelter vets. Though the staff put extra time into training and exercising him, he bounces up and down on all fours in his kennel. He's clearly miserable. I get down on my knees one last time and scratch him until my fingers nearly break. As the steely January skies roll in, the staff take Happy into the auditorium for a game of fetch one morning. They feed him a cheeseburger. Then, seven months after he arrived, seven months from when he thought pigeons were fun and women with big purses were terribly interesting, they put Happy down. No one knows what could have been done, but everyone, volunteers and staff, is filled with remorse. I regret introducing him to Scott, which led to the quarantine. I ponder what I could have done differently as I stand in his empty kennel, which no one had the heart to clear out right away, and look at his toys scattered on the floor and his name in bold letters on his kennel door: "HAPPY."

When people say to me, "I don't know how you do it," or tell me, "I'd adopt all the animals in the shelter," I joke, "Then you would be an animal hoarder." But what I think is, You don't know the half of it. When I signed on to work with the red dogs, I unwittingly agreed to work with the dogs most at risk of being put down for their behavior. I agreed to step into a shadow, to give my heart to dogs I might never see again for the most final of reasons. Of course the staff have made the same choice, though I wonder if some of the young women who take shelter jobs understand exactly what they have signed up for. I don't know how they give their hearts away. I don't know how I do, either. All I know is that we do.

Best Friends has become a kind of mecca to shelter volunteers, so, like a pilgrim, I went there. I flew to Las Vegas and drove a rental car with the horsepower of a lawnmower four hours west and three thousand feet up. As the engine of my economy rental whined its way across a high plateau under the watchtower cliffs, it dawned on me that maybe this would have been a drive better made in the light of day or at least in a sturdier car. But once I had my mind set on going to Best Friends, I couldn't get there soon enough. I wanted to see what it felt like to work with homeless dogs without the shadow of death lurking over my shoulder. Some people I'd known had had what seemed like an almost religious experience there. I can't say that I did in the end, but I relaxed in a way I didn't even know I needed to. A tour guide told me that there's a healing power in the canyon, and though I'm not one for that kind of thinking, I couldn't deny that I left in better shape than I was in when I arrived. Certainly there is power in a place created from the best of ideals that just happens to be set amid one of the world's most startling landscapes.

Geologists liken the study of rock layers to reading a book. In those bands of sedimentary rocks—the "pages"—you can read the earth's story. Most everywhere else, those pages are hidden by trees or mountains or oceans. Or else, glaciers essentially ripped out the pages and scattered them here and there. In southwestern Utah the pages are laid bare and in good order. All that layer cake, all the striated turrets and clefts of rock, recount six hundred million years of history. You are looking at time, magnificent and endless. It seems terribly presumptuous to think that you could buy a chunk of this unique landscape, but that's what a loose group of twenty-eight like-minded friends did in 1984. They scraped up enough between them and bought a three-thousand-acre family ranch in a canyon just north of Kanab, a small, sun-blasted town of wide roads. They renamed this cleft in the land Angel Canyon and began hammering together pens and kennels, though most of them had never built much of anything. Now Best Friends is a national leader in the sheltering world, and the largest no-kill sanctuary in the country. Some seventeen hundred horses, pigs, parrots, rabbits, cats, and dogs live here. Most of the animals are adopted, but if they don't find a home, they can continue to live here, where time is boundless.

Best Friends sprawls so much like a campus that it's hard to get your bearings at first. The dogs, as many as four hundred at a time, live in kennels with yard-size or bigger outdoor runs. There are jumpy-mouthies from shelters across the Southwest. There are dogs with complicated medical problems, such as Hamlet, a young border collie–like dog whose back feet knuckle under inexplicably. A steady stream of puppies comes from a half dozen nearby Native American reservations. Hummer, a chow-like dog with one ear up and one down, was rescued from Hurricane Katrina. Black-nosed Joy came from the Missouri

500, a massive, multistate dogfighting ring that was busted in 2009. Six of Michael Vick's dogs still live here. The sanctuary took in twenty-two of them, many of whom were adopted. I met one, the chipper Sugar Ray, as his owner led him through the lunchroom where I was devouring a mountain of salad. I put down my fork so I could rub his graying muzzle.

Like nearly all the visitors, I came to Best Friends to help. If you watch a video and sign some paperwork, you can work with any of the animals. I was tempted by the potbellied pigs, especially by the idea of brushing their golden, bristly coats, but dogs, as always, called my name. My first day, just before 8:00 a.m. I report to puppy school, where four other volunteers and I grab a seat on the floor while some rez puppies shyly pad into the room. We will be among the first humans these little ones will have met. Our goal is neither to overwhelm nor to scare them, which is why the young trainer declares, "No petting. Just let them check you out." I can keep my hands to myself because, as much as I love dogs, my dirty secret is that I can take or leave puppies. For the other volunteers, keeping their hands to themselves proves a tall order. One stout woman in a hoodie sweeps a white puffy pup into her arms like a lost lover. "Please put down your puppy," the trainer instructs. Yakima, a milk-chocolate pup, gingerly sniffs me. He tucks in his tail and then sticks his front paws on my thigh. He laps my chin with his small tongue. Across the room, a puppy wails and whines as if it's being pinched. A moony-eyed middle-aged woman has plunked the complaining pup into her lap. "Please don't pet the puppy," the trainer commands.

I leave behind the four volunteers trying not to pet the puppies and head for my soft spot, senior dogs. The oldies' files are inches thick with medical notes. Squinting in the Utah sunshine, I walk a milky-white American bulldog with bad hips, a lumpy Lab mix, and a Dalmatian with an arthritic neck. None of them, however, has the aches and pains of a bright-eyed Lab mix named Delaney, my hands-down favorite. Despite heart-worm, a bum leg, a fused spine, and other ailments, she smiles at me as we amble down the red earth road. I smile back, and we look into each other's eyes for most of the outing except when we pass Klaus, a dog whose back legs stopped working for some unknown reason. Two trainers pull Klaus in a wagon. As he rolls by, he growls at us to stop our silly smiling.

After lunch, I rush over to a building filled with young jumpy-mouthies. It has the feel of a public high school. There I meet Spekk, Stymie, and Rigby, all young, brawny goofballs who bark as a hobby and can pull on their leashes like holy hell. There's also Wallie, a whitish bulldoggy mix who carries rocks in from his morning outings. The keeper, a slim, extraordinarily calm young woman in big glasses, puts the rocks in a basket labeled "Wallie's Rocks." The keeper, like a good high school teacher, does not abide any hijinks. The second the kennels grow too raucous, she shushes the dogs down using treats or putting some in their outdoor runs, bringing the others into their kennels. She'll light a stick of incense by Wallie's Rocks. It might not help them, she says, "but it helps me."

After I exercise a number of the rowdy youngsters, who steer me along a looping trail and across the remaining patches of March snow under a summerlike sun, the keeper asks me if I would take Tahiti out. "She needs practice meeting new people." The nearly all-white Australian shepherd with one eye lined with black quietly stands at the front of her kennel. Tahiti doesn't quite fit in with the rest of the ruffians here, because she's older and far more composed. She used to live in the sanctuary's roomy outdoor runs but found that overwhelming. When she quit eating, the staff moved her here, where there are fewer dogs and where chances are she will always live. Despite her demure appearance, Tahiti bit her previous owner's wife and the wife's friend. She also ripped their German shepherd's face open. She couldn't abide sharing her owner with anyone. She's up for adoption, but really only a hermit would be the right fit for her. Chances are Tahiti will always live here.

The trainer tells me Tahiti will make it clear if she doesn't like me the second I crack her kennel door. I don't want to seem like a chicken and do want to help Tahiti, so I muster all I know about canine behavior and banish thoughts of the women this beauty sank her teeth into and push open Tahiti's door. I'm looking for any sign of stiffness in her posture or a glare, what is called a "hard eye." Tahiti stays put and looks as welcoming as the best southern hostess. She waits for me to hook her leash on and then sashays out ahead of me. On the trail, Tahiti takes the lead and doesn't look back. She stops only to pee and to throw her beautiful self into a crunchy bed of sparkling snow. Then, as we near the kennel building, she turns around as if she's thought of something to say to me. She looks at me with a relaxed, friendly face. I stroke her neck. She moves closer to me, pushes her back against my shins, then plops her bottom down on my feet. As I rub her shoulders, lightly running my thumb along the edge of her shoulder bone, that dark dread rolls over me. What will happen to her? Then I remember that nothing will happen to her. This may not be a true home for a dog, but it's a life. She'll have a life.

• • •

Best Friends may not have any better answers to kennel stress, but it has more resources. They have a staff of trainers. The dogs go to play groups and splash in kiddie pools. They nap in offices and behind reception desks. When I was signing all my volunteer paperwork, a pittie snoozing behind a reception desk opened one eye to see who was there and then closed it tight again. I came across an odd white thing named Kiwi surveying the laundry room as a volunteer folded sheets. The volunteer told me she had to wear rubber boots at first because Kiwi bit her feet. Many of the dogs have outdoor runs any city pooch would envy, and they can frolic together or lounge under the Utah sun nearly year-round. In many ways, the dogs at Best Friends have a richer daily life than many pets. Sherry Woodard worries sometimes that they may have too much of a good thing, that Best Friends can be a little too exciting.

Woodard is a small woman who cuts a big profile with her mane of straight blond hair and a large parka that rustles as she strides. When Woodard first moved to this corner of the world, she guided rafts through the wonders of the Grand Canyon. In 1996 she traded in her paddles to become one of the first paid employees at Best Friends. She oversaw all the dogs for eight years and then became a traveling expert, advising shelters across the country on how to improve their behavior programs. One of her bugaboos is the overemphasis on walking dogs in shelters, what she calls "mindless marches." Mindless marches are dogs just plunging along, never looking back, while you cling to the leash, what volunteers across America are doing as you read this. Dogs need more than exercise, Woodard says. They need to think. Training them actually uses more of their energy, she points out.

I talked with Woodard off and on for two days as she guided me around Best Friends, dog crates jangling in the back of her SUV as we bumped over potholes left by a spring snowstorm. We periodically stopped by her stucco house on the grounds so she could dash in and check on her ferret, Skippy, who'd recently had emergency cancer surgery. He'd had his spleen, adrenal glands, and part of his liver removed. Woodard had sat up with him the night before I arrived. She spent those dark hours monitoring his temperature and trying to get the ferret to drink water. Woodard likes, maybe even thrives on, challenges. She helped during Katrina. She has pulled dogs out of hoarders' houses. She's fostered and adopted wolf hybrids. Whenever I mentioned dog behavior problems, she had a suggestion, even a handout or two. Woodard doesn't give up easily, especially on dogs. At Best Friends, she doesn't have to. And not having had to, she's seen the miracles training can work for some dogs, how many "untreatables" can be made adoptable. I asked her what I could do while I was there that might really help a dog. "The best thing you can do is take a dog away from all of this," she said, motioning to the outdoor runs and trails.

For a night, I could do that. If you volunteer with the dogs, you can take one back to your hotel for a sleepover. When I ask the extraordinarily calm keeper with the big glasses whom she would like me to take, she points to a hunk. Guy is a one-year-old with the physique of a boxer, the chunky head of a pittie, a smooth coat the color of a new penny, and greenish eyes lined with black like Cleopatra's. Despite his good looks, Guy has spent most of his young life in a shelter in New Mexico and now here. He's never gone with a volunteer for an overnight. This is why: Guy recently mouthed the keeper so hard he bruised her arm badly. If he bounds on me, the keeper says, I should hold still.

"Are you worried?" she asks me. Kind of, but I shake my head no. When I tell the staffer who organizes overnights which dog I want to take, her face sinks.

"Are you sure?" she asks me. I'm not, but I nod my head yes.

If he does okay with me, he can go with other volunteers on sleepovers. So I pack the juvenile in the back of my pathetic rental car, which I'm not supposed to have dogs in. The keeper cinches a seat belt leash around him so he can't leap into the front seat with me. This may be his first car ride. It certainly will be his first hotel stay. She hands me a bag of toys, and off we go.

We zoom down a two-lane highway to the far end of the Best Friends property, where the horses, goats, and potbelly pigs live and where a row of hotel suites overlooks a paddock. Watching out the car window as we drive in, Guy looks a little bug-eyed at the horses but he sits quietly on the backseat. Inside my suite, he quickly inspects the rooms as he snorts softly here and there. Though I've spent the afternoon with Woodard, I do exactly what she pooh-poohed. I take Guy for a mindless march—well, half-mindless. There is, it turns out, a lot to bark at along our route: horses, goats, the wild turkeys that noodle along the edge of a road, and a small herd of deer that freeze when they spot us. Guy strains hard on his leash and pulls my arm a few inches longer as we march for an hour or more through the fading evening past all these animals. I tough it out because I want to tire him enough so he won't jump on me. Eventually I'm too tired to keep tiring him out, and we return to my suite. I'm also starving. I pry the plastic lid off a grocery store salad as Guy puts his paws on the kitchen counter so he can watch. He watches everything I do (getting out silverware, turning on the faucet) with intense wonder, though he occasionally has to dart back into the bedroom to look at himself in a full-length mirror. I manage to eat my salad while tossing treats to Guy on the couch. Then I turn on the TV. Guy jumps like a cartoon character but then climbs onto the couch next to me and falls asleep for two hours while I try to figure out how the satellite channels work. Finally, I give up on the mysteries of the remote, and we head out for last call. The horses are already old news for Guy. He doesn't even turn his head at a goat coughing in a barn or when a bunny bounces through the dark in front of us.

Inside again, Guy puts his front paws on the bathroom sink so he can better watch me brush my teeth. I turn to him and say, "See?" When we climb into bed together, Guy finally gets a little mouthy, so I grab a rope toy to stuff into his maw. I hold that with one hand and a hardback book with the other. He leans over me slowly, mouth open, as if to swallow my novel. I close the Man Booker prizewinner and call it a night. Guy paces around briefly, knocks his head into the metal blinds a few times trying to look out the window, then pulls his lug of a self onto the other queen-size bed in my room, and begins to snore as any dog would.

Guy never lived up to his reputation. The next morning, I returned him with a grade of A+. Despite a year in a shelter, despite his behavior there, he easily began to become a pet in just twelve hours. I sang his praises loud and clear as I handed his leash over to the calm keeper. She walked off with him, and Guy looked back at me with those Cleopatra eyes, with a look that said, "Aren't you coming?" Seeing that I was not, as had been the case with so many people in his short life, he turned away and walked on. Standing amid all the everlasting beauty, I felt my heart, like old stone, crack some. He can live here, I told myself. He has all the time in the world. I didn't have to worry about him, but I did. I still do.

I've never told my friends about Happy—nobody wants to hear those stories—but I have told them about Harmony. Her elbows were rejiggered. She was transferred to a German shepherd rescue to recover in a foster home while she was on crate rest for months. One January morning, a matter-of-fact woman with a station wagon drove off with my funny girl. That left Bridget.

Now one year old, Bridget has become harder and harder to harness because she bucks like a pony. Her behavior is reevaluated. The lower the score on the test, the better. In the fall, she scored a fifteen. This time, when the trainer tries to touch her food bowl with the plastic hand on a long stick, Bridget sinks her teeth into it. When the tester runs across the room, Bridget grabs at her clothes. She scores a thirty-four. A score of thirty-five or above usually means the end is in sight. We repeat the usual refrain: "If only she'd been adopted right away." Miraculously, a family does take Bridget home at the end of March, nearly five months after she arrived, but she's back before we've even stopped worrying about her. She's growled at the wife and mouthed the husband when he tried to dry her feet. She didn't puncture his skin with her teeth but left scratches and red marks.

Now Bridget needs all the help we can give her. The staff take her into their offices during the day. We red dog volunteers organize our schedules so one of us goes in to work with Bridget nearly every day. We are careful with her, especially around men, because we know one more mishap might mean her end. Still, when she digs in her heels as we pass a gay bar on our walk, riveted by the happy buzz and the smell of steaks, I let her look into an open window. She suddenly puts her front paws on the sill and leans in. "YEAH!" the roomful of men calls to her. Bridget wags her tail and happily lets her tongue roll out. Yet a few days after leaning happily into that gay bar, she springs at a male staff member. That's the last straw. The shelter staff are too worried that she will bite someone. There are so few potential adopters who can handle a big dog like Bridget. Maybe a trainer who lived in the country would adopt her, but that is pie-in-the-sky thinking. On a Friday, the staff e-mail the few volunteers who have worked with Bridget to tell them that she will be put down the following Monday. They want to give us a chance to say good-bye.

Early that Sunday morning, I slip into the shelter's door like a thief. I get Bridget as quickly as I can. I don't want to see anyone or talk to anyone. I might sob. I might scream. Outside, I open the door to the backseat of my station wagon. Bridget dives in, and off we go. I pull onto the South End's empty streets. The usual insanity of Boston traffic finally ebbs on a Sunday morning. I worried that Bridget might knock around the car excitedly while I drove or try to wedge her bulk into the front seat, but she is a natural. She sits upright on the backseat. I open the windows so she can stick her yellow head out into the wind. Her ears blow back. Her nose quivers. I steer us past the Back Bay's row houses and then over the still Charles River and into quiet Cambridge, where I loop Harvard Square several times. I shoot along the river on Memorial Drive so Bridget can smell the goose poop on the banks and hear the slap of paddles on the water. We ride over the bridge and dive into the tight streets of my neighborhood, Charlestown. "This is where I live," I tell her.

This the best I can do for my Hollywood girl: give her a car ride, show her the world she has seen so little of, let her be like a pet dog if only for an hour or so. That it is so little yet Bridget is so clearly enjoying her car ride makes me even sadder. It also makes me keep driving. I watch her in the rearview mirror as often as I can. At red lights, I take pictures of her head out the window. As I drive down Memorial Drive for the second time, Bridget licks the back of my head, a heartfelt lick that dishevels my hair. We drive on to Watertown, and then back along the river, which she seems to like best. Anyone passing us would have thought, Look at that woman with her huge, yellow pet dog.

That Monday evening as I stood in the dim, dusty light of a pottery studio half-listening to my teacher talk of clay slabs and coils, slip and glaze, as I tried to turn my mind to the inconsequential joys of turning the earth into a cereal bowl, my phone vibrated against my thigh. I delicately pulled it out of my pocket with my clay-coated hands. Another red dog volunteer had left me a voice mail, I supposed about losing Bridget that day. I didn't want to talk about losing her. I couldn't. I shoved the phone back into my pocket. I watched my bristle-haired teacher pound clay out on a table and then roughly smash it with a rolling pin. My phone rattled again, another time, then a third time. I stepped away from the thumping and angrily wrested my phone out again.

My screen lit up: "They found a rescue in New Hampshire, in the country, that would take her. Bridget is alive."

Ned
(courtesy of Jackie MacMillan/HSSV)

9

MATCHMAKING

Blanca has a broad, round face and spaces between her teeth. She has a quiet, almost solemn manner at first but warms up quickly. She is from Guatemala but has lived in Boston since she was a child. Her parents recently moved back to Guatemala for six months, to work on the house they still own there, but Blanca and her brother, who goes to community college, are staying put. Blanca doesn't attend school or work, she tells me, because she has bipolar disorder. She lives off disability payments. Her therapist suggested she get a dog to keep her company. She's never had one before.

Fay is a seemingly purebred Maltese. Her dark eyes are punched into her little white face like black buttons sewn tight on the face of a stuffed animal. Maltese look like toys and, with their silky fur, which slips through your fingers, feel like toys. Fay came into the shelter with a passel of Maltese dogs who'd been confiscated from a breeder who kept them in a room at the Red Roof Inn, or that's the story. Word is there are more Maltese where these came from. The next group, I've been told, are so inbred they don't have fully formed skulls. Fay's group is just skittish, but when I take a seat on their kennel floor, they quit spinning and yapping and pile into my lap. That is why I've asked Blanca to sit on the ground of the ARL's play yard with me. When she does, the poof of fur that is Fay, the dog who snapped at my hand when I first tried to leash her, hops into the young woman's crossed legs.

"Don't pet her just yet," I say, because Fay quivers nervously. "Let her smell you some."

I've become a matchmaker. This is where the urge to walk homeless dogs all those years ago has led me. Now I have a hand in a dog's fate and a person's fate. It's thrilling, yet quite a responsibility. Mostly it's more satisfying than I ever expected, especially making people happy. I never meant to help people, and what I've seen at the shelter did nothing to enamor me with my own species. I've petted a cocker spaniel whose belly was covered with such thick mats that he couldn't fully stretch out his back legs. I've walked dogs so thin they had to wear jackets in the spring because they didn't have enough body mass to keep warm in sixty degrees. "I hate people" is a common refrain in the halls of shelters every-where. I've said it myself. But Bridget made me realize that I had to do more than just try to keep the dogs sane while they endured shelter life. Since the ultimate solution to kennel stress is to find the dogs homes, I would help find those homes.

I've learned to chat with prospective adopters casually while keeping an eye on the dog's body language, asking people personal questions without seeming as if I'm interrogating them, and sneaking in information about dog behavior here and there. I want people to listen to me, but primarily I want them to fall in love. Like any matchmaker, I have my tricks. I once read a study that found that people were more inclined to adopt a dog if he lay down near them. That is why I take people looking at lapdogs to the Real Life Room and ask them to settle down onto the stained rug. I hand them treats or toys, whatever might make that dog nuzzle up to them. That same study essentially found that adopters also like dogs who will play with them. So I lead outside anyone looking at a pup who likes a good game of fetch. Fetch is like a love potion, especially if the dog drops the toy at someone's feet, especially if those feet belong to a young man. My goal is always to get a dog to pay attention to an adopter, which is exactly what Fay is doing. As we shelter folk say, Fay "shows well." While Blanca and I talk, the cotton ball of a dog scoots up on her shoulder. That makes her laugh. Then Fay squirrels into her lap. "You can pet her," I tell Blanca, "long, slow strokes on her back." She does exactly as I suggest, which is one of the reasons I love first-time dog owners. They listen to me. The ones who grew up with a golden retriever think they know everything about dogs, even though, as their parents would probably tell me, they never lifted a leash. For a first-timer, Blanca looks like a natural the way she's handling Fay. As the Maltese begins to fall asleep in her lap, I tell Blanca about the little dog, about the weirdo breeder, about the breed. Blanca tells me about her family, her mental illness, and how little she has to do. She gazes down at Fay and says, "I could help this little dog," and smiles. She's falling—maybe fallen. This might seem an odd match, a needy dog with a needy woman, but it strikes me as perfect. Blanca needs a purpose. Fay needs attention, love, and patience. When we are done talking, I fill out a form and next to the question that asks if I would recommend this person for this dog, I write: YES.

As a volunteer, I don't have final approval over an adoption. All I can do is recommend somebody, but if I don't, then maybe no pooch for you. I've yet to not recommend someone, because the people I've had doubts about typically have decided against the dog. A pushy man who told me he adopted shelter dogs, trained them, and then sold them stormed out of the lobby when he found out he had to fill out some paperwork. The nerve of us! The man who told me he wanted a dog who could stay in a crate *at least* twelve hours a day left when I politely informed him that none of our dogs could do that. I cringe at those occasionally snarky newspaper columns about how hard a time the writer had adopting a puppy from a purebred Australian cattle dog rescue or the like. We make it as easy as we can at the ARL. Like a growing number of shelters, the ARL has what is called an open adoption policy, which is to say, we give you the benefit of the doubt. You might not have the perfect home, but you have a home. There are reasons the ARL would exclude someone, such as if they are planning to keep their dog outside on a chain. The ARL is highly unlikely to adopt out a dog who guards his dinner bowl to families with small children. The shelter does not require that your backyard be fenced in, nor will they come check out your home, as some rescues will. Nor do they insist that every member of the household come meet the dog, though they strongly recommend it. They know that love can overcome only so many hurdles.

I'm a matchmaker, but I'm also a salesperson, a salesperson who's likely not to have what you are looking for, which likely would be an exact replica of your last dog or the one you grew up with. So many people who are looking for a dog are, in fact, trying to reinvent their childhood. If you grew up with a shaggy cocker spaniel-looking thing, I have a shot. If you grew up with a golden retriever, I'm dead in the water, though I may direct you to an overweight chow mix with all the shiny aplomb of a golden. I also will have to deliver a discouraging "not now," which really should be "next to never," to all the people looking for puppies. Puppies under four months hardly put their soft pink pads on the ARL's hard floor before they are whisked away, even at $450 a pop. I tell the person who asks if we have any French bulldogs (as popular as babies in Boston just now) that we'll get bigfoot before we get a Frenchie, though pugs show up. We had one not long ago. He was blind. And ten. And he didn't like cats.

I give anyone walking through the kennel door high marks if he only looks at one of our dogs, but sometimes I just want to yell, *"Folks, this is an animal shelter!"* You don't find a brand-new Porsche in a custom color at a used-car lot. That's a crude way to put it, but shelters are in the business of selling secondhand dogs, some lightly used, some with the fender off, so to speak. Despite their flaws (or maybe because of them), they are all lovable, wonderful, but they are last year's models to purebreed-obsessed Americans. They are the "product" we must move in what is a highly competitive market. According to the American Pet Products Association, that market includes breeders, from whom a third of pet owners buy their dogs. Another 20 percent get them for free from friends and relatives, and then a smattering buy them from pet stores or take in strays. The rest, about 35 percent, go to a shelter or rescue organization. That is a historic high, but there are still more dogs than homes. That would change, according to Rich Avanzino, if every shelter and rescue organization adopted out four more animals a week. Four animals is a strato-spherically tall order for some shelters, and we aren't talking about widgets but living beings. Still, every business, especially what is essentially a retail business, needs a sales goal.

This retail mentality makes zealots grind their teeth, but it is transforming how shelters find animals homes for the better. To increase adoptions at the Animal Humane Society in the Minneapolis–St. Paul area, volunteers roam the airy adoption floor with iPads in hand, ready to answer questions, show you animals, and do your "paperwork" on the spot. Tony La Russa's Animal Rescue Foundation in California relaxed its return policy to tempt people to take a chance on an animal. Adopters can get a refund of their adoption fee for up to six months. That might horrify some people, but with that new rule in place, adoptions shot up by 25 percent, and returns increased by only 7 to 9 percent. The San Francisco SPCA built a series of slick tables and benches for counselors to meet with would-be adopters. It installed acoustic tiling to dampen the sound so people could hear themselves think. It hung two hard-to-miss signs that read, "DOGS" and "CATS," the clearest I'd seen in a shelter. Codirector Jason Walthall, who had a long career in retail before he came to the SPCA, told me that customers need to know easily where to go. "When you walk into a store, you don't have to ask where the shirts are."

The most extreme example of a shelter applying the ideas of retail I found in Los Angeles, but as extreme goes, Adopt and Shop makes perfect sense. After a somewhat wearying morning at the city's enormous South LA shelter (which, despite its general tidiness and landscaping, still resembles an outdoor prison for dogs), I swung open the glass doors of Adopt and Shop in Culver City and immediately perked up at the brightness, the bold colors, and all the fun stuff I could buy. I picked up a Frisbee with a stuffed squirrel attached to it, pulled out my wallet, and began to feel like myself again. Across the shelves of silly squeaky toys and bags of pricey dog food, I heard an emphatic bark. Squirrel Frisbee in hand, I followed the demanding woof and came upon Zeppelin, a white hound with patches of apricot and an impatient expression, as if a waiter had forgotten his order. The one-year-old was one of the dogs in a row of glassed-off rooms. Down the row, I found Chelsea, a border collie pup, napping; Willard, a young black-nosed mastiff, also snoozing; and wide-eyed Ox, an outgoing pittie who liked hiking, running, biking, and camping. Around the corner, I found kennels built into a wall and framed like paintings. In one of these kennels, two small dogs were so entwined that they resembled one furry blanket. It was hard to see whose tail belonged to whom. All these dogs needed homes.

Adopt and Shop is the brainchild of the innovative Found Animals, a nonprofit animal welfare organization started by billionaire surgeon and inventor Dr. Gary Michelson. In 2005 the Philadelphia native started several philanthropic organizations, Found Animals being one of them. Michelson hired self-described workaholic and animal lover Aimee Gilbreath to lead the organization. Gilbreath came from the world of R&D and big-time management consulting. In what little spare time she had, Gilbreath had walked shelter dogs and, like me, was a bit nervous at first about taking out the pitties, but obviously got over her fears. She adopted Rufus, a then-one-year-old pittie with a blaze of white down the middle of his shiny black face. His head might be larger than hers.

Found Animals is about ideas, ambitious ideas that could have far-reaching effects on animal homelessness. Studies have found that many people don't put ID tags on their pets. When pets without identification are lost, they are rarely reunited with their owners and end up in shelters. This inspired Found Animals to start a free national microchip registry and an educational campaign to convince people to hang ID tags on their pets' collars. (Even an animal who has a microchip needs a tag because it can be read instantly by the person who finds the dog or cat. A microchip requires a scanner to find the animal's contact information, which usually means it has to be taken to a shelter.) Next, Found Animals offered the equivalent of $25 million to a scientist who creates an affordable, nonsurgical way of sterilizing pets, one that could be used around the world. Then Found Animals took on the shelter model itself, specifically, the out-of-the-way locations (by the town dump or in some far-flung office park), and the noisy kennels that can resemble jail cells. Michelson wanted to make shelters less intimidating and put home-less animals smack in the middle of life, where they'd be harder to ignore. In a country of shoppers, where better to do that than in a shopping mall or plaza, and where better to put animals who need homes than near merchandise?

The first Adopt and Shop opened next to a Costco, in one of the country's largest malls, the epic Lakewood Center, which draws shoppers from a half dozen or so communities south of Los Angeles. In its first full year, the small shop in the megamall placed six hundred dogs and cats. The much bigger Culver City store opened along busy Sepulveda Boulevard in the spring of 2014. That store is not in a mall but there's a Starbucks and a Chipotle up the road and a bus stop just across the street. The 405, LA's central artery, rushes by just two blocks away. The Culver City store also provides grooming and doggie day care, giving people even more reasons to come by and, maybe, check out animals such as Ox. Half the people coming through the door are there to buy modern pet necessities, such as a foot-long braided rawhide, or to pick up their Goldendoodle from day care. The other half, including a woman with apricot-colored hair who came in with her daughter, are there looking for a soul mate. She'd brought her own apricot-colored terrier to meet a blonder but still apricot-tinted slip of a mutt. A few people have been known to stop in for a bag of dog food and leave with a new pet. By the end of 2015, this store had found homes for more than two thousand cats and dogs. Lots of people mistake Adopt and Shop for a pet store, which are, in fact, illegal in Los Angeles. (In 2012 the city banned the selling of animals from commercial breeders—in other words, puppy mills.) The staff doesn't mind the confusion. They are happy to explain why the animals are there amid the plushy toys and bottles of puppy shampoo. Maybe after you pay for your cockapoo's raw food, you'd like to meet Zeppelin or Willard or Chelsea.

The ARL in no way resembles a boutique. Despite the beds, blankets, and toys, dogs can still look as if they are in jail, especially the sad sacks. The sadder a dog looks, the fewer people will ask about it, though they will tell me, "That dog looks really sad." A good salesperson never says, "Duh," though I'd like to sometimes. I'm used to how desperate or crazy the dogs can look. I'm also used to the loud chorus of whines, howls, and barks. The people who parade through on a Saturday are mostly not. If the din is especially raucous, some people duck in and out before I can even shout a hello. The ones who stay, who walk from kennel to kennel, can get to looking a little shell-shocked. "The dogs rile each other up," I holler apologetically. "What kind of dog are you looking for?"

There must be some strange law of fate that dictates that people who have cats want the dog who would swallow a kitty like a canapé, or the people who already have a dog cast loving eyes on the one pooch who loathes his own kind. Couples with one-year-olds go for the burliest, nuttiest juvenile, the one who would accidentally take a toddler down in a nanosecond. Young tech workers who pull sixteen-hour days tell me they want a dog with the energy of a border collie to run with them on the weekends. I divert these people as best I can to better fits, but once someone falls for a dog, it's hard to talk sense into them. Many, having learned nothing from their own love lives, fall hard for the wrong reason—for looks alone, especially if that dog happens to have fur the same color as their hair. A quiet young man with pale blond hair asked about Chance, a loony, Lab-like pup with pale blond fur. As I leashed Chance up to meet the guy, I told the pup, "You, my friend, are going home." And he did.

Helping with adoptions has uncorked an inner salesperson in me I never knew existed. I'll take dogs to the lobby to meet people, especially dogs such as Stella, the black-tongued shepherd/chow/whatever who raged in her kennel but who was a perfect lady outside it. "Would you like some free love?" I'll ask people as they step in the door. This makes some titter, but no one ever says no. As I lead smaller dogs through the cat kennels on our way outside, I'll sing out like a peddler, "How about a cat trapped in a dog's body?" The cat volunteers think this is only kind of funny. Sometimes I get in the kennels with the dogs who look intimidating but are anything but, such as Max, a chunky young pittie usually sprawled quietly on his bed. For months, people passed by this wonderful boy. Someone told the staff at the front desk that he looked "really scary." To me, Max looked as if he wished he had a good book to read, something meaty, such as Proust. Around month four, I started lying on the floor in Max's kennel and leaning my head on him. "Are you looking for a pillow?" I asked people as they passed. "Ha, ha," they would laugh and hurry along. Before I could think of a new sales strategy, maybe put my head in his mouth like a lion tamer, a well-heeled couple in their early sixties swept in, saw Max for Max, and took him home to live with their two other pitties. Later, they posted a photo on Facebook of Max in a life jacket on their powerboat racing off into the Atlantic Ocean.

Rudy is our best dog by far just now. He's sweet, gets along with other dogs, walks well on a leash, and is housebroken. When people tell me they want an easy dog, I take them to his kennel first and say, "Here you go." Some politely demur, saying he's not their "type." A few frown at him. One woman recoils as if she has smelled death itself and spits out, "He's really, really old."

Rudy is ten, which is really almost middle age for a Chihuahua. Unfortunately, he looks twenty. He's a bit underweight, which makes his head look big. His ears stick out like an old guy's. His muzzle has whitened. What nobody can see are

Rudy's charms. When I took this little guy home for a night, he gamely played with toys, zipped around the condo, and was more happy-go-lucky than my own, somewhat pampered dogs. Rudy was anything but delicate, which is partly why my husband blanched when I pulled out the girlie fur-lined hoodie the shelter had sent with him. "Don't do that to Rudy," he begged. But as ridiculous as the coat was, Rudy owned it.

Matchmaking has taught me what is hard to sell. People are put off by skin conditions, such as the bald patches of mange or even nasty scars such as the great inexplicable black blot on one mutt's back. Female dogs with droopy teats are another. Women with children will moan in pain when they see those long nozzles, even protectively wrap their arms around their own breasts. Men are horrified and perplexed. I have explained to men how teats work more often than I ever expected to. Any problems around the genitals or the rear end can be a near deal breaker, too. As one shelter worker put it, "People don't like to think about anuses."

They don't like to think of old age, either, which is why old dogs have a hard time getting adopted in shelters. Numbers are hard to come by, as they always are in the animal shelter world, but it's safe to assume that seniors do not find homes at the rate younger dogs do. This ageism really steams Sherri Franklin, and is exactly why she founded Muttville, a shelter and foster organization in San Francisco just for seniors. Well into her fifties, Franklin could easily pass for the lead singer in some überhip band. In fact, she resembles a more polished Patti Smith. Among shelter workers and volunteers, who seem chronically underdressed in drab T-shirts and jeans with mysterious stains, Franklin easily stands out. On the December day I met her, she had on orange velvet skinny pants, a cardigan splattered with posies, and chunky Doc Marten boots. As she led me on a tour of Muttville, the force of her long stride blew back her straight black hair. She immediately stopped in her tracks, though, when she came across a tubby blond terrier mix named Lucille. Lucille had arrived at Muttville so fat that her gut dragged, which made her not want to walk. Now she danced around Franklin's feet.

About fifty or so of Muttville's dogs live in foster homes, and another twenty or so bunk in the organization's homey offices, tucked in the SF SPCA's original building. The seniors, most needing at least a good teeth cleaning, if not surgery, come from shelters in the Bay Area and beyond, even as far as Los Angeles. There is never a shortage. Muttville gets about one hundred requests a week but can typically accept only fifteen dogs. It looks less like a shelter than a shabby youth hostel. In one bright, airy room, small dogs pile on a mishmash of human and dog beds covered with quilts and sheets. Others busily pace the bright linoleum floor, such as Blitzen, a sparkly white terrier barking at a volunteer. "Didn't you just go out?" the volunteer in an apron asks her. Behind her, a dog with cataracts quietly humps another. Franklin leans over Savannah, a beagle flopped on her side on a bed, and pulls back a chest harness to show me a fleshy, grapefruit-size tumor drooping from her chest. Savannah calmly studies us with one eye. "We'll get that taken care of," Franklin says.

We swing our legs over a Dutch door into the next room, where larger dogs, such as Dolly Parton and Marilyn Monroe, bunk. The two friendly, shaggy mutts accompany us through their digs, and then we swing our legs over another gate and into Muttville's main office. When Avanzino became director of the SF SPCA, this was his office. Now Franklin and three of her staff type and chatter while a half dozen or so dogs, mostly the more infirm ones, sack out under their desks or wander about. Dustin Hoffman (Franklin likes celebrity names) has lost his fur to alopecia. They are calling him a hairless Mexican mix. Blind and deaf McDreamy, a fourteen-year-old Chihuahua blend whom they have dubbed a pocket golden retriever, slumbers on a footrest in his own deep silence.

At a heavy wooden table, a man dreamily

clutches a limp Pomeranian to his chest as a counselor hands him adoption forms to sign. Someone carries in Baby, a transfer from the San Jose animal control, who's estimated to be seven. Like many of the Muttville dogs, Baby became homeless when her senior owner developed a serious illness. Franklin renames the Havanese-looking pooch Valerie, for the actress Valerie Harper, and places the newly dubbed pooch, no worse for her faded celebrity name, on the floor. She pads after snaggletoothed Gumbo as he parades from desk to desk announcing his presence. The workers type on despite Gumbo's nonstop and emphatic protests, but the noise rouses one of the sleeping dogs. He walks to a desk, lifts his leg, and leaves a puddle on the floor where Avanzino once waited for office furniture and then went on to rethink sheltering, dreaming of the day when dogs like these sick, old, goofy ones would find homes.

When I asked Franklin what she did with her time before Muttville, at first she can't remember. "I guess I shopped and traveled." She also cut hair full-time. Back then, the 1990s, she was scared to death to go into a shelter, but some mice in her home changed that. She needed a cat. So she braced herself and marched into the SF SPCA to adopt one. The experience was as upsetting as she expected—all those sad animals—but she had an epiphany. "You can say you love animals, but if you aren't doing anything for them, what good is that?" she tells me. She signed up to walk dogs and then left with Conan, a neutered male cat with a gash in his head, whom she renamed Jah Kitty. Franklin started going once a week, then twice, then five days a week. She began fostering animals, paying their medical bills, and adopting them out of her home, usually by spreading the word through her hair clients. "I have a big mouth."

The "old down-and-outers" were the ones who broke her heart. They'd come into the SF SPCA because their owners had died or gone into a nursing home. At first the oldsters would be so hopeful, Franklin says, happily greeting everyone who passed their kennel. Then, she says, it would start to sink in, as person after person walked by without stopping—they weren't going anywhere soon. Franklin wanted not only to find these old guys homes, but to show that it could be done, though she admits she wasn't sure it could.

Since starting Muttville in 2007, one of the first (and few) organizations devoted to old dogs, Franklin and her crew have sent senior after senior to new homes, even dogs with at best a year or even months to live. Now the group averages about seven hundred adoptions a year. Franklin found a way to do what most in the shelter world once thought impossible: convince people to adopt dogs such as Tesla, a dachshund whose skin is flaking from Cushing's disease and who had to have half his teeth extracted. Franklin pulls this off, she says, by lumping the seniors together. That way they don't have to compete with the shiny young things. This tactic also gives Muttville a niche and a brand, so to speak. Franklin has done for seniors what places such as Animal Farm have done for pitties—made them fun and sexy and debunked myths around them, such as the very old saw that an old dog can't learn a new trick. (Tell Franklin that one if you want to get a rise out of her.) She's also created a specialized market, as with the purebred rescues. You go to a greyhound rescue for a greyhound. You go to Muttville for a senior. Franklin believes this could be the way to find more dogs homes, by sorting them not just by breed but also by type and age and energy, and thus making it easier for adopters to find exactly what they are looking for. What Muttville adopters are looking for is a mission, and they find that amid the ravages of old age. Dogs teach you your limits, and those might include doggie diapers or giving your heart to a pooch who may pass through your life only fleetingly. This can be too tall a bargain for some people. Others not only can make that deal, but want, even need, to.

Franklin throws on a deep-blue coat with swirling satin appliqués to walk the few blocks to the San

Francisco Animal Care and Control, a rather dour municipal pound that houses row after row of dogs. Franklin had been told that there was an Australian cattle dog there who might be right for Muttville. Franklin, her fashionable coat flaring out behind her, dashes past one kennel after another in the gray light. She glances at each label, reading only the ages of the dogs, not really looking at the dogs themselves. I struggle to keep up with her because I can't quit looking at the faces, the friendly eyes, and the cocked heads. I catch up with Franklin only because she suddenly stops at a kennel. "Hello, baby," she coos, and steps inside. A brown Lab who's been napping on the cement floor struggles to his feet. He wags his thick brown tail. Cataracts flash from his warm but somewhat confused eyes. He has the rough coat of an outside dog. Franklin kneels on the floor, her coat falling around her knees. She waves her hand back and forth before his eyes. "I'm not sure he can see this." The rickety guy leans forward and licks Franklin on the cheek.

This obviously isn't the cattle dog, but at fifteen, he's plenty old enough. His name is Prince. He was confiscated. He'd been kept in a back-yard, probably his whole life. Backyard dogs are Franklin's bailiwick. She helped pass a 2005 ordinance in San Francisco guaranteeing that they have fresh water daily and a doghouse with a roof. Prince creaks out with Franklin, his long toenails curled under his pads, and we make our way back to Muttville. With Prince at Franklin's side, she moves the slowest I've seen her all day. Once at Muttville, she helps the old-timer up the steps. She wants to see if he gets along with dogs. Prince, half-blind but game for an adventure, wags his tail at everyone, cinching the deal without ever knowing there was one to be made. A few days later the dog who spent his life outside moves into a foster home, where he begins to sneeze from a case of kennel cough he probably caught at the city pound. In his website listing, Prince sticks his tongue out comically. His estimated age has been lowered to thirteen, so he might have another year or so to live. No matter. An older couple see a kindred spirit in Prince's murky eyes and take him home.

I admit that the one time I went into a nursing home, which was only because I was attending a meeting there about starting a neighborhood dog park, it took all my willpower not to sprint through the lobby past the wheelchairs, the tubes, the purplish skin, the slack, moist mouths. I'm not proud. So how do I explain that my day at Muttville was one of the cheeriest, and Savannah, the beagle with the grapefruit-size tumor, provided the highlight? When Franklin and I returned from the pound, I retreated to a desk in the sunny room with beds to work on my notes among the diminutive dogs milling about. Savannah soon planted herself at my feet and pawed my knee forcefully. I realized she wanted in my lap. Thinking of her tumor, I ignored her, even moved my legs under the desk so she couldn't get at my knee, but she wasn't having it. She kept scratching my leg. She stared at me with those pleading beagle eyes. Still, I have my limits, and they include not wanting to make some dog's tumor explode. When a volunteer walked through the room, I asked her if I could pick Savannah up, hoping she would say no. "Yes," she said. "Just be careful." I set down my pen and sighed, then leaned down, wrapped my arms around Savannah, and gently lifted her. I braced for a yelp, for the tumor to pop like a balloon, but she seemed unbothered, and happy to be in my lap looking down on all the tiny yappers. I felt relieved and silly. I tried to keep working by reaching around Savannah. Finally, I set my notebook aside and stroked her long ears, which seemed the best way to make a bit of difference for one old, homeless dog in Muttville.

Helping with adoptions, I have learned, finally, to wait—to wait for that one person to come through the shelter door and change a dog's life. You don't know who that person is or when he will come, only that sooner or later he will. I've been waiting with Greg for months. Greg's markings look like a tuxedo, all charcoal black except for a bib of white. He's maybe one year old or younger. I refer to him as "my boyfriend," as in when I say to my husband, "I'm going to see my boyfriend." Greg has been dubbed a pittie, but he has the pricked ears and long, square muzzle of a Great Dane. He was a long-time stray who was so fearful he had to be trapped. When he arrived in the fall, his paws were bald in spots and he was so thin that his spine bumped along his back. I was the first volunteer to walk him. He shied away from me in his kennel, but I was able to leash him, and we quickly became friends despite his shyness. Since then he's come out of his shell—a little too much. Like Gwen Stefani, Greg lives for fetch and has her same Olympic athlete's stride as he chases a ball down in the play yard. He may be even faster than Gwen, and he can also leap atop the A-frame in one stride. He wants to fetch and run outside all day long. That's why when I reach to leash him to leave the play yard, all hell can break loose. He cocks an eye at me as if he's got a better idea than going back inside. Then he mouths my arm or my hand or the leash. Though I have techniques for handling this, he has still managed to knock my watch off my wrist, rip my down coat, and bruise my arms. He's a lot of dog. Most people would not love him. I do. When Christmas comes, there's no way Greg is posing with Santa. He bucks on his leash when he sees the ogre in red and white. I pull an elf hat on him to pose with me instead. When I show my mom the photo, she says, "You look so happy."

I want to adopt Greg, but I can't. His rambunctious energy would drive Penny Jane and Walter Joe berserk. Six months have gone by. I'm so worried about Greg that I go some days only to see him. I whiz a tennis ball across the auditorium. He snatches it and then, as he likes to do, takes a flying leap onto the folding table, *KA-BLANG*. We tour the South End. If it's snowing, Greg jumps up and catches the flakes in his mouth. He snaps at them so hard his jaw cracks loudly. On a slow night, we sit in the adoption lobby. He drapes himself across my lap and looks, deceptively, like a calm dog. I hope someone will happen in, notice him, and then, *BINGO*. But everyone strolls past the athletic dog with upright ears and the woman holding him. Usually a staff member will look at the two of us and say, "You should adopt him."

"I can't," I say.

One Saturday, someone finally asks to see Greg. A middle-aged couple and their two adolescent children have driven in from the suburbs to meet him. They are middle class and have a house— what we dream of for our pitties. They've even had a pittie before. I rush Greg out of his kennel. I'm afraid if he plays fetch with the kids he's going to knock them down by mistake, so I take the family to a small office to meet with him. After everyone takes a seat, Greg, who's been afraid of some men, warms right up to the father, a burly former police officer with a naturally soft touch. This gives me hope, but the wife rattles on and on about their previous pittie, listing everything she taught him, the kinds of treats he liked. She stops talking about her dog-training prowess only to yell at the kids, "Say something!" The silent children look up briefly, as if startled, and then recede into their quiet blankness as their mother winds up again. Greg wiggles past them, holding a stuffed lobster toy in his mouth. Both kids look scared of him, even though their mother has yelled at them, "Don't be scared!" The father is perfect, but I now have serious doubts about the rest of the family. I want Greg to go home, desperately, but I feel myself switching from sell mode to discourage mode. As I'm thinking about what to say to get this family to pass on Greg, the chatty mom calls him over.

"I want to put my hand in your mouth," she says to Greg.

"I wouldn't do that," I say, but Chatty jabs her plump hand right into Greg's mouth. He looks confused at first and then realizes what a gift from the gods this woman is. She is asking to be mouthed.

"Owww!" she cries and jerks back her hand. Both kids jump. "You are a bad dog!"

Chatty bats Greg on the nose and waves a

pointed index finger in his face. Greg starts to cock an eye at that finger. I quickly take his collar and apologize. Luckily her hand is neither scratched nor bleeding. I hustle Greg out of the room. "I think he's had enough," I say as cheerily as I can. As I rush him down the hall, away from Chatty and her family, I pat him and say, "Good boy."

The weeks go by. No one asks about Greg. Then, one night, as he lounges in my lap in the adoption lobby, a tall young woman with a head of blue-tinted dreadlocks steps through the door. She's come to meet Greg, just Greg. She saw him in November, but she couldn't have a dog where she lived back then. Now she can. Her name is Natasha. She's all of twenty. A very, very young renter, she's not whom we dream of for our pitties, but I immediately notice how she looks at Greg.

"I can't believe he's still here," she says.

She's brought her roommates, two soft-spoken, lanky guys, Greg's type. He coyly sniffs their hands and then stands next to me as I go over his story, his shyness with men, his jumpy-mouthiness. Natasha quietly listens to everything I say but never takes her eyes off Greg. I've got to get him to stop clinging to me, to focus on her. "If you take him home, he'll be this way with you," I tell the dreadlocked girl and pass her a fistful of treats. She kneels down and holds out a few to Greg. He approaches her, nibbles a few biscuits, steps a little closer to her, and gingerly licks her on the cheek. Natasha keeps still while he wiggles around her. She strokes his smooth back. He likes her, so much so that when she stands up, he cocks his eye and grabs her shirtsleeve. "Drop some treats to distract him," I tell her. Natasha remains calm and does exactly what I suggest. Greg lets go of her sleeve to vacuum the goodies off the floor.

"I love this dog," she says.

Natasha is our Princess Charming, the one whom Greg and I have been waiting for all these months. She's as smitten with him as I am. When I fill out the adoption form, next to where it asks, "Do you recommend this adopter?" I write the word *yes* in large letters and circle it. Then I walk out to my car and surprise myself by bursting into tears.

After Greg went home with Natasha, I felt a bit adrift. I didn't know any of the dogs nearly as well as Greg, and some not at all, such as the beagle puppy named Luigi. But you don't always have to know a dog to be its matchmaker. The first Saturday that Luigi was on the adoption floor, a family rushed into the kennels and pressed up against his door. One of the boys yelled, "Dad is he the one? I think he's the one!"

"He's the one!" the other boy yelled.

This would be easy, but like any good matchmaker, I still had a strategy. I took them into the play yard so the puppy could chase the boys and the boys could chase the puppy, while the bewitched parents watched. Then we went to an office so the mother could snuggle with him. On cue, the little beagle hopped into Mom's lap.

"I think this is the one! I think this is the one!" the boys chanted, bouncing up and down in their seats.

The couple had had a beagle, so I didn't have to give them my beagle spiel. They lived in a house, so it didn't matter if the beagle barked, as many beagles do. They had a fenced-in yard. They had successfully housebroken dogs before. I sat back and let the magic happen. Luigi was everything they wanted—except for his name. They bandied new ones about. Maybe Harrison. Maybe Harry. "What about Harry Potter?" one of the boys exploded. The mustachioed dad shook his head. The names kept bouncing around. The family seemed to be just one name away from taking the little guy. I wanted to close this deal.

"What about Jimmy?" I ventured.

The father's eyebrows shot up. "That's it. JIMI HENDRIX!" he shouted.

A cheer rose in the room. "He's the one! He's the one!"

I grabbed the puppy's leash and we stampeded into the hall and rushed downstairs so Jimi Hendrix could go home as soon as possible.

Jared Leto

10

THE GREAT MIGRATION

As my small pack and I head toward Boston Harbor on our morning loop, a man and his puppy block the brick sidewalk on a late winter day. The houndy-looking pup with a coat of black, white, and caramel splotches wiggles and whines to meet Penny Jane and Walter Joe. I pause, though my dogs could mostly take or leave their own species, especially the younger members. Penny Jane and Walter Joe are a party of two, but they deign to sniff and be briefly sniffed by the soft-eyed newcomer, who has pretty nice manners for a puppy. At the other end of her leash, the bespectacled man beams. Where is this pup from? I query, though I have a good guess.

"I rescued her from Tennessee," the man says, and smiles proudly like a father. "I saved her from a kill shelter."

"Of course you did" is what I want to say. And what he wants me to do is hand him a halo or pin a medal on his down coat. Instead, I ask how old his pup is, and pose a few more polite questions. Penny Jane and Walter Joe strain at the end of their leashes, ready to recommence our routine, eyes fixed down the block, toward the harbor park, where someone has taken to leaving peanuts out for the squirrels. I don't let on how much the man's proclamation sets my teeth on edge, but the moment I turn to leave with my small pack, I start thinking about why this person, who's ultimately done a good thing, struck me as such a jerk. Obviously there was his New England smugness about the South, not to mention his obliviousness. There I stood with my two mutts, and it never occurred to him that he was bragging to the choir. What nagged at me the most, though, was that his doe-eyed pup had been shipped hundreds of miles to Boston, which has its own homeless dogs. Why didn't the bespectacled man help the ones in his own backyard? And is that even a fair question to ask? I don't know.

Trucks and vans packed with crates of homeless dogs ply America's highways each day. What was once a kind of Underground Railroad movement has gone very much aboveground. During the 1980s and '90s, networks of animal lovers and a few shelters began shipping dogs from regions with far too many, such as the South and Southwest, to regions with many more adopters, such as the Northeast and Northwest. Wherever the dogs were headed, most of their wet noses pointed north. Then Hurricane Katrina raked the Gulf Coast in 2005 and made legions of pets into strays overnight. Many of these lost dogs ended up at the Expo Center in Lamar Dixon, Louisiana, where an army of shelter workers from around the country converged to help the hurricane refugees. As shelter staffers from points north, south, east, and west frantically worked long hours side by side, they also made friends. Those friendships became partnerships, and in the barky, barely controlled chaos of that expo hall, countless transport networks were born. What once was largely a grassroots effort grew exponentially. Moving dogs here and there became a standard, if still controversial, way to find dogs homes.

That is why Madison, a terrier-like mutt with the pricked ears of a fox and a belly of knobby teats, sits quietly, if a bit confused, on an exam table while a curly-haired vet tech with a high, singsong voice pulls the dog's top lip up. Madison's pink gums glisten. She squints in the glaring lights of the vet bay. After a seven-hundred-mile truck ride from Oklahoma, Madison arrived at the Animal Humane Society in Minnesota yesterday. So far today she has passed her behavioral evaluation with flying colors. When the vet tech, testing for food aggression, plunged a plastic hand on the end of a stick into Madison's dinner bowl, she wagged her tail. When the vet tech gave her a kind of rough massage, something I'd not dare give a dog I'd just met, the petite female wagged her tail again. Madison tips the scales at eighteen pounds, neither too thin nor too fat. She has a round sore on her front right ankle, but that should heal quickly. The only hitch so far is with her teeth, which are noticeably worn, the bottom front ones just a row of nibs. The vet tech lifts Madison's back legs and bends them this way and that, to check her joints. She darkens the room and waves a blue light over the pup, looking for the telltale glow marks of ringworm. Madison, who doesn't glow, remains pliant and cheerful in the eerie light. Afterward, she lies down prettily for her photo, her two front legs straight in front of her.

"You are so cute," the vet tech trills. "You are going to go fast."

When Janelle Dixon went to work at Animal Humane in 1991, the shelter, like all shelters then, had far more dogs, Minnesota dogs, than homes for them. Then people quit dropping off squirming litters of puppies. By the early 2000s, for a long list of reasons, Animal Humane had far more kennels and potential adopters than it had dogs. Dixon, by then director, cast her thoughts beyond Minnesota's border. Animal Humane could do something she had never dreamt of back in the trenches of the 1990s—fight dog homelessness on a national scale.

Now a truck or van of dogs pulls up to Animal Humane every day. The shelter brings in as many as seven thousand animals from other states each year, making it one of the largest shelter transport programs in the country. Animal Humane trucks in dogs of all ages and types, except, like most transport programs, pitties. The Twin Cities have enough of those. Animal Humane also won't take dogs with either severe behavioral or medical problems. The last thing Dixon wants to do is to import euthanasia. What she wants is to have a good mix of dogs for the excited people who crowd the adoption lobby on Saturdays and Sundays, if there isn't a Vikings game on TV. Like a good store manager, she wants to have enough inventory for her customers, but she isn't a store manager trying to turn a profit. She wants to have what potential adopters are looking for so they won't go elsewhere—say, to a pet store or the Internet, both of which might sell dogs from puppy mills. She wants to make it easy for people to do a good thing, to adopt a homeless dog.

About two weeks after I saw Madison under the blue light, the terrier from Oklahoma went up for adoption. The shelter had decided not to scrape the tartar from her teeth, a procedure that would only have delayed her finding a home. The vet tech was right. The Oklahoma gal with bad teeth and pricked ears stepped into an adoption kennel on a Friday and by that Sunday she was in her new home, maybe in time to see her first Vikings game on TV. All it took to find her a home was moving her seven hundred miles.

It's hard to argue against Madison finding a home. Or is it? Rich Avanzino worries that transporting cutie-pies like her into a shelter distracts adopters from local pooches in need. He also worries that it diverts staff time and funds, and keeps shelters from what he believes is their true calling: "to sell the public on the idea that the big, old, ugly, sick, injured, and poorly behaved deserve to be saved." Should a shelter's goal be to save as many dogs as possible, to shoot for the highest number, or to help the dogs in its community, which might take more resources for a much smaller number of animals? Avanzino says the latter always comes first. Dixon has answered his question by saying yes to the highest possible numbers and the homegrown dogs. She also believes, like many shelter directors who bring in dogs from other states, that the often more desirable imports ultimately help the sometimes shaggy locals. A wider range of pooches to choose from draws more adopters, she says. More feet through the door translates into more locals going home. That seems logical, but one of the few studies to test that theory found that the presence of Madison and her ilk seemed to have no effect, good or bad, on the homegrown dogs. The latter didn't get adopted faster or slower, which is good news of a sort.

You can't argue that the good-looking imports are helping the locals if you only bring in dogs from other states, which is what some shelters and many rescues in New England do. I worry that this great migration of homeless dogs to our corner of the country gives New Englanders the wrong idea: that there are no, or next to no, homeless dogs in their backyard. I cringe each time someone pronounces dog overpopulation solved here, and that's why we can absorb all these needy pups from the South. It's true that New England has a spay/neuter rate to crow about. Yet, though pet overpopulation and pet homelessness are linked, you can still have the latter without the former, which is why private shelters and municipal facilities around New England are still regularly filled with Yankee dogs. The reason these animals find homes is that New England shelters work so hard and so relentlessly. They cannot retire anytime soon, which a brief stop on my way home from Stockbridge to Boston once made clear. I pulled off the highway to check out the Worcester Animal Rescue League in Massachusetts. From the outside, WARL, which resembles a little clapboard ranch house, gave the impression that it might have a mere dozen kennels. Inside, however, I found *eighty,* nearly all of them full of Massachusetts dogs. In Portland, when I stopped by to visit the Animal Refuge League, the director told me| that her shelter was in no position to import dogs. If it could, she would help the beleaguered shelters not in the South, but the ones in far northern Maine.

Beyond the philosophical questions of transporting homeless dogs around the country is a long list of practical problems, the scariest one being the risk of importing contagious diseases such as distemper or parvo. Sick dogs will force an entire shelter into quarantine and endanger the animals already there. One northeastern shelter reportedly brought in a puppy with a vaccine-resistant form of rabies. Another ended up with a pup sick with a tick-borne disease unknown in the Northeast. In the early days of the puppy transport program at Sterling Animal Shelter, a private nonprofit outside Boston, director Leigh Grady says she didn't think to require that the animals be vaccinated before they were sent north. Back then, the staff would excitedly welcome the new arrivals only to have half of them die of parvo. Even after Grady began insisting that the puppies be dewormed and given a series of vaccines before being shipped to Sterling, a handful from Virginia showed up with distemper, a wildly contagious virus that is often deadly. The puppies, deathly sick, exposed as many as four hundred dogs to the disease, some of whom had already been adopted. Grady says she lost forty pounds that summer trying to manage the outbreak. "I called it my Distemper Diet."

Many states have responded to the flow of dogs across state lines with laws requiring veterinary exams, quarantines, and healthy transport conditions—obvious things such as fresh drinking water and potty breaks. Receiving shelters such as Animal Humane in Minneapolis insist on vaccines and behavior checks. None of these safeguards, however, will help you if you are picking up your pooch in a parking lot somewhere. Some rescuers, desperate to save dogs' lives, do not always follow rules or common sense. Some rescuers aren't rescuers at all, but are posing as such while they sell "rescue" dogs for a profit. Transporting dogs, in theory, sounds like such a simple solution to homelessness—which of course means it isn't.

In 2004 Marlene Walsh, a Wisconsin native who began her shelter career hosing out kennels in high school, was asked by PetSmart Charities, then the largest source of grants for animal welfare societies, to launch a model transport program. In response, Walsh created Rescue Waggin', which eventually grew to a small fleet of vans and trucks moving six thousand to seven thousand dogs a year among twenty states. Waggin' set a standard for how animals should be moved. The trucks were air-conditioned. Music was piped into the back for the dogs. The trucks stopped every ten hours at a minimum for a potty break (unlike some transport trucks that don't stop at all). Still, Walsh, who left the program in 2012, doesn't consider Waggin' a success. Source shelters were expected to graduate from the Rescue Waggin' program, to use it only as a stopgap measure while they solved the core problem of why they had too many homeless animals. They were supposed to improve their spay and neuter rates and increase adoptions, for example, and PetSmart Charities gave them grants to do that, at least in the beginning of the program. None of the shelters, Walsh says, ever "graduated," however. They just kept sending dogs north. "I don't think moving animals from point A to point B is the answer," she tells me.

Walsh is now the director of the Bay Area Humane Society in Green Bay, Wisconsin. Though she is still ambivalent about transport, the Bay Area Humane Society imports dogs from Alabama and Arkansas, and sometimes Texas. If they didn't, she says, they would have only large dogs and pitties, neither of which a lot of families want. From the South, they can get smaller dogs and puppies. A group of puppies who'd just walked in the door were already on hold. "That's all fine and dandy, but we have local dogs that have been here for two weeks to three months."

There is a pink Quarantine sign on the door to the small kennels at the ARL. When I peek through the window, I can't see anything, but I have a good hunch who is in there: Chihuahuas from California. Maybe once or twice a year, a shelter in Pasadena ships a half dozen or so of the peewees here. This precious cargo crosses the great width of the United States, sailing over the Rockies and zooming over the Great Lakes, and touches down at Logan Airport along the Atlantic's very edge. They are then quarantined for two days, per state law, after which volunteers can walk them, though I usually don't. Being one of the few volunteers trained for the hard-to-handle dogs, I feel it would be a waste of my time to take out these hanky-size critters. Besides, for most of my life I have not considered myself much of a Chihuahua person, whatever that means exactly. Besides, most of them will be adopted before I can even spell *Chihuahua,* while my beloved pitties wait and wait. I confess I used to resent the squirts; this resentment filled me with guilt because they are, after all, still dogs. What with all my conflicting emotions, and considering what a pain it is to hook a leash to the tiny rings on their tiny collars, I usually avoided the shrimps—until I learned that the breed that Boston city slickers crave is the one most likely to be euthanized in California.

The Chihuahua, if it's not already obvious, is the world's smallest dog breed. They weigh between four and six pounds, less than my purse. Because dog eyes are close to the same size no matter the breed, Chihuahua eyes bug and look inordinately large in their diminutive faces. That, plus their domed foreheads, lends them a slightly extraterrestrial look. Other than as TV or movie dogs, Chihuahuas can't claim much of American history. Though our presidents are famously dog crazy, I could not find one who'd had a pet Chihuahua. Still, these dogs have a history far deeper than our Labs and goldens. Images of Chihuahuas and their precursor, the Techichi dog, emblazon pots unearthed in archaeological digs across Mesoamerica, including in their namesake, the rugged and immense state of Chihuahua.

While I was in San Francisco, I saw Chihuahuas, lots of them, at every shelter I visited. At one, they had their own play yard. At another I met a blind one named Figaro who had had a rectal prolapse. Though his bottom had been repaired, no one had asked about Figaro. I saw by far the most Chihuahuas at the San Jose Animal Care Center, a mammoth municipal shelter with eighty dogs up for adoption plus uncountable rows of dogs waiting out their stray holds. The director, Jon Cicirelli, an upbeat, fast-talking man with a dimpled chin, showed me to a hallway that shot the length of the building to impress upon me the building's scale. The end of the hall was blurry, a football field or two away, or at least that is how it felt. On the adoption floor, I followed Cicirelli down a row of kennels as he chanted, "Chihuahua, Chihuahua, Chihuahua." The little dogs clustered and twirled like leaves blowing in the wind. They barked nervously, excitedly. Chihuahuas, Cicirelli told me, are easy to take care of. You can put four or five in a kennel. They can be shy with people, but Chihuahua play group improves their confidence. From where I was standing, I could see a courtyard where a tall, slightly stooped volunteer with an apron towered Gulliver-like over the Lilliputian mob racing around his feet. The only problem with the dogs, Cicirelli said, is that there are far too many of them, so many that they all start to look alike, especially the blond ones. Cicirelli, who said he'd once not liked small dogs, was considering adopting one for himself and his young son.

"How will you pick one?" I asked as we stared into a kennel of dogs running in a circle.

"I have no idea," he said.

Only Ned stood out in the kennel. Ned is what they call a Chiweenie, a Chihuahua who's been stretched like taffy by being crossed with a Dachshund. Ned was scrawny looking, with a bump of a tail and pointed feet. His bottom canines jutted over his top lip. The two-year-old's teeth made for an odd little smile, until he barked. Then he became all clacking fangs. He's in fact a cuddler, but you could mistake him for a Gremlin from hell.

"What about Ned?" I asked. Cicirelli shrugged a "maybe," and we turned to look at more Chihuahuas.

About 40 percent of the some seven thousand dogs the San Jose facility takes in each year are Chihuahuas. Nearly all of them are strays, though that term, Cicirelli says, can be a misnomer. They are often community dogs, ones people feed but whom no one "owns." The Chihuahuas are anything but scary, so people don't report them to animal control. When they do, Cicirelli, who started his career as an animal control officer, says the dogs are hard to catch because of their size. They know all the back alleys and can slip through holes in fences. Cicirelli blames the smooth-talking Taco Bell Chihuahua and Paris Hilton, with her designer purses full of dogs, for the tidal wave of Chihuahuas that rolled in about ten years ago. He also blames human nature. On a large map in his office he has taken a red marker and outlined the five zip codes where most of the Chihuahuas come from: all poor, largely Latino neighborhoods. There they don't tend to fix their dogs, whether because of cost or their culture, and often let them run loose, he says. The result is more and more Chihuahuas in those areas. Cicirelli says there is one sure way to get fewer and fewer: spay and neuter. San Jose Animal Care and Services has joined with the Humane Society Silicon Valley to offer free spaying and neutering for any Chihuahua in the outlined zip codes, and together they have fixed more than forty-five hundred dogs so far. That seems to be making a dent in the number of stray or unwanted Chihuahuas coming out of those neighborhoods. Still Ned and his ilk sit in kennels waiting for someone to take them home.

The thing about spaying and neutering is that it doesn't help the dogs who need homes now. That's why Cynthia Karsten, a vet at UC Davis, packs Chihuahuas in planes headed northwest, bound for shelters in the cold climes of Madison, Wisconsin; Toronto; and Minneapolis. One Chi adopted in Minneapolis, the dainty Marigold, reportedly wears a sweater September through May, Karsten tells me on the phone. As Karsten describes the logistics of packing up Chihuahuas for a cross-country flight, I hear an off-key chorus of barks rise in the background. Karsten explains that her dogs are riled up because a repairman is fixing her garage door and excuses herself from our phone conversation, and hollers, "Hey! Quiet!"

The barks diminish slowly, with a few last, defiant woofs here and there, as if to say, "Don't you get that there is a stranger in the garage?" Karsten lives in a household of mostly mini dogs. Three of her four are Chihuahua mixes, but she was once like me, maybe worse. A skier and hiker, she thought Chihuahuas were "useless." Still, she couldn't resist a hospice case she came across during a veterinary internship at a Denver shelter. She took home Millie, an old long-haired Chihuahua mix who had seizures, to live out what little time she had left. Karsten assumed Millie had a brain tumor, but when she changed her food, the seizures stopped. Then Karsten brought home Peter, a senior Chihuahua mix with a severe heart murmur and a condition that made his penis protrude, which freaked out potential adopters. Peter as well as Millie lived far longer than Karsten expected. Also, Peter turned out to be an athlete of sorts. Karsten and her husband took him on ten-mile hikes. He ran beside them as they cross-country skied. If he got tired, Karsten would simply tuck him into her back-pack. "We need to let people know these dogs can do anything a big dog can do, but they eat less and poop less."

Karsten doesn't believe that Paris Hilton and her Hollywood compatriots caused the glut of Chihuahuas. She mostly blames poverty. When Chihuahua owners in poorer neighborhoods lose their pets, they often have no idea where to find them, she says. They might not be able to afford the redemption fee. Sometimes a shelter's adoption fee can cost less, making it less expensive for them to get another Chihuahua rather than pay to get their own dog back. If the owners are undocu-mented workers, they may fear a shelter might ask for their papers. "We need to communicate to them that we don't care about their papers," Karsten tells me.

She found a surplus of the pip-squeaks in Denver, but nothing on the scale of what she discovered in California, where she moved in 2011 to work for UC Davis's well-respected shelter medicine program. While she toured a city pound in Clovis, an old railroad town at the foot of the Sierras, someone mentioned that a few of the Chihuahuas had been there for a year. This shocked Karsten, who knew these dogs would be snapped up in her native Wisconsin. The Chihuahuas didn't have health or behavior problems, Karsten realized, just a location problem. All they needed, essentially, was a lift. Karsten organized her first transport in 2012, flying six Chihuahuas from Clovis to Madison's Dane County Humane Society. Nearly all the dogs were adopted as soon as their paws touched Wisconsin soil. Since then, Karsten, working on her own or with other organizations, has helped send more than twelve hundred dogs northwest. When I spoke to her, she had just spent the weekend before packing up eighteen Chihuahuas from Stockton's city shelter, yet another under-funded and overwhelmed city facility. It was December. The dogs, bound for Toronto, left on a Sunday, tucked into the pressurized, climate-controlled compartment of a red-eye connecting through Atlanta to Buffalo, where a van would meet them. After an eight-hour flight and then a two-hour drive, they arrived in Canada's largest city that Monday. Within a week nearly all the Chihuahuas were adopted—and probably dressed in one, maybe two, sweaters, possibly teeny down jackets. "I know we aren't fixing the overall problem of too many Chihuahuas," Karsten said, "but we fixed it for these dogs."

When those Chihuahuas left Stockton behind, they left a city voted the most miserable in the country by *Forbes* magazine in 2011. Where people struggle, animals struggle, too, and both do mightily in Stockton, which rests at the northern tip of California's great Central Valley. That long sweep of rich farmland produces mountains of fruits and vegetables and wide swaths of poverty. This is where you'll find some of California's most bedraggled communities, such as Stockton, Fresno, and Visalia. It's also where you'll find thousands and thousands of homeless dogs and cats. Fresno's Central California SPCA took in more than 12,500 dogs in 2015, nearly all strays, few wearing any kind of ID. In Visalia, a city a fifth the size of Fresno, the Valley Oak SPCA cares for about eight thousand animals a year, many of them covered in ticks or suffering from parvo and distemper.

The number of dogs put down in Stockton's municipal shelter has dropped dramatically in recent years, but that's because the SF SPCA has adopted the facility and poured major resources into it. Rather than just import animals, the SF SPCA is addressing the problems that have produced so many homeless dogs in Stockton. The SF SPCA is one of the only private nonprofits in the country to deploy a full-time team to work with a municipal shelter, and their aim is to create a new model for helping over-whelmed shelters beyond importing dogs from them. The SF SPCA working with Stockton Animal Services has tackled root problems there, by shortening lengthy quarantines, improving cleaning methods, and adding a full-time veterinarian to the staff. Stockton, which once managed to save only about 30 percent of the animals in its care, now saves over 80 percent. But Stockton is just one city in the Central Valley. An estimated forty thousand dogs are euthanized there each year. "We're more like Alabama," a shelter director in Visalia tells me. "We're years behind."

That's why many Bay Area shelters, unlike ones in Minneapolis or Boston, don't have to look beyond their state lines for dogs. That's why I had to drive only sixteen miles west from San Francisco to Tony La Russa's Animal Rescue Foundation (ARF) to meet dogs from the Central

Valley. The day I went, I drove through such heavy rain that the cars ahead of me became gray smudges, and I was wholly at the mercy of the spectral directions of my phone. Though I couldn't see much, I could feel the land open up as the buildings and roads dwindled and the foothills rose. By the time I reached Walnut Creek, the fog had lifted and I could see bike trails and soccer fields and art centers, all signs of the well off and college educated—pretty much what most of the Central Valley is not. Yet the Central Valley has something Walnut Creek does not: litters and litters and litters of puppies.

Puppies have vanished from most American shelters, but they are exactly what many adopters want when they walk through a shelter door. Most shelters need only post a little one's photo on its website to get it adopted, but first they have to have a puppy. The youngsters are a dying breed, so to speak, in parts of the country, such as New England or the Bay Area, anywhere pet owners religiously spay and neuter their animals. Shelter leaders actually fret that one day, when spaying and neutering reign supreme, there will be no homeless puppies, period. For now, though, shelters hungry for youth need only look to regions where dogs run loose and where next to no one fixes them, usually poor or rural or both, such as the Central Valley.

Every Monday, ARF's van plunges into the

Valley, visits county-run shelters, and returns with as many as fifty dogs. When I arrive on a Tuesday, I find forty new arrivals from the Central Valley, twenty-four of them puppies. Pacific, a black hound-like mom with pleading eyes, stands to greet me at her kennel door. As she wags her tail, her hungry pups, all ten of them, grab for her raw-looking, swollen teats. One latches on to the tip of Mom's tail and tries to suckle it. Pacific, all ribs, somehow ignores the melee. Next door, I find a doughy pile of young terrier types smashed in a corner while their mom takes advantage of the quiet and grooms her feet. A green note on the kennel board reads, "Coccidia," a parasite that causes diarrhea. That's why within a day or two, these families will move into a foster home before ARF staff lose their self-control and handle the youngsters even though there is a sign on the kennels that reads, "Don't Handle the Puppies."

That these puppies are here, that this tidy, cheerful shelter is here in Walnut Creek, is the work, oddly, of one stray cat. During a televised 1990 game between the Oakland Athletics and the New York Yankees, a tortoiseshell cat dashed out of the bullpen and onto the field. Play stopped. Baseball players watched as the kitty rounded the outfield. The crowd of thirty thousand in Oakland Coliseum roared as the kitty frantically looked for a way out. When she ran toward the A's dugout, Tony La Russa, the A's manager, herded the kitty there. She hid in a corner for the rest of the game. Afterward, La Russa and his wife searched for a shelter that would promise not to euthanize her. When they couldn't find one, they rehomed the kitty, whom they named Evie, after the A's cofounder, Evie Hass. A year later, the La Russas started ARF. In its early years, ARF was a foster home network that was largely devoted to cats, but over time it took in more and more dogs.

In 2003 ARF built the plush Walnut Creek shelter, which has a classroom full of stuffed dogs and cats that kids can "adopt" as they learn how to care for pets. The shelter has space for more than one hundred animals, but many more are sent to foster homes, some of which are brave enough to take whole puppy litters. Given its no-puppy-left-behind policy, ARF always has plenty of those.

When the ARF van pulls up to a Central Valley shelter, it takes adult dogs, but only after it has taken every puppy it can. That—I know it's hard to believe—is controversial. It's controversial because shelters that specialize in puppies naturally end up with very high adoption rates and, usually, very low to no euthanasia rates. Shelters that admit a lot of pitties or older dogs or nutbar juveniles will often have less stellar numbers. That can cause some resentment between shelters. It shouldn't, says ARF director

Elena Bicker. She explains the math of puppies to me. ARF can put as many as eleven puppies or more in one kennel as compared with adult dogs, which are typically one to a kennel. Because puppies can be housed together, and because they are adopted so quickly, ARF can save many more lives. ARF is going for numbers. Looking at those snub-nosed faces, especially the noodle trying to get milk out of his mom's tail, I find it hard to argue with that.

I eventually crossed on Chihuahuas thanks to Rudy, the geezer Chi who rocked the silly white jacket. Volunteering at a shelter has taught me that all it takes is one dog to change your mind about any breed, any type, any size, any age. Only the dog's personality, his individuality (not his size or the color of his coat, not how you will look walking him), matters. Yet to adopt a Chihuahua would mean I would probably need to adopt a dog who had been transported to New England. My heart is with the locals, Avanzino's "old and uglies and misbehaved," who are in my own backyard. I can, unlike a lot of people, handle freaked-out farm dogs such as Penny Jane or terriers clacking their way through the shelter such as Walter Joe. I understand that not everyone wants a dog he or she can't touch. Some, like Muttville's adopters, are better suited for the aged or infirm, for pill cases and doggie diapers. Some people want to do more than just give a dog a home. They want to "save" one from a "kill shelter." Who wouldn't when it's put that way?

I've come to realize that, for now, there are more than enough homeless pups for every kind of adopter. When people ask me about puppies at the ARL, I tell them about Sterling. When people ask me about rescuing from the South, I warn them off adopting dogs over the Internet. I point them to area shelters that import southern dogs, where they can meet a potential pet in person. If their heart is set on a Chihuahua, I check to see if any are due in at the ARL. The last time I came across yet another man in my neighborhood with a dog from the South, I did not grind my teeth, or not as much. When he happily proclaimed to me he had saved his dog from "Tennessee," I pointed to my dogs and said, "Maine!" and "Massachusetts!" He paused, seeming confused that someone could have "rescued" dogs from New England, from his own backyard—and they weren't even pitties. How could that be? Then he said, "I see you shop locally," and we both laughed while our dogs patiently waited for us to walk them home.

Trigger

11

KEEPING DOGS HOME

As Titan the Airedale steers me out of the shelter, we pass the large windows of the intake office. Though Titan strains on his harness, his black nose already twitching at the smell of fresh air just beyond the door, I manage a glance into the office where pets are given up, where they become homeless. I can't help looking to see if anyone is standing in there holding a leash or a carrier, even though I feel like an intruder doing so. Typically, there are one or two people (a couple or a mother and son), but I've seen what looks like whole families crowded into the boxy room to give up their cat or dog or gerbil. Sometimes the owners cry under the glare of the fluorescent lights. Some look angry. Their eyes blaze. Sometimes their faces have that incredible blankness of deep sadness. If our eyes meet, we all quickly look away. I've caught them at such an awkward moment. For most of my years as a volunteer, I can't say the crying ones have inspired much sympathy. What I want to do is open the door, lean in, and ask, "How can you?" Today a lone man is bent over the tall front desk filling out paperwork, a cat carrier at his feet. I avert my gaze as Titan briskly tugs me along. The lordly Airedale was adopted from us two years ago and then returned this spring by his adoptive owner for fighting with her other dog. That was his fourth home in his two short years. He's enormous, as if they had been fattening him to eat for a feast. As I push open the heavy door for the big boy, I wonder if he is racing outside to let loose a puddle of pee or in the hope that his last owner, who walked the Airedale into the ARL's intake office just weeks ago and handed over his leash, might be standing outside waiting for him.

People who surrender their pets have long been considered the enemy by the shelter world, an enemy so reviled that no one bothered to understand them, not to mention help them, other than by taking their pets off their hands. They were nonpeople or, at least, people who did not deserve their animals. They were irresponsible, maybe even liars. Allergies, moving—yeah, right. The thinking was (and is) for many shelters, if you are willing to forsake your pet, who should be the love of your life, that animal is better off in a shelter. That couldn't be more ironic, since in the not-so-distant past, that nearly always meant the pet would be euthanized. In fact, back then the thinking essentially was that an animal was better off dead than in an imperfect home. Logic hasn't always been the shelter world's strong suit.

When it comes to animals, logic has never been humans' strong suit.

In 1998 a study (albeit a small one, but one of the first of its kind to be published) demonstrated that "the enemy" might not be the irresponsible jerks everyone assumed. They might just be people, regular people who make bad decisions, plan poorly, have bad luck, and get tripped up by life's many demands and vagaries. Dr. Gary Patronek, then and still a lead researcher in the shelter world, had studied the reasons people give up their animals to shelters, but the veterinarian wondered if the one-word answers they scribbled on intake forms represented the whole story. Patronek and fellow researcher Arnold Arluke enlisted Natalie DiGiacomo, a graduate student at Tufts University, to interview people who were surrendering animals. DiGiacomo had worked at her hometown shelter in Youngstown, Ohio, throughout her undergraduate studies in field biology. She thought she'd become a marine biologist, but shelter work made her set aside dreams of wet suits and dolphins. She debated going to vet school, but decided on Tufts's public policy program instead because she wanted to help homeless animals, which she has. DiGiacomo, who lives with seven pets, has spent her career working in shelters and for the Humane Society of the United States.

When I called her nearly twenty years after the

study, DiGiacomo still vividly recalled how much she dreaded the project at first. Like me, she had no love for anyone who would give up a pet. She bought the study's premise intellectually, but this meant she would have to sit down with people who had done the unthinkable to her, even be friendly to them. She worried that her disapproval, her rage, would leak through. She worried they'd yell at her. She worried that no one would talk to her, or if they did, that the whole conversation would be painfully awkward, the way any con-versation is when a person in the right asks a person in the wrong to explain himself.

At a suburban shelter outside Boston, DiGiacomo asked everyone who gave up a pet if they would participate in the study, even the people rushing out the door, even the people who were crying. A few people choked out a no, or just walked off, but to her surprise, most everyone said yes. They seemed relieved to talk. As they did, long, complicated stories unspooled that the one-word answers they had given the intake desk had barely hinted at. One woman told DiGiacomo that she had suffered from bad allergies for five years from her cats. She had lived with wheezy lungs and tearing eyes, but then one of her two cats started spraying the furniture. She couldn't figure out which one was the culprit. She couldn't keep up with the cleaning. She couldn't afford to have them both neutered. She had tried everything she could think of and, as a last resort, had brought them to the shelter.

Not only were people's reasons for giving up their pets complicated, but the people had spent weeks, months, and, in one case, close to a year procrastinating, racking their brains for other solutions, or, as humans are inclined to do, hoping things would somehow just work out. An elderly couple, each with health problems, explained to DiGiacomo that they'd been told when they adopted their puppy, a shepherd mix they'd fallen in love with, that he wouldn't grow much more. He grew so brawny that neither of them could easily handle him. The young dog playfully pounced on them, knocking them to the floor. He tugged so hard on his leash that he would pull them down onto their hands and knees. Still, the couple kept the ever-expanding apple of their eyes. When the husband became too ill to walk the dog, they realized the wife alone could not exercise him enough. They had no choice but to bring him to the shelter. As the couple talked, DiGiacomo says, the man kept looking through a window to the adoption floor, hoping to see their dog already walking out the door with someone who would love him as much as they did.

These weren't the impulsive, thoughtless decisions DiGiacomo and the shelter world had assumed. Many of these people wished they could keep their pets but just couldn't figure out how. Maybe they hadn't tried things she would have, DiGiacomo tells me, but they didn't know about the resources she did as a longtime shelter worker. DiGiacomo began to think that if the shelter world, the experts, helped these people figure out how to keep their pets, maybe they would. There was only one problem. By the time most people came to a shelter, DiGiacomo found, their minds were already made up.

The conversations did take odd turns that might have confounded even Freud. People would claim that they had not been told their pet might be euthanized when DiGiacomo knew for a fact they had been. When she brought up that possibility to one man, he became so upset that he abruptly left. People criticized other people for giving up their pets even though they had done just that. Someone who brought her cat in because of allergies would tsk-tsk over someone signing a puppy over because he was moving. People told DiGiacomo that they could never work in a shelter because they would adopt all the animals. A they left the room, they would often wish her good luck. They hoped her study would stop people from giving up their beloved pets to shelters.

By 1998 no one had thought much about how to keep people from giving up their pets. Shelters had traditionally fended off animals by keeping them from being born. They sponsored educational campaigns urging people to fix their pets, and starting in the 1960s and '70s, began to oblige adopters to sign agreements that they would have their new pets fixed. People being people, a lot of them never bothered to, then let their unfixed dogs nose around the neighborhood and deposited the resulting puppies at the shelter. There was one way to stop that unending cycle. Shelters started fixing animals before they could be adopted, which has become standard practice. Many of the shelters I visited have surgical bays that are devoted exclusively to spaying and neutering. The San Jose Animal Care Center fixes about thirty-five hundred dogs a year. At Tony La Russa's, I walked by dogs wrapped in blankets on the floor who were sleeping off the anesthesia while others waited quietly in nearby kennels for their turn under the blazing light of the surgical table.

That shelters can fix this many dogs is a relatively recent development, and is the result of how the surgery has changed. Until the 1940s, most veterinarians worked with farm animals, pulling open horses' mouths and palpating pigs. They knew the insides of these domestic animals, with their softball-size hearts and organ-like stomachs. The comparatively delicate anatomy of a dog or cat was terra incognita. Many vets didn't think twice about leaning into a cow's abdomen up to their shoulders during surgery, but they weren't as adept at the finger work required for a Yorkie's itty-bitty innards. This changed after World War II, as more and more Americans got purebred puppies, and more and more veterinarians moved from farm to suburban practices. Sterilization did not start to become part of standard veterinary care until the 1970s, and then took years to catch on. That is why for twenty-five years the ever-tan, ever-smiling Bob Barker closed every *Price Is Right* by looking at the camera, pointing his index finger at all of America, and saying, "Help control the pet population. Have your pet spayed or neutered." His replacement, Drew Carey, continues the tradition to this day, though the forever-pale comedian often looks like he's muffling a giggle as he chants the line.

Better technology, as so often happens, made it easier for humans to do the right thing. In the old days, when you dropped your female dog off to be spayed, you might not see her again for four or five days. That's how long it took for the effects of the anesthesia, typically a syringe of sodium pentothal, to wear off. Dogs often spent the first two days after surgery out cold, then one to three days vomiting and wobbling around. Now dogs are knocked out like humans, with a cocktail of intravenous drugs. They are given IV fluids, and their vital signs are monitored during the procedure. The pups I saw wrapped in blankets on the floor at Tony La Russa's would wake up in thirty minutes. They would have dinner that night, go for a short walk. Their chances of developing a postoperative infection were much lower than in the past. Vets now wear surgical masks, gloves, and sterile gowns during the procedure, which is a relatively recent development. Incisions are closed with dissolvable sutures that lead to far less inflammation than the old catgut variety. Less inflammation means less licking, which means less infection. Their incisions are often closed beneath the skin, so there are no stitches for a dog to worry, unlike in the past. One last change in the surgery made all the difference for shelters. The procedure was once considered dangerous for a dog under six months old, which forced shelters to adopt out unfixed puppies. In 1993, the American Veterinary Medical Association proclaimed the procedure safe for dogs as young as two months old. Finally shelters could fix every dog before adoption.

About the only way to improve on the surgery now would be essentially to get rid of it, to find a nonsurgical means of sterilizing male and female pets that costs little and involves next to no recovery. Despite the $25 million prize offered by Found Animals to the scientist who creates such a magic potion, no one has yet. The FDA has approved Zeuterin, a zinc solution that is injected into a male dog's scrotum to kill the sperm and gum up the tubing. The procedure does not require general anesthesia, which most men may have trouble believing. What some might appreciate is that the dogs will appear intact, which is why inside their flank is tattooed a *Z*. Most people, however, do not appreciate a male dog who looks intact, and that may be one reason Zeuterin has not sold well.

I can't remember the last time I saw a dog with balls on the streets of my neighborhood. Maybe that is why Drew Carey seems nearly to smirk—urging people to fix their pets seems almost ludicrous today, when an estimated 83 percent of Americans do. All my neighbors' dogs, all my friends' dogs, are spayed or neutered. If I want to see an intact male dog, I go to the ARL. Shelters exist in a parallel universe in this respect. According to one report, only one out of ten animals entering shelters has been fixed. They don't remain that way for long.

If you want to surrender your dog at the ARL, you should make an appointment. That's the case at Animal Humane in Minnesota, too, but they'll be sure to make you wait a few days, even if they have room in their kennels right then. The operator will politely ask you a lot of questions about why you want to give up your dog. If you take your dog to the San Jose Animal Care Center the staff might just shake their heads. The municipal facility does not accept owner surrenders when its kennels are close to full. It will direct you to the Humane Society Silicon Valley or another private nonprofit shelter. At Silicon, you will have to fill out a questionnaire, bring your dog in to be evaluated, and then maybe wait weeks before he is accepted. Giving up your dog isn't as easy as it used to be.

For most of the last century, shelters would readily take an animal off your hands almost no questions asked. Many didn't charge surrender fees. Some were open twenty-four hours. They put cages in their lobbies where people could leave their pets in the dark of night. Shelters feared that if they didn't make it easy for people to give up their pets, they'd ditch them at the local park or, as with Gwen Stefani, leave them tied to a pole. Shelters ran like emergency rooms, open to all comers at all hours, but this assumed that someone who wanted to give up a puppy because it was too active constituted a crisis.

This was a nutty, stressful way of doing business, and made it impossible to help many animals. Dogs came in with contagious diseases, and a few coughs later, everyone had kennel cough or, worse, distemper. The dogs deposited in the cages in the lobbies arrived with no histories, no details. They might as well have been strays. Shelters ran out of room, which meant other animals had to be euthanized to make space for the newbies. Imagine being admitted to an overflowing hospital where the only way the doctor can treat you is if he rips the life support off someone else. This mind-set was born in the nineteenth century, when mangy, wormy, starving strays crammed many city streets, when the thinking was that a dog was better off humanely put down then left to fend for itself in what was often a cruel world. Given some of the strays I've seen in Mexico, I can understand this way of thinking, but times have obviously changed in the United States.

Spaying and neutering have stemmed the flow of puppies into shelters but not adult dogs, and they are who fill shelters today. The average age of a shelter dog now is about two. They are not unwanted puppies. They are largely unwanted pets. One way to find these dogs homes is to keep them exactly where they are—in their current homes. One way to do that is not to make it so easy for owners to surrender them. In 2002 the Oregon Humane Society (OHS) did just that. The Portland organization was one of the first shelters to require people to make an appointment to relinquish their pets. The OHS, northwest of Portland on what was once ten acres of farmland, is one of the country's largest shelters, finding homes for eleven thousand animals a year, as well as one of the oldest humane societies. A doctor founded the OHS in 1868 after he saw a horse brutally beaten. Despite its many years, the OHS became a national leader only in recent decades. When Sharon Harmon joined the staff in 1989, only 26 percent of the shelter's animals were adopted. The rest were euthanized. Harmon, who became director in 1998, says her sole goal was to save more animals. She did what she could by loosening adoption restrictions. That helped, but the OHS still had to euthanize for space. Harmon and her board of trustees decided to make a leap and stop putting down dogs and cats because they didn't have room for them. To do that, the OHS couldn't take every animal that came through the door, especially when its kennels were already full. It could take in only as many animals as it could care for, period. The mere act of making people phone ahead to make an appointment, the staff decided, might make a difference. As DiGiacomo found, by the time people arrive at a shelter, they have already made up their minds to surrender their dog. By making people call ahead, the shelter could catch people before that fateful decision. Shelter staff could ask what the problem was, offer behavior advice, tell the owners about resources, such as low-cost vet care, or explain how they could rehome their pet themselves. Did they just need a bag of food? On the phone, they might be able to change people's minds, to give them ideas for how they could keep their pet.

As sensible as this idea sounds, it was radical, even upsetting to many people in the shelter world. It meant that the animals might be better off where they were, not in the loving, knowledgeable hands of shelter staff, that humans might not be as awful as shelter workers assumed. Barbara Baugnon, at the time the OHS's relatively new PR person, admits she was one of the early naysayers. She was sure people would just dump animals on the society's sprawling property. She worried that it would look like Oregon Humane was turning animals away. How would she explain that to newspaper reporters?

None of her fears materialized. Dogs weren't abandoned by the dozens on the OHS's fields. People called and made appointments. That first year the new policy was enacted, the society took in two thousand fewer animals. However, it appeared many of those pets were driven to the county facility, which took in an extra two thousand animals that same year. Still, the OHS quit putting down dogs for space. The dogs, cats, bunnies, and horses could stay as long as it took to find them a home. But the OHS didn't want to become a no-kill facility by pushing its animals down the road to the county facility. So, in 2006, it and nine other Portland-area shelters joined together to save more animals throughout the county. To do that, nearly all the organizations in the coalition would take only animals for whom they had room. Even the county facility, which must accept every stray, injured, and abused dog, draws the line at owner surrenders if its kennels are too full. The only way managed intake really works, Harmon says, is if it is a regional effort. Otherwise, the animals one shelter won't take can just end up at another one.

Ten-plus years after the OHS took the plunge with managed admission, it has become common practice for shelters, especially private nonprofits, to require people to make an appointment to give up their pets. In Boston, the ARL asks people to call ahead and to fill out a long form about their dogs in advance. The afternoon I sat in the intake office, there were three appointments scheduled. Reading the 1998 study and talking to DiGiacomo had had a profound effect on me—profound enough that I had decided to quit peering through the intake office window and to step through the door for a few hours. For most shelter volunteers and probably a lot of staff members, the people who surrender pets are nameless and faceless. All we see are the dogs they leave behind, which makes it so easy to think the worst of the people. I wanted to put faces to them.

The first appointment of the day, a woman bringing in her Yorkie, didn't show, which was worrisome. A judge had ordered the Yorkie to be boarded because the woman's estranged husband had threatened to kill the dog. When the woman had called to make her intake appointment she said she couldn't afford the boarding anymore and needed to give her Yorkie up. Who knows what she did?

Then a couple, downcast and teary-eyed, brought in an injured mourning dove they had found along a road. They had placed the bird in a cardboard box. Inside, the dove blinked, fluttered slightly. The bird was injured so badly it needed to be euthanized. The couple held hands as they left.

At 5:00 p.m. nearly on the dot, a slim young man with large round eyes and the pallor of a drug addict slipped through the door holding a plastic carrier. He had made the appointment to give up his ten-month-old kitty, Lulu, because he was too allergic to her. He smelled of cigarettes and unwashed clothes. His teeth were gray and caked with plaque. He was so thin I wanted to buy him a burger. Yet he was clearly not high, and far more thoughtful than he looked. He had brought a bag filled with Lulu's toys. The lovely tiger, Lulu, had a shiny coat and bright eyes. The man sat down and carefully filled out the intake form. While he did, I remembered how Ruby had come into my family's life. I'd gotten her for free at a farmers' market in Madison, Wisconsin, where I was in college. Back then I had only the vaguest idea of how to take care of a puppy—I tied her up out in front of my apartment when I went to class—and my landlord did not allow dogs. Within a few weeks, the landlord busted me.

Either I had to go or Ruby did. It was midterms. My mother agreed to take my puppy, but what if she hadn't? I had been so stupid but, in the end, lucky. This young man did not look lucky. He pulled out a wad of bills to pay the fifty dollars for Lulu's surrender. He asked to be called if the ARL was going to euthanize her. He'd come back for her. He blew hard on a tissue and then coughed something into it. "Sorry, I have asthma."

Not long after he left, a woman who'd just been evicted phoned to see if the shelter could come get her dog, another Yorkie. The woman was staying at her friend's place, but her friend wasn't allowed to have dogs. The rescue van could go the next day but not that night. She couldn't wait, but didn't have money for the subway or the bus to get to the shelter. The constable had locked all her things in her apartment, she said, including her purse. Her entire life was a mess.

How can you keep a dog caught in the middle of such chaos in its home? I went to Los Angeles to find out.

The South Los Angeles Animal Shelter, which resembles a kind of modernist bunker from the front, is one of the busiest and largest of the city's six facilities. Some five thousand animals, most of them strays or lost pets, land here every year. The shelter is on an out-of-the-way street that is lined with a mix of blocky industrial buildings and a large parking lot of school buses as bright as daffodils. It's the kind of treeless, hard-edged street where people, especially walking, look out of place, but not far from here are block after block of small bungalows, nearly all of them packed with people struggling to pay their bills. The dozen or so mostly Latino neighborhoods the shelter serves are some of the densest and poorest in Los Angeles. Nearly fifteen thousand people squeeze into a square mile of South Los Angeles (compared with Beverly Hills' roomy six thousand). Jammed in with all those people are countless pet dogs, typically two or more per small bungalow.

A quiet young man with a flop of heavy black hair falling over his inexpressive face has come to the shelter on a sunny December day to retrieve Sheba, his young shepherd mix. She escaped over his family's backyard fence, which is higher than his head. This is the second time animal control has caught Sheba running loose, so the redemption fee to retrieve her is $107. He has $30. In the past, the clerk would have just shrugged her shoulders and said, "Sorry," and Sheba would have stayed put in one of the shelter's 250-plus kennels. Now the clerk picks up her phone and calls for Amanda Casarez to come to the shelter's imposing front desk.

Casarez is a short, broad-shouldered woman with a natural air of authority. She grew up in

Watts and still lives there with her husband, two sons, and a houseful of dogs. She refers to her Chihuahuas as her "gangster dogs." Her job is to keep other people's pets out of the South LA Animal Shelter. In the case of the shepherd mix, that will be relatively easy. The young female is spayed and licensed, which Casarez rarely sees. She won't have to explain the importance of doing either. As Casarez asks about his fence and how often he walks Sheba, the young man stares off as if he wishes he were somewhere else. He answers once a day for fifteen minutes. She suggests taking her out more often, tells him about free training classes nearby, and explains the redemption fees. She starts to write out a voucher to cover the difference between his thirty dollars and the rest of the fee so he can take Sheba home.

"I don't actually have thirty dollars," the young man says. "It's more like twenty-eight."

Casarez crumples that voucher and quietly starts again.

Casarez works for Downtown Dog Rescue (DDR), a private nonprofit run by volunteers that helps dogs in Los Angeles' toughest neighborhoods. Three years ago, DDR began a pilot project with funding from Found Animals to keep pets out of the South LA shelter. When people bring in animals to surrender, the shelter clerk suggests they talk to Casarez first. A large portable plastic file folder by her side, Casarez can help people with vet care, spay/neuter surgery, or redemption fees. She can arrange for a free dog run to be delivered to someone's house. She will call a landlord to negotiate a pet security deposit. If the animal really needs a new home, Casarez will find a foster home or rescue network that can take the dog. The point is to keep the dog out of the city's overtaxed system. The first year's goal was to fend off four hundred animals. That took only two months. By the end of the first year, the program had diverted two thousand animals, most of them dogs.

The program is the brainchild of Lori Weise, the founder of Downtown Dog Rescue, a woman who is as slender as a ballerina but as tall as a basketball player. She runs a furniture factory that crafts sleek mid-century designs, the desks, couches, and chairs you'd see in the photos in stylish magazines. When Weise first began working at the factory in the 1990s, it was near LA's Skid Row. As Weise drove to work past boarded-up buildings, she passed people camped on the sidewalks and under bridges. Many of them had dogs. She wanted to help these people and their pets somehow. She convinced some of the Skid Row inhabitants to get their dogs spayed and neutered and arranged a free clinic. She bought dog food, leashes, and collars. Without addresses, the homeless people couldn't license their dogs, so Weise let them use her home address. At one point some three hundred dog licenses listed Weise's address, as did lots of microchips. When animal control officers picked up those dogs, they would call Weise, who would find the owners and drive them to the city pound to retrieve their pets, where she'd pay the redemption fee.

Weise had started a surrender-prevention program before there was even a name for it, but more than that, she was keeping dogs in "homes" few people would have approved of. Most animal advocates would have "helped" these dogs by taking them away from the homeless people and rushing the pups directly to the nearest humane society. Not Weise. She thought it was better for the homeless people to keep the dogs, their best friends and often their protectors. It was better for the dogs, too, who were often rough around the edges, so rough that they would have had a hard time getting adopted and would likely have been euthanized in LA's strained city shelters. These dogs might not have had a picture-perfect life on the streets with their homeless guardians, but it was a life, a home.

Weise's efforts eventually grew into Downtown Dog Rescue, an organization dedicated to tackling the problems of poverty that led to animals' becoming homeless in the first place. DDR runs a small shelter of its own for about thirty mostly large, rowdy dogs, a network of foster homes, and the program at the South LA shelter. Downtown

Dog Rescue also holds vaccination clinics in South Los Angeles, which is why, on a Saturday morning, Weise bounded down block after block in a mostly Hispanic neighborhood. Fair-skinned, her long red hair waxing gray, Weise cut a striking figure, a stack of two hundred flyers in her freckled hand. The flyers were for a vet clinic that would be held the next day in Gilbert Lindsay Park, a wide stretch of green amid a sea of small houses. As I broke a sweat to keep up with Weise's long stride, she scanned dusty front yards for dogs or listened for barking and then left flyers on those fences. She asked people inspecting tables of CDs and toaster ovens at tag sales if they had dogs, cheerily sputtering "la vacunación" in her limited Spanish to anyone who didn't speak English. She interrupted a woman reading her Bible in the sun as her Bichon Frisé, dressed in a Santa sweater, napped at her feet, to hand her a flyer. We crossed the street here and there to avoid loose dogs giving us the eye for being on their turf. On one block, two dirty, matted small dogs raged at us from behind a fence. Weise wrote down the address. She would have Casarez come later to talk to the family about how to care for their dogs. As we passed by, a man tending a sizzling grill of whole chickens in a sidewalk stall waved his spatula at Weise and asked for a flyer. Another man ran across the street to catch up with her to get one. "There are jerks, but not as many as you think," she says.

The next day, South Angelinos began lining up at 9:00 a.m. by white pop-up tents erected in a parking lot not far from a soccer field. Whole families walked to the park with their dogs. Kids cuddled puppies as they waited. By the end of the day, 125 dogs had been vaccinated and microchipped.

The morning I spent at the South Los Angeles Animal Shelter with Casarez was what she would call a good one. She had to help two people at a time, not four or five. On a busy day, she might keep as many as sixty dogs out of the shelter by solving their owners' sundry problems. Those are mostly Saturdays. This was a Friday. After beautiful, if dirty, Sheba was reunited with her owner, a smiley woman showed up clutching a Chihuahua to her breast. Another one on a leash stood close to her feet. She said she had a third in her car. She was there not to give them up but to ask if the city shelter offered low-cost vaccines. Casarez told her about DDR's free clinic that weekend. She also warned the smiling woman that city law required that all dogs be spayed or neutered. If she didn't fix hers, she could be ticketed. The animals could even be taken away from her. The woman was surprised. She had never heard of the city law. Without hesitation, she agreed to have all three fixed at the clinic the ASPCA runs out of the city shelter.

As a poker-faced Casarez filled out the paperwork for the procedures, two elderly men, one hook-nosed and heavyset, the other soft-faced with a thin gray mustache edging his lip like an old-time movie star's, waited for her. Afterward, Casarez sat down with them together so she could see who needed help most urgently. The heavyset man described in a high, nasal voice how his old dog, Rico, was whining and panting from pain. He needed to go to the vet immediately. Casarez recognized the man, but the man claimed he hadn't talked to her before. She turned to the mustachioed man. He had a calico cat in a kennel who couldn't quit drooling or licking herself. He'd paid to have all her teeth removed, yet the vet had left a few in the front for some reason. He thought that was the problem, but he had no more money for a vet to find out. He'd brought the cat to the shelter hoping that if he gave her up, she would get treatment, but he had been told the shelter would euthanize her. "I don't want her to die," he said, leaning forward, his voice breaking. "She's my family."

Casarez asked him to get the kitty out for her to see. She was too thin. Her calico coat was patchy and glistened from her constant licking. There was more wrong with her than her teeth. Casarez quickly called ahead to the vet clinic to explain the case, handed the man a voucher, and sent him on his way. "God bless you," he called as he hurried out the door. While she arranged the cat's vet visit, Casarez had asked the clinic about the heavyset man's dog. As it turned out, she had talked to the man just a few days ago. She had given him a voucher then to see the vet, who had given him pain medication for Rico's arthritis. The man had lied to her, she suspected, hoping she wouldn't remember him and send his suffering dog right back to the vet, no questions asked. Instead, Casarez explained that it would take time for the painkillers to take effect. He admitted he couldn't get Rico to take the pills. As Casarez demonstrated to him how to give the pills with baby food, a family of three arrived with a lumbering gray pittie with one ear so swollen it stuck straight out from his head. He couldn't help loudly flapping the uncomfortable ear. The family explained that they fed him grain-free food for his skin allergies, but they hadn't been able to afford the food in recent weeks. Since then, their dog had been scratching a lot and then his ear had swollen. Casarez gave them a form to fill out while she dialed the vet clinic again. The teenage son, who had dark, thick hair and unusuall close-set eyes, wrote in the pittie's age, six. He asked his mother how to spell the dog's name. She didn't know. Nor did the father. The family giggled when they realized none of them did. Was it Sakumy or Zakumy or Zakumi?

Not long after the family left, Casarez was called to the intake office, where a woman with a knit cap pulled tight over a tangle of braids held a squinty-eyed golden dog. The Chihuahua, a pup of six months, had thrown up as much as a person, the woman sadly told Casarez. Also, she had some blood in her stool. The pup had gotten one parvo vaccine but hadn't finished the series of three yet. The woman had the dog's sister in the car, who'd had all three. Parvo is often deadly, and is viciously contagious. For that reason, the South LA shelter will euthanize a dog with parvo. Casarez asked the woman not to set the dog down and to come outside. The puppy, Casarez told the woman, had a fifty-fifty chance of surviving. She would give the woman a voucher for the vet clinic, but there was only so much they could do. As Casarez wrote out the voucher, the woman's partner, a tall man with bad teeth and worried eyes, lumbered over to ask why the Chihuahua was breathing so hard. Casarez explained how painful parvo is, that the dog's intestines were tightening like a knot. She told the couple to clean the floors of their apartment with bleach every day to keep the other dog from getting parvo. "You see," the man said, "just now we are living in a hotel."

Most people in the shelter world want to help animals, only animals, but Weise says that if you want to do that, you have to help people, especially poor people. The program at the South

LA shelter makes that obvious. Casarez estimates that 98 percent of the people she's offered help take it. About a third of the people need help with fees, such as Sheba's owner. Another third need help with bills for pet care, everything from the vet to dog food. Some people just need their fences repaired so their dog won't keep escaping. Often people have a tangle of problems that Casarez has to tease out like a social worker. They need help with the fee for not having their dog fixed and help to pay for the surgery. Maybe their car was impounded and now they don't have a way to get to work, which means they have no money to feed their dog. One day, a woman in dark sunglasses came to give up her Chihuahua. She had no place to keep her but wouldn't really explain why. She was short with Casarez, almost rude. Finally, the woman lifted up her sunglasses. She had black eyes. Her husband had beaten her and threatened to kill their dog. Casarez found a women's shelter for her and her daughter. Her Chihuahua was surrendered to the animal shelter, but a few weeks later the woman returned for it. She was moving to San Francisco to live near her family. Casarez wrote out a voucher for the redemption fee so the woman could take her dog with her.

When Casarez began working at the South LA shelter, the program, which is funded by Found Animals, was going to run for only two years.

Now Weise says it will run indefinitely because of its success and because as long as there is poverty in South Los Angeles, which might be always, there will be people who need help to keep their animals, people such as the couple living in a hotel with a deathly sick puppy they love. Not long after Casarez sent the couple to the vet clinic, they called her to say their puppy had survived.

A few days ago a truck driver noticed a young dog with funny front legs slowly walking, almost crawling, up a street in Fitchburg, an old mill town near the New Hampshire line. The driver called the police, who scooped the dog up, and now the puppy is with the ARL. "Wait until you see him," a staff member calls after me as I head to the back kennels. I am so worried about Titan the Airedale, who's now been with us for months, whom only a very few of us volunteers walk, that by the time I reach the kennels I've half forgotten about the puppy.

Then, as I lean over to say, "Hello there," to Titan through his door, a little face with curious dark eyes appears next door. Rugby's front legs are kicked out like a grasshopper's. They bow out so awkwardly that they look like they might snap. His thin chest is not far from the floor. The cutie has a rather serious expression for a puppy. Rugby is a pittie but with a real boxer look, given his camel-colored coat. His ears flare back as if caught in a breeze. Black outlines his curious eyes. But it's his strange buglike posture that stands out. He can hardly walk but has toddled up to see me.

Who would abandon a dog on the street in the soggy chill of April? Once I had an easy answer to that question: a heinous cretin. Now I don't. It might have been a heinous cretin. It might also have been someone who is mentally ill. It might have been someone who in a backward way thought that abandoning this dog was helping him. I don't know. That's the point. Sitting in the intake office at the ARL and visiting the South LA shelter showed me how much I don't know about other people's lives.

I don't usually take puppies out, but I can't help myself from scooping up this one. "Hold on," I say to Titan. When I lift Rugby, his front legs hang straight out and look normal. When I set him down outside on the lawn, they go all grasshoppery again. The spring sun has finally dried out the ground enough so that I can sit down cross-legged next to him in the grass. Rugby clumsily pulls himself into my lap. Nearly all dogs are better off in their homes. If we can keep them there, we can help the ones who truly need to be in a shelter, such as this pup with goofy legs who is falling asleep in my lap.

Rugby

12

WHAT TO DO WITH RUGBY?

I can't get any clear answers about what's wrong with Rugby's legs or what the plan is for him. One staff member tells me she hopes they don't have to amputate his front legs. Another tells me his leg bones may be growing too fast. His computer file says he has carpal laxity syndrome, which means essentially that his wrists bend too much, but I can't find any notes on how the ARL plans to treat his elastic joints. As a volunteer, I can have trouble getting the whole story on a dog. What is clear to me is that Rugby could be in his shelter kennel for a stretch. He's a puppy, maybe four months old, about the age at which his young brain will become less accepting of new experiences. So far, his youth has been less than ideal, but luckily he likes people and other dogs. He is a curious boy, even intrepid, always greeting people at his kennel door. Still, he needs to learn the ways of the world, everything from car rides to ceiling fans. If he grows up in a shelter, even with the volunteers taking him out constantly for walks—or, in his case, crawls—he'll learn little about what life will be like as a pet. That could make him into a neurotic, even unruly dog.

Penny Jane doesn't like puppies. Rugby isn't housebroken, and my husband doesn't like accidents in the house. I have lots of nice things, including an orange leather couch that a puppy would like to chew. But the clock is ticking on Rugby. He needs a taste of life in a home *now*. A week after Rugby arrives at the ARL, Scott meets me there to collect him for a sleepover. He lifts Rugby into the crate we've put in the back of our station wagon. We throw stuffed toys and a rawhide in with him and click the crate door closed. After everything that's happened to him, he seems unfazed, even game. He's quiet as we drive home through the spring twilight, the crate door jangling as we go.

There are so many big-picture ways to help dogs, to find them more homes—new ways of thinking, fresh ideas to fill a crisp three-ring binder, long lists of training techniques—but I'm just a shelter volunteer. All I can do is help these dogs one by one in the relatively short time I have, with a stroll, a game of fetch, some people-watching, or just a chance to be themselves. One night, I walked Annika, a large, pewter-colored pittie as sleek as a seal. She had bumped from shelter to shelter. She was, sadly, used to having no bond. She hardly looked at me, even when I proffered handfuls of treats. I was just another faceless human holding the other end of her leash. Her life had become one endless, mindless march. We paused by a shop window that for some reason had a stuffed woodchuck in it. The woodchuck stood on its haunches and peered into the distance. Annika threw her paws onto the windowsill so she could better see this wondrous mystery. Her golden eyes widened. Her face relaxed. She bobbed her head back and forth. She looked me in the eye for the first time that evening as if to say, "Can you believe this!" You could argue that being a dog, Annika needed a brisk-paced walk, but, being Annika, she needed that woodchuck more. It was obvious how I could help her right then. We gazed at the woodchuck with its expressionless, glassy eyes for a good fifteen minutes. Passersby chuckled at us. "What is that woodchuck looking at?" I asked Annika. She looked at me, looked back at the still critter. I ended Annika's reverie only when I realized the shelter would be locking up at any minute. I planned to take her back to the woodchuck in the window, but the next time I went to the ARL, I found that the pittie had been transferred to another shelter. Who there would know, I worried, that Annika liked stuffed woodchucks?

I get discouraged over how little I can do, how I have no say over what happens to these dogs I give my heart to. Sometimes I've gotten so discouraged and frustrated that Scott, who has listened to me rage over dinner or found me crying in our bedroom, suggests that I should stop volunteering or, at least, take a break. "Maybe so," I'll whimper. But then I'll think of specific dogs, such as Greg or Gwen or Harmony, and the force of their needs will crowd out my sadness and frustration, and off I go. The next thing I know, I'm asking my husband if we can bring home a puppy for the night. "He can hardly walk," I'd told Scott. "He should be easy."

Scott carries Rugby from the car, over the street's rough pavement, and up the stairs to our second-floor condo. As Scott sets him down on our thick Oriental rug, Rugby's front legs bow dramatically beneath him. The puppy stands for a moment, quietly taking in the room. Then he is off. He churns his front legs like paddles and his back legs rush him along. He makes quite a racket as he flies down our long hallway. He races into and out of both bedrooms. He clatters as he goes. "I thought you said he could hardly get around," Scott says. "He can't," I call as I run after Rugby to make sure he doesn't grab our silk throw pillows or leather shoes. I hadn't picked up very well, assuming he'd move slower than a turtle. Rugby kicks up rugs as he runs. He tips over the bathroom trash can before I can grab it. A confetti of used dental floss and tissues hits the floor. I herd Rugby back to the living room as Scott rushes around, closing doors. Rugby makes a clumsy leap at our leather couch, but luckily can't bound high enough. He bounces off the front. We quickly empty our toy basket on the living room floor. Rugby digs into the heap, tossing toys this way and that, squeaky ones rising to the ceiling. I turn to walk into our small kitchen for a glass of water. A commotion follows me. I feel a hard pinch on my ankle. "Ouch!"

For the rest of the night, anytime I move, Rugby comes after me. If I sit down, the puppy leaves me alone, lies at my feet, or snuggles in my lap. The second I move, though, Rugby, the canine sled, shoots at me. If I am lucky, he just grabs my pant leg or hovers right under my feet, which makes it impossible to cook dinner. If I'm not lucky, he chomps my ankle. He doesn't mouth me hard enough to break the skin, but it hurts. He is a jumpy-mouthy who can't jump, so he is just a mouthy. Still, he snoozes the night away in his crate. He eats with the other dogs without a problem. Penny Jane is not thrilled, but Rugby gives her wide berth. When I carry the puppy outside in the morning, he reverts to the gentle creature I knew in the shelter. I tote him up to the Bunker Hill Monument park, where he gets in my lap to watch the busy tourists pointing this way and that as they tromp the steps to the great spike of granite.

We brought Rugby home once or twice a week for the rest of the spring, even though after each time, we compared bruises and agreed that it

would be his last visit. We dubbed him the Beast. We wore long pants and boots when we had him with us, even as the temperatures tilted toward summer and we sprang our windows wide. We didn't
take him out of his crate in the morning until we were both out of our PJs and fully dressed. We'd learned the hard way what the Beast's canines felt like on our bare feet. We had meant to show Rugby the ways of the world, but now we had a more serious job: we had to calm down his hard mouthing. Someone might adopt a dog with crummy front legs, but no one would want a baby barracuda. When he went for our feet and ankles, we froze and asked him to sit. When he wouldn't snap out of an overexcited mouthy fit, we carted him down our back steps to our small yard, where, under the sky, he would immediately mellow. The outside world seemed to awe him, maybe because his first venture into it, crawling down that road in Fitchburg, had been so overwhelming. More and more, we could manage his mouthiness, but as he grew, carrying him, which we had to do on steps and on the street when he became weary of the hard pavement, got harder and harder. Once, I had been able to lift him with one arm. Now I had to hoist him with both, like a bag of garden mulch. I feared for my discs. At least he liked to be picked up and went still in my straining arms.

In the meantime, the shelter sent him to physical therapy. There, Rugby solemnly stumbled along a treadmill in a water tank. At the shelter, he got regular nutritious meals and many walks each day. At the shelter, he was all sweetness, so volunteer after volunteer took him out. Then something wondrous yet awful happened. His front legs started to straighten. His left one tightened up first. His wrist was still knobby, but he began to stand flatly on that paw. His right leg still curved like the letter *C,* and when the pup was tired, he would step on his foreleg instead of his foot, but he could walk better. What was awful about this was that now the Beast could jump. He began to leap at volunteers, even nip them. He bit his physical therapist on the breast. He left a dark blue tattoo on my forearm. He leapt onto our leather couch and nearly tore a button off it. He peed on it.

One day, Scott and I took Rugby with us to our favorite beach, a great crescent of gold along a narrow harbor that opens wide to the Atlantic. The sand was mostly flat, and the water was shallow, perfect for a dog with a bad gait who had never swum before. The May sun shimmered by the time we pulled into the beach's enormous parking lot. We couldn't resist going barefoot, though we had a baby barracuda with us, so we carried our shoes with us, just to be safe. Penny Jane and Walter Joe sprinted as soon as we took their leashes off. They ran in great curlicue paths of joy, raising their tails to the day. Rugby trundled along on the forgiving sand, yet he still wasn't stepping squarely on his right foot, and his gait had an odd hop to it. By the time we reached the water's edge and rolled up our jeans to wade in, he needed a break. He stretched out on a patch of cool sea grass and happily watched dogs gallop across the great tidal flats that reached as far as we could see.

Rugby didn't seem up to strolling the length of the beach, so I stayed with him while Scott ambled off with our two dogs weaving around him. Rugby stood and whined as he watched them go. He strained at his leash. For a moment I thought of catching up with my pack, but didn't. Instead, I pulled Rugby toward the dry heat of the sand. My feet were going numb in the saltwater's chill. I took only a few steps before Rugby nipped my ankle hard. I stopped to ask him to sit. He did, his face brightening as I popped a treat into his mouth, and I turned to go again. He munched the same ankle. I asked him for another sit and then turned once more. He pounced on the back of my legs and grabbed my jacket, which I'd tied around my waist. He mashed my foot. I'd been so stupid to take my shoes off and roll up my pants. I grabbed his harness and held the Beast away from me with a stiff arm as I hurriedly padded out of the water and to the beach on my numb, sore feet. There I sat to pull down my pant legs and put on my sneakers, but with only one hand free, I couldn't hold Rugby far enough away from me to do either. He mouthed one arm hard and then the other. I stood up. I asked for sit after sit, hoping to snap him out of his obsession. Then I ran out of treats.

As dogs ran here and there and boats puttered by, I grabbed Rugby by the harness and, under the glory of the spring sun, pushed him to the sand with all my might. I held him there as I waited for Scott, and my spirits darkened. By the time my husband and dogs returned, Rugby had snapped out of his mouthy attack and was lounging by my side as I stroked his smooth back, which is why Scott was so surprised by my frown and then my tears. I cried not because Rugby had bruised me, but because I didn't see how this baby barracuda could ever find a home, bum legs or no.

"I think you should take a break from the shelter," Scott said on the drive home.

"Maybe," I whimpered.

Over the past few years my office has become a de facto library on dogs. Stacks of books teeter on the shelves. Magazine articles and studies pile up on my desk. We have given man's best friend more than his due in ink. Yet I found, as I plowed through this literature, that I was reading mostly about my own kind, over and over. We humans see dogs not for who they are but for what they can do for us. For aeons they hunted, herded, and guarded for us. Their "history" is just one long story of wondrous ways they helped our species flourish, accompanying our explorers into the wilderness and sitting on the battlefield with injured soldiers, as Sallie did. Our expectations have only grown. Now we use them to make us healthier and less lonely. They soothe battle-weary veterans. They find illegal drugs and homemade bombs. Countless dogs have given their lives so ours can be better. What we have done for dogs makes for a comparatively short reading list.

As I interviewed shelter leaders for this book, I always asked them what they thought was the one thing that needed to change to find homes for more dogs. Some answered more spay/neuter programs. Some said more foster homes. As I asked people to give me an answer, it became clearer and clearer that there isn't just one answer. There rarely is for any problem, and if there is, you can count yourself lucky.

Finally, I put that question to myself. What would I change?

What if we balanced this out-of-whack relationship? What if rather than always asking what dogs can do for us, we flipped the question around? Not just for our own dogs, but all dogs, these creatures whom we take epically for granted even though they seem to have magically sprung out of a fairy tale. If we thought about what we owed dogs for their loyalty and service, we'd be better people for it, though that would be yet another self-serving reason to do right by them. I could live with that if it meant that all of us, not just people in the shelter and rescue world, felt obliged to help *Canis lupus familiaris* in whatever small way we could. If we gave thanks for this devoted companion with whom Mother Nature has endowed us, and if each of us asked ourselves how we could help this species, Rich Avanzino's dream might come true, that in his lifetime no dog would die for lack of a home.

Tired of rarely knowing the rest of the story of all the dogs I'd given my heart to, I went on a tour of sorts. I started by driving up the coast to the very tip of Cape Ann, Massachusetts, to Rockport, an old New England fishing village of white clapboard buildings that now has more tourists than lobster boats. When I saw Gwen, she had, of course, a tennis ball in her mouth. She and Silvana, her extroverted, dark-haired owner, stood on the corner in front of Silvana's jewelry shop on a July afternoon. Sunburned families hoisting shiny creamy whips and knocking paper shopping bags against their legs wove around the twosome. Most smiled at Gwen or patted her as they passed. One woman took her child's hand and pulled her into the street to avoid getting close to the pittie with the tennis ball. Silvana shrugged. Off and on, Gwen would drop the ball, watch it roll, and then drag Silvana, sandals flapping, toward it as it bumped into the street. Silvana didn't seem to mind. "Oh my God, I LOVE HER," she sang out like a town crier. Her shop employees teased her, she said, because of how much she fussed over Gwen.

When I kneeled down, Gwen came right up to me and wagged her tail, but she didn't overdo it. She might not have made much of a display of remembering me, but I was sure she did. Dogs always remember. That's not why I had come, though. I had come to see her in a home, the home we had all worked so hard to find her.

We walked through the village to a small, shaded park. There Silvana unhooked Gwen's leash and dug several more tennis balls out of her voluminous purse. Gwen trembled while waiting for a toss. Silvana lobbed ball after ball while she walked around collecting the ones Gwen had left here and there in the grass. Gwen stopped playing only to slip into the bushes. She peeked out between the leaves while she pooped. Gwen, Silvana, explained, likes her privacy.

"Come on, Momma!" Silvana hollered. Then Gwen raced over and did something I had never seen her do at the shelter. She threw herself down onto the grass and rolled on her back to allow Silvana to rub her belly.

Natasha, Greg's owner, brought the once nervous stray to me. I waited for them by the ARL's parking lot. They live with Natasha's boyfriend about an hour's drive south of Boston, in a town of lakes and cranberry bogs. When their small car pulled into the lot, I could see Greg sitting in the front passenger seat next to Natasha's boyfriend. I saw Natasha only when Greg got out of the car. He'd been sitting in her lap, and his Marmaduke head had blocked hers. Greg was no Gwen. He put his paws all over me. We took him into the play yard so we could take off his leash. When I sat down on a bench, he licked my face so hard I couldn't see. His tongue seemed to almost go up my nose.

Natasha told me that when she first brought Greg home, he would grab her dreadlocks, but eventually she got him to leave her hair alone. He never mouthed her now. Still, he was weirder than she expected. He loves traffic cones and picks one up whenever he sees one. Natasha's boyfriend, a freckled young man with earrings the size of thimbles, showed me a video of Greg methodically destroying a young tree, grabbing, bending, and pulling it. They'd take him swimming and kick water at him so he could bite at the splashes. Natasha had Greg designated as an emotional support dog so she could take him everywhere with her. She renamed him Trigger, after Roy Rogers's faithful horse. Greg/Trigger licked my face hard one more time, and then the threesome piled back into the small car and drove off into a world of traffic cones and saplings.

Brody was larger than I recalled, even imposing, and his widow's peak of dark fur seemed to have faded ever so slightly, yet he was the same happy-go-lucky dog I remembered. One ear was up, one was down. Jenna, the low-key young woman who had adopted the punk, had suggested we meet at her parents' snug house along a small lake. There, Brody climbed onto the couch next to Scott, who wrapped his arm around the shepherd. They sat there, side by side, while Jenna and I talked.

When she first brought Brody home, Jenna said, the microwave chime scared him. So did ceiling fans. He was afraid of thunder and would curl up in a corner of the room during storms. He still balls up blankets so he can suck on them during the night. For their first two years, Brody and Jenna were nearly inseparable. She took him along to the kennel where she worked. She'd taken the job after college because it was all she could find. She finally went to work as a research analyst, and Brody had to stay home. Jenna and her husband adopted a stray beagle named Chiky, hoping the two would play the day away. Instead they napped, which is why Brody had gotten chunky. The extra weight had had no effect on his mischievousness, however. If they got him really riled up, he would still throw himself at them.

We walked outside to the grassy yard, which tumbled down to the water's edge. A fall breeze rippled the surface lightly. Brody spied a kayaker paddling by and dashed into the lake. He barked and then lumbered back out. Scott, the man who wanted to buy a house so we could keep this big guy, did something he would have never dared doing while we were fostering this then-jumpy-mouthy. My husband, his hair just graying, ran like a teenage boy after Brody, and the two chased each other in ever-growing circles.

I went to see my lovely Nervous Nellie by myself. Harmony's owner told me she was still very shy around people, even ones she had met before. And sure enough, she shook violently in a spacious crate when Karen led me into her living room. "She'll settle down once we start talking."

Karen got her first German shepherd as a teenager. She runs German Shepherd Rescue of New England, the all-volunteer group to which the ARL had transferred Harmony. Harmony was a slip of a thing then, only fifty-two pounds, and spent her early weeks at a trainer's house while she recovered from more surgery on her wonky elbows. Then the long-legged gal moved to a foster home, but shortly after the move, her foster mom caught pneumonia and Harmony ended up at the rescue's kennels, where she struggled. Karen brought her to her hilltop house twice a week to play and relax. She couldn't adopt Harmony because she already had two German shepherds, an elderly female and a young male who hated other dogs. For a year, Harmony's photo languished on the group's website. The rescue could not find what they thought was a suitable home for such a skittish girl. Then Karen's elder female German shepherd passed and Karen adopted Harmony even though she worried about taking in such a young dog, who was barely two then, when she herself was in her seventies.

Harmony had stopped shaking, so Karen let her out. Harmony draped her front legs across Karen's lap and studied me from that safe distance. The dog who once happily bounded all over me, carefully leaned over far enough to sniff me with her long nose. I ignored her. Her eyes relaxed, but then she startled when I pulled a marker out of my purse. The room was so warm that I wanted to take my sweater off, but I didn't want to scare Harmony. I broke into a sweat as Karen told me about how she had gotten Harmony's weight up to seventy-four pounds by throwing chicken or cheese into her food bowl. Killian, Karen's German shepherd who doesn't like other dogs, had decided Harmony was okay. Karen and her husband walked the striking twosome through their five wooded acres every day. As Karen described these outings, Harmony tentatively stepped toward me as if to interrupt and ask a question. Then she gave me a lick or two on my right hand as I wrote with a marker in my notebook. Karen said that this was more than what she would typically do. Maybe through the veil of her fears, Harmony recognized an old friend.

There was another dog I had to see. Scott and I packed Penny Jane and Walter Joe into the back of our station wagon, and the four of us headed west. Our pups napped as we zoomed out of the city on the empty highways of a Sunday morning. We opened the car windows on an early fall day |as we barreled through town after town until we finally turned into a woodsy cul-de-sac. We parked by a red clapboard house and walked around it to a beautifully landscaped backyard. There stood Rugby.

Even after that day on the beach, we hadn't

stopped bringing Rugby home for sleepovers until, against all odds, he was adopted by Maddy and Pam, a longtime couple who already had three dogs and two cats, and no plans to get another pet. They had seen a local TV news story, a real tearjerker, on Rugby, with his odd legs and bright eyes. Their friends called to tell them they should adopt that dog on TV. "My friends think I'm Dr. Dolittle!" said Pam. They told their friends someone would surely adopt such a cutie after his star turn on TV. So they were surprised when, the next day, they came across Rugby at Boston's closest thing to Mardi Gras, the annual Gay Pride Parade. Rugby trundled along on his improving legs through the jubilant throngs with an ARL volunteer, who told Maddy and Pam that no one had called about him. A few days later I got word that Rugby was going home that after-noon. I rushed to the shelter to say good-bye. The Beast sat in my lap calmly while Maddy filled out the paper-work. Within a week, she e-mailed me a video of Rugby splashing in a blue kiddie pool.

Scott and I fell to our knees so Rugby could lick us. He put his paws on our legs and shoulders but did not munch us. Those days were behind him. His front ankles were knobby, but that was the only sign of his past troubles. He runs with Maddy and has turned into a squarely built dog, which is why they have nicknamed him Tank.

Rugby got kicked out of day care for playing too rough, but he lets one of their cats bat him on the head. Every morning, Rugby makes a beeline for the garden pond, where frogs have gathered overnight. He circles the water, gently touching his black nose to one slippery back after another, methodically making frog after frog leap into the pond.

We ate thick wedges of quiche and drank deep mugs of coffee on Maddy and Pam's porch while Penny Jane, Walter Joe, and Rugby milled around us, sniffing here, sniffing there. We told stories about them and laughed so hard we swatted the table. We toasted these dogs who once had such dim prospects. Rugby, Penny Jane, and Walter Joe had loving homes, what every dog needs, what every dog deserves.

Author's Note

Portions of this book are told from my own perspective. I've described shelter dogs as I knew them, which may not represent the same experience other volunteers or staff members had with them. I've also relied on my memory to tell some of the stories within these pages. I have checked those memories against records and other sources whenever I could, but I've often had only my own recollections to go on, and, as everyone knows, recollections are not foolproof. I have found that I have a much sharper memory for animals (one of my earliest is of sitting in my family's front yard with our mutt Curly), but years of meeting dog after dog has blurred some of them. Still, I fudged only one name that I could not recall. When I couldn't remember one pittie's name I dubbed him Baxter, a very common name in the shelter world. Maybe he was actually Baxter.

Acknowledgments

This book was made possible, in essence, by an entire field—the shelter and rescue world. In my time as a journalist I have rarely come upon a profession so open and willing to help me understand what they do and why. To the whole heroic profession I say a big thank you. Amid that world a long list of people lent me a hand, foremost Rich Avanzino. I count myself lucky not just for his immense help but also for his inspiring me, as well as many other people, to think big. Not much would ever change in this world without the likes of Rich Avanzino to lead the way.

I had many other guiding lights within the shelter world: Mindy Naticchioni, Sharon Harmon, Lori Weise, Amanda Casarez, Jon Cicirelli, Janelle Dixon, Sharon Harvey, Sherry Woodard, Mike Kaviani, Aimee Sadler, Jennifer Pimentel, Patsy Murphy, Natalie DiGiacomo, Kristen Collins, Emily Weiss, Pamela Reid, Elena Bicker, Paula Zukoff, Stacey Coleman, Sue Schellhous, Sherri Franklin, Cynthia Karsten, Marlene Walsh, Carol Novello, Kelly Krause, Sharon Fletcher, Jennifer Scarlett, and Jason Walthall. I owe special thanks to Patricia

McConnell, who not only has always been generous with her time, but also gave me a deeper understanding of dogs with her thoughtful writing long before I was lucky enough to interview her.

Sheila D'Arpino not only answered my endless questions but also set the ball in motion for this book long ago, well before I'd ever thought of writing it, by creating a team of volunteers to work with the more challenging dogs at the Animal Rescue League of Boston and inviting me to join that group. My fellow team members— Mal Marme, Maria Uribe, Kate Hanson, and Michele Smith—have been an endless source of encouragement. The entire ARL staff, who fight the good fight day in and day out, deserve many thanks, especially Deborah Vogel, Dot Baisly, Carolyn Curran, Claire Humphries, Michele Polin, and Brittany Monteiro. A number of my most formative influences have moved on from the ARL but not from my mind: Kim Melanson, Laney Nee, Marianne Gasbarro, and Naomi Stevens.

I'd also like to thank the people who adopted dogs at the ARL, never expecting a journalist to come trailing after them, and gamely invited me to their homes and kept in touch with me: Silvana Costa, Madelyn Bell, Pamela Rivera-Bellino, Jenna Shepard, Natasha Wilson, and Karen McCall. Without them I would have never gotten to see the result that I had worked so hard for—dogs in the homes they deserved.

I was lucky enough to find an agent, Alice Martell, and an editor, Jennifer Barth, who are both far smarter and more talented than I, and who love dogs as much as I do. Both understood the goal of this book immediately. I hit the jackpot. Speaking of which, thanks as well to all the hardworking staff at HarperCollins who made this book happen and look so stunning.

My husband, Scott, looms large between these pages. I had the great fortune to marry a dog lover, and together we have explored the depths and lengths of that affection. It's been the most rewarding adventure to share. Along the way, he became a de facto shelter volunteer, gamely helping me walk dogs and always welcoming them into our condo, even the ones who jumped on his head while he tried to sleep late on a Saturday morning. Behind many shelter volunteers are spouses and partners quietly helping in the background and not always getting their due. We volunteers, not to mention the dogs, would be lost without them.

And then there are the dogs, my own (Dixie Lou, Penny Jane, and Walter Joe Jr.), the ones in this book (far too many to list), the entire fabulous species, *Canis lupus familiaris*. This is my third book about animals, and I find I can never fully express my debt of gratitude to the world's creatures, especially to dogs, these creatures who devote their lives to us. How I owe them. So rather than say thanks, I'll show my gratitude by continuing to help them however I can until the end of my days. It's the least I can do.

About the Author

Amy Sutherland is the bestselling author of three previous books, most recently *What Shamu Taught Me About Life, Love, and Marriage.* She writes the popular Bibliophiles column in the *Boston Globe*'s Book Section and has contributed to the *New York Times, Smithsonian, Preservation,* and other outlets. She lives in Boston with her husband and two rescue dogs, Walter Joe and Penny Jane.

Center Point Large Print
600 Brooks Road / PO Box 1
Thorndike, ME 04986-0001 USA

(207) 568-3717

**US & Canada:
1 800 929-9108**
www.centerpointlargeprint.com